New Songs from a Jade Terrace

Also by Anne Birrell

Erotic Decor: A Study of Love Imagery in the Sixth-Century AD Anthology 'Yü-t'ai hsin-yung' ('New Poems from a Jade Terrace') (Columbia University, 1979; University Microfilms International)

New Songs from a Jade Terrace

*An Anthology of Early Chinese Love Poetry,
Translated with Annotations and an
Introduction*

by ANNE BIRRELL

London
GEORGE ALLEN & UNWIN
Boston   Sydney

**George Allen & Unwin (Publishers) Ltd,
40 Museum Street, London WC1A 1LU, UK**

George Allen & Unwin (Publishers) Ltd,
Park Lane, Hemel Hempstead, Herts HP2 4TE, UK

Allen & Unwin Inc.,
9 Winchester Terrace, Winchester, Mass 01890, USA

George Allen & Unwin Australia Pty Ltd,
8 Napier Street, North Sydney, NSW 2060, Australia

First published in 1982

British Library Cataloguing in Publication Data

New songs from a jade terrace.
   1. Chinese poetry – Translations into English
2. English poetry – Translations from Chinese
I. Birrell, Anne
895.1′12   PL2518
ISBN 0-04-895026-2

Set in 11 on 12 point Baskerville by Grove Graphics, Tring
and printed in Great Britain
by Mackays of Chatham

To the memory of
Suzuki Torao (1878-1963)

Acknowledgements

My sincere thanks go to Burton Watson, Chih-tsing Hsia, Denis C. Twitchett, Angus C. Graham, and Piet van der Loon for their thoughtful comments on my manuscript and helpful suggestions. I am particularly indebted to Michael Loewe who, besides reading various sections with valuable insights, provided generous encouragement and sound advice at critical stages of my work. I am also grateful to my editors, Michael Radford, who brought painstaking critical acumen to bear on my manuscript, and John Hardy, who with never-failing courtesy adroitly steered my work through the Scylla and Charybdis of publication. My last word of thanks goes to many friends, especially Brigadier Philip Moran, Sir John Brooke, Miss Elizabeth S. Blair, and Ewen G. Cameron, for their good-natured interest. It is no exaggeration to say that without Mr Cameron's continued support this work would never have been realised.

Foreword

Some works of literature we prize for their universal and timeless qualities. Regardless of when or where they were created, they seem to speak directly to us today, their freshness and power unaffected by the passing of centuries. Others appeal to us for a quite opposite reason, because they so richly and vividly reflect the particular period and society that produced them; because in effect they are so unlike the literature of the present. Like artefacts from an old tomb, they tell us of customs and beliefs that have now vanished, of a way of life that fascinates us with its foreignness. They are witnesses not of the fundamental emotions common to all mankind, but of the infinitely varied ways in which those emotions find expression in different ages and climes.

The *Yü-t'ai hsin-yung* or *New Songs from a Jade Terrace,* an anthology of Chinese love poetry compiled in the sixth century AD, in a way belongs to both these categories. Many of the poems in it, especially those that appear to be of an earlier date, depict the joys and sorrows of love, and above all the sorrow of separation, in terms that are immediately understandable and moving to the reader of today. They reflect the timeless aspects of the anthology. But the reader, in addition to assuring himself that the Chinese heart in love beats much like hearts in that condition the world over, is at the same time intrigued to observe the particular conventions that governed courtships and romantic involvements in traditional China and the particular images and epithets that its poets employed in portraying the object of their affections.

And how different indeed are the conventions of love poetry in different lands and times! If men and women everywhere alike fall in love, each culture seems to have its own unique manner of giving expression to the feeling. Or so the poets would suggest. The ancient Greeks and Romans wrote of love with a frankness and exuberance that brought blushes to their cultural successors in later centuries of European history, and would most certainly have done the same to readers of traditional China. The troubadours of southern Europe, whose works had such a profound influence upon the European literary tradition as a whole, seemed to take a perverse delight in depicting lovely ladies who are cruelly chaste, forever demanding tokens of devotion from their hapless lovers while withholding favors. How far removed are these chill mistresses from the voluptuous beauties of Sanskrit poetry, with their hair and clothing in disarray and their flesh battered and bruised from the violence of their lovemaking, or from the fretful Japanese ladies of the *Man'yōshū* who wait impatiently for a lover who slips into their room at night and slips away again at dawn. And, as the reader will presently discover, the lovers and loved ones of the Chinese tradition are different again from all of these.

Long before the compilation of *New Songs from a Jade Terrace,* the Chinese had had an earlier body of love poetry dating back perhaps as far as the ninth, eighth, or seventh century BC. But these ancient love lyrics were preserved, unfortunately perhaps, in an anthology that was believed to have been compiled by none other than the venerable sage and moralist Confucius. Since it was assumed that Confucius would not have been interested in anything so frivolous as romantic love *per se,* the Chinese scholars concluded that there must be weighty moral or political lessons hidden beneath the surface meaning of the poems, and set about with all the exegete's characteristic ingenuity and zeal to dig them out. Such an approach had the additional advantage that it allowed the scholars to gloss over what appeared to be indecorous passages in certain of the love poems, whisking them out of sight behind the curtains of allegorical interpretation before anyone could ask just why Confucius would have included works of this kind in his compilation in the first place.

But, if these earliest love songs were fated by circumstance to be thus forced into a didactic mold, no such treatment befell the poems of *New Songs from a Jade Terrace.* They were the products of a later age, one less dominated by Confucian concepts of morality, that frankly admitted its decadence and dared to take an interest in literature for its own sake, believing that love and physical attraction, whether that of a high-born lady of the aristocracy, a peasant girl or a professional prostitute, were fit subjects for poetry. These are the poems that laid down the patterns for later Chinese love poetry, and in many cases remain among the most popular and poignant treatments of the theme in the Chinese language. And now, thanks to Dr Birrell's excellent introduction and translations, the English reader can for the first time enter into and appreciate the world of *New Songs from a Jade Terrace,* savoring both the peculiarly Chinese charms and conventions of that world, as well as its more universal aspects. He can see for himself how the Chinese poet's depiction of love compares with those put forward by poets of other cultures, and in doing so perhaps acquire some fresh insight into the nature of both love and poetry.

BURTON WATSON
Osaka, May 1980

Contents

Chapter Two — Poets of the Wei and Chin Dynasties (third and fourth centuries)

Chapter Three   Poets of the Chin Dynasty
(third and fourth centuries)

Chapter Four   Poets of the Southern Dynasties
(early fifth century)

Chapter Five   **Poets of the Southern Dynasties**
                               (the decades AD 490–510)

Chapter Six   Poets of the Southern Dynasties (early sixth century)

Chapter Seven   Royal Poets of the Liang
(the Hsiao Family)

Chapter Eight — Twenty Poets of the Liang Dynasty (sixth century)

xix

Chapter Ten **A Treasury of Short Love Poems**
(from third to sixth centuries AD)

xxii

xxvi

Chronological Table

(Dates and names prior to 841 BC are traditional)

The Age of Culture Heroes and Sage Kings	?2852–?2206 BC
Yellow Emperor	
Emperor Yao	
Emperor Shun	
The Golden Age of the Three Dynasties	
Hsia Dynasty	?2205–?1767
Shang (Yin) Dynasty	?1766–?1123
(beginning of archaeological evidence *c.* 1300 BC)	
Chou Dynasty	?1123–221
Western Chou	?1123–771
Eastern Chou	771–256
Spring and Autumn Era	722–481
Warring States Era	403–221
Ch'in Dynasty	221–207
The Han Empire	202 BC–AD 220
Former (or Western) Han	202–AD 8
Hsin Dynasty (Interregnum)	9–23
Later (or Eastern) Han	25–220
The Three Kingdoms	221–280
Minor Han Dynasty	221–265
Wei Dynasty	220–265
Wu Dynasty	222–280
Chin Dynasty	265–419
Western Chin	265–316
Eastern Chin	317–419
The Period of Disunion	317–589
(also known as the Six Dynasties, namely	
Wu, Eastern Chin, Liu-Sung, Ch'i, Liang, Ch'en,	
or the Northern and Southern Dynasties)	
The Northern Dynasties	386–580
The Southern Dynasties	420–589
Liu-Sung Dynasty	420–478

Ch'i Dynasty	479–501
Liang Dynasty	502–556
Ch'en Dynasty	557–589
Sui Dynasty	589–618
T'ang Dynasty	618–907
Five Dynasties	907–959
Sung Dynasty	960–1279
Yüan (Mongol) Dynasty	1280–1368
Ming Dynasty	1368–1644
Ch'ing (Manchu) Dynasty	1644–1911
Republic of China	1912–1949
People's Republic of China	1949–

New Songs from a Jade Terrace

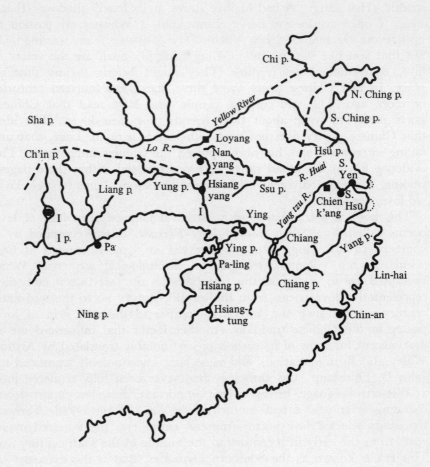

The Southern Dynasties

Introduction

'Who can stop love once love happens?' (Yen Yen-chih). 'Autumn will come when all things wither, / And touch her body with nature's stealth' (Hsü Ling). 'A bed of love stares at its lonely shadow' (Hsiao Yen). 'I offer my love to her eyebrow kohl, / Whisper my passion to lipstick on her mouth' (Shen Yüeh). 'The sad way I am wasting / Is not that you like slim waists!' (Wang Seng-ju). Such are the voices of love, contradictory yet credible. They might belong to any time or place. In fact Chinese poets wrote these lines some fourteen centuries or more ago. This will surprise people who have read that Chinese poets prefer to write about their friends, not their lovers. The idea that Chinese poetry does not deal with love is a myth. Love, that un-failing interest of man, has also captured the Chinese imagination. The evidence lies in the broad range of love expressed within these pages: wooing, marriage, divorce; celebrations, obsessions, laments; new love, old love, dead love.

This book is a translation of a medieval Chinese anthology of love poems called *New Songs from a Jade Terrace*. It was compiled by a court poet, Hsü Ling, in about the year AD 545. It consists of 656 poems in ten volumes arranged in chronological sequence. What prompted me to undertake this translation is the fact that it embodies representative love poems from the second century BC to the mid-sixth century AD. As such the anthology testifies to the rich vein of love poetry in the Chinese tradition. Another factor that influenced me is that, except for some of its earliest pieces (notably translated by Arthur Waley and Burton Watson), and some later ones (notably translated by John D. Frodsham), this anthology has never been fully rendered into a Western language before. More important, however, apart from spanning seven and a half centuries *New Songs from a Jade Terrace* represents selected love poems from an entire era, the hundred or so years from the early fifth century to the middle of the sixth century AD. This era is known as the Southern Dynasties, that is the dynasties of the Sung, Ch'i, and Liang. Numerically speaking Southern Dynasties love poems dominate the anthology. It was in this period that a new poetic style crystallised from the royal patronage of Southern Dynasties courts, especially of the Liang Dynasty. The new vogue was dubbed at the time 'Palace Style Poetry', what we would term today the love poetry of Southern Dynasties court poets.

This volume of translations, therefore, serves a manifold purpose. First it will redress the balance regarding China's alleged dearth of love

1

poetry. It will also show the development of a major literary theme over several centuries. Furthermore, it will demonstrate the mature features of the new Southern Dynasties 'Palace Style Poetry'. As a corollary, forgotten poets and their poetry will be rediscovered. Lastly, this anthology will provide a necessary link between the more familiar landmarks of ancient China and the later medieval period of the T'ang Dynasty. Clearly, much of the originality claimed for T'ang poetry has to be put back where it rightly belongs – to poets of the Southern Dynasties.

Historical Perspective

Poets in general speak the language of their time and reflect something of the changing nature of their society. *New Songs from a Jade Terrace* appeared at a favourable juncture in time, during a period of relative present peace poised between past war and future political strife. This collection was a literary product of the Liang Dynasty, ruled by Emperor Wu from the southern capital of Chienk'ang, modern Nanking. It was the literary inspiration of his son, the Crown Prince Hsiao Kang. In about the year AD 545 Hsiao Kang commissioned the court poet, Hsü Ling, to compile these love poems. The majority of them date from the fifth and early sixth centuries AD, when China was ruled in the south by a succession of Chinese dynasties, and in the north by foreign invaders. Men of the Liang Dynasty looked back on three hundred years of divisive warfare. Their ancient Han empire which for four centuries had dominated the Orient east to Korea, west to Turkestan, and south to Indo-China, collapsed in the year AD 220. China became a divided country. Reunification was only achieved after the passing of the Liang Dynasty in AD 589. The three and a half centuries between AD 220 and 589 were characterised by rivalry among regional warlords and foreign invaders. The crisis came in the year AD 317 when foreign tribes conquered the ancient Chinese capitals of Ch'angan and Loyang and drove the Chinese rulers and their court south into exile. Until reunification in AD 589 Chinese territorial power was eclipsed to a shadow of its former size and grandeur.

A major source of continued strife was the lack of coherence within the ruling groups of China. Powerful family warred against family for supremacy in the political sphere. Even within the great families internecine rivalry for power superseded the desire to achieve concerted dynastic aims. During these centuries there were twenty-nine different dynasties in north China and six in the south. This historical period is variously known as the Period of Division, or the Six Dynasties, or the Northern and Southern Dynasties. The result of this inter-family and intra-clan struggle was the proliferation of power bases among a number of great families, rather than the concentration of power in one central dynastic house. The southern dynasty of the Liang itself was founded by an act of usurpation by Hsiao Yen when he destroyed the Liu-Sung royal house of which he was a member and proclaimed himself Emperor Wu of the Liang. He went on to enjoy a long and peaceful reign lasting fifty years. His son and heir, Hsiao Kang, was not so fortunate. He ruled for a mere two years before being assassinated by a Tartar general from the north.

The historical era of *New Songs from a Jade Terrace* was aristocratic. The southern Liang court was based at Chienk'ang and Emperor Wu conferred upon his numerous sons and relatives aristocratic rank and administrative power. The twenty-three provinces of his domain were ruled by civil and military governors related to him. Often they were figureheads enjoying the wealth, status, and privilege that went with their noble rank and official title. Actual governmental duties were carried out by educated men of the middle ranks of society. These imperial policies of conferring hereditary rank on members of the royal family and of recruiting officials from lower bureaucratic echelons meant that many men from great and illustrious aristocratic families were bypassed in political life. In some cases they directed their energies to the literary life of the capital and provincial courts.

Court Patronage of Literature

One of the striking features of southern aristocratic society was the system of literary patronage that operated in the imperial court at Chienk'ang and the minor courts of princes in the provinces. Much of the literary efflorescence of this era was lost when the capital was sacked and its libraries and cultural treasures destroyed in AD 555. *New Songs from a Jade Terrace* survived the holocaust. It owes its creation to one of the great men of early medieval China. Promoted to Crown Prince in AD 531, Hsiao Kang succeeded to the throne in 549, and is known to history as Emperor Chienwen. Like many Chinese dynastic rulers he managed to combine a political career with literary and intellectual interests. While he was Crown Prince he assumed the role of patron of the arts in his own court at Yung, west of the capital. His literary circle was attended by nobles, courtiers, and educated men of the gentry class. The composition of the anthology testifies to his royal patronage: of its ten volumes one whole volume is devoted to poets of the Liang royal house, and, of the 502 poems by fifty-one Southern Dynasties poets, Hsiao Kang is represented by seventy-six poems, his father Hsiao Yen by forty-one, and the Liang royal house as a whole by 166 poems. A nice case of flattery on the part of Hsü Ling, the compiler, who modestly included only four of his own poems.

3

In this aristocratic society the poet was not a special class of person. He was very different from the romantic Western image of a wild-eyed, unbuttoned, tousle-haired poet, an independent spirit moved by the divine muse to express himself in original verse. The Chinese poet of this era was more like a Victorian poet laureate who was also a civil servant. In order to be recognised the Chinese writer had to gain entry into the central or provincial court through family connections, imperial preferment, and literary talent. Once admitted, he was required to perform official duties and attend numerous court functions. On such occasions as formal banquets he was not only commanded to participate in poetry competitions, but also presented with a mandatory theme for competitive extempore composition. A number of poems in the anthology have tagged onto their titles the formal phrase 'At His Highness's Request', or 'Commissioned by His Majesty', or 'Composed at His Majesty's Banquet on Such-and-Such a Theme'. In this sense poetry was not simply an art, but also a form of social intercourse, and more importantly a means for official promotion and literary recognition.

In such an environment where literary success was dependent upon royal patronage it was natural for courtier poets to offer their compositions to their social superiors, albeit artistic peers. The honorific tag 'Respectfully Submitted to His Highness' appears in many poem titles of this period. Another way the court poet consolidated his official and literary career was to imitate the poems of his superior. Not only was the theme imitated, but more often the rhyme scheme of his superior's admired poem was matched. That this technique was extremely popular is evident in the large number of poems in this collection bearing the tag 'Respectfully Submitted to His Highness, Matching the Rhymes of His Poem'. The proliferation of these dedicatory titles in the anthology indicates the extent to which court poets felt the literary weight of royal patronage.

The Anthologist's Purpose

T. S. Eliot claimed with understandable poetic licence: 'Few things that can happen to a nation are more important than the invention of a new form of verse'. Certainly, poets of the Liang era would have glumly agreed as they witnessed their dynasty disappear into ashes. The most significant factor of court patronage of poetry was the development of a new form of love poetry. Historical annals credit various people with the invention of 'Palace Style Poetry' – Hsiao Kang, Hsü Ch'ih (Hsü Ling's father), Yü Chien-wu, and his son Yü Hsin. Regardless of who the actual innovator was, the last three names

4

were associated with Hsiao Kang's literary court. In his capacity of patron it was Hsiao Kang who set his seal of approval upon the new poetic vogue and thus ensured its success. The prevalence of imitation in poetry circles and the trend toward dedicatory verse meant that the fashion legitimised by a royal patron was destined to become popular. By commissioning Hsü Ling to garner the gems of the earlier tradition of love poetry and glean the finest contemporary models, Hsiao Kang was instrumental in immortalising this new form of verse.

Anthologies by their nature are in some respects ephemeral literary things. They are often based on literary views and sets of values which sum up an attitude to the past and present held at a particular moment by a particular person or group. *New Songs from a Jade Terrace* was for China in AD 545 what Francis T. Palgrave's *The Golden Treasury of Songs and Lyrics* was for Victorian England in 1861, essentially a contemporary collection. Of the 656 poems in the Chinese anthology 75 per cent are of the century or so before and up to its compilation. That is to say they were modern in their own day. Modernity is but one aspect of the word 'New' (*hsin*) in the anthology's title. Another is the compiler's personal predilection for poems representing the new poetic vogue. Linking these two aspects of modernity and fashion is the new aesthetic preoccupation of Hsü Ling and of his patron Hsiao Kang.

Although at first glance it seems that Hsü Ling selected love poems from the vast timespan of seven and a half centuries in order to demonstrate the richness of Chinese love poetry down through the ages to his own day, he did in fact make two important omissions in his selection. One was the body of love poetry among the 305 poems in *The Book of Songs,* traditionally believed to date from the ninth to the seventh centuries BC. The other was the corpus of erotic and elegiac rhapsodies of *The Songs of Ch'u,* dating from the fourth century BC to the second century AD. The reason for these glaring omissions cannot be said to be metrical, for both their metres, the archaic tetrasyllabic and the *sao*-song metres respectively, appear in Hsü Ling's anthology. The reason has more to do with a radical change in literary values in the sixth century AD.

In the early part of the Han dynasty (202 BC–AD 220) *The Book of Songs* was elevated to the status of a classic, together with four other works associated with the teachings of Confucius, and Confucianism was espoused by the state as official doctrine. The idea gained currency that Confucius had edited the 305 poems of this classic from an earlier collection of over three thousand poems. Authorities were appointed to supervise each of the five *Confucian Classics* and Han scholars began to write commentaries on them. Adhering to the belief that Confucius had edited the songs, these writers insisted that the sage

5

had implicitly editorialised in making his selection. Consequently, these scholars evolved elaborate explanations and interpretations of quite innocent songs, giving them a didactic tone. Thus a marriage song becomes an allegory for the exemplary marital relationship between a ruler and his consort. Or a lovers' elopement becomes an allegory for dissident peasants fleeing to another country. *The Songs of Ch'u* suffered a similar fate at the hands of exegetical writers. Its early poems written in a highly complex symbolic language were reduced to more prosaic allegory of a political, moralising nature.

The result was that later generations of scholars and writers extended the didactic values attached to these works, especially *The Book of Songs* as a state classic, to literature in general. The function of literature, they persuaded, was to edify and improve; literature was to provide a mirror of personal conduct. It was only some fourteen centuries later, when the forthright philosopher Chu Hsi (AD 1130–1200) punctured the pious excesses of Han and post-Han scholarship, that these allegorical distortions of classical poetry and literature in general were deflated and Confucian doctrine on the didactic value of literature was diminished.

In this context Hsü Ling and Hsiao Kang were avant-garde writers. When Hsü Ling compiled his anthology of love poems, didactic views of literature had long held sway. In his Preface to the anthology, however, he makes it quite clear that his purpose in literature is to give pleasure rather than instruction. Tilting obliquely at dour academics who managed to find moral meaning everywhere, Hsü Ling mischievously pictures his readers as women indolently passing days and nights in luxurious harem boudoirs. He archly states: 'The palace lady takes no delight in idle hours, / But devotes her mind to the latest verse'. Tongue-in-cheek, Hsü Ling brags about the popularity of his volumes of poetry among this female audience, who after preening themselves in their boudoir nonchalantly tuck his volumes under their pillow: 'They will always be tucked away in vermilion pillows'. He claims that ladies will 'for long hours be diverted behind their reading drapes, / My book always open in slim hands.' Hsü Ling ends his Preface with a series of humorous disclaimers: 'Certainly my book will be quite different / From Empress Teng's study of *The Spring and Autumn Classic,* / For a scholar's attainments are hard to acquire!' Empress Teng was famous in the Han Dynasty for her single-minded pursuit of knowledge, conning the *Confucian Classics* all day long, solemnly and earnestly. Finally, to make sure that his view of literature as entertainment is perfectly understood, Hsü Ling sardonically notes that poetry is better than drugs, such as 'the flower of oblivion', for alleviating boredom: 'For poetry can / Be a substitute for the flower of oblivion / And can banish the disease of ennui.' This ambience of boudoirs, cosmetics, pillows, and palace ladies is a world apart from the solemnities

6

of exegetical scholarship. It is an urbane acknowledgement that art is lightly to be pursued for art's sake.

Conventions of the Love Poem

Art and artifice were the hallmark of literary products in the Southern Dynasties era. To be successful the courtier had to be an accomplished artist in many different forms of literature. Not only must he compose correct memorials to the throne, obituary notices and eulogies for his superiors, treatises and epistles, but also works in various forms of verse for specific occasions. The diverse functions and forms of writing were appreciated quite early in the literary tradition. In the third century AD the poet Ts'ao P'ei, known to history as Emperor Wen of the Wei Dynasty, made a list of eight genres in his *Essay on Literature* (*Lun wen*). By the sixth century Hsiao T'ung, Hsiao Kang's older brother, had compiled an *Anthology of Literature* (*Wen hsüan*) which contained examples of no fewer than thirty-seven different forms of literature. Each of these literary forms had recognisable rhetorical, structural, and stylistic differences. Many of them were composed for a special social or official occasion. Success or failure depended to a large extent on whether the writer conformed to a particular literary model and had displayed technical virtuosity in its execution. It was no good confusing the diction and allusions of a prose obituary with those of a treatise, still less muddling the diction and allusions of a poem about a hermit with those about a lover. The genre was the thing in the writer's composition and in his critics' appreciation.

Depending on the different genres and sub-genres, therefore, the writer employed different systems of rhetoric. When he composed in the love poem genre, and especially in the sub-genre of 'Palace Style Poetry', the court poet not only respected the appropriate devices of rhetoric, but also observed a strict code of poetic convention governing subject, theme, mood, and attitude. This well defined system of conventions was an implicit agreement between the poet and his literary circle to impose certain restrictions upon and to take certain liberties with his treatment of the theme of love. These courtly conventions were strongly influenced by earlier love poems in the literary tradition – anonymous folk-songs, ballads, so-called ancient style poems, and the poems and rhapsodies of *The Book of Songs* and *The Songs of Ch'u*. Many features of these types of poetry were borrowed and adapted according to the dictates of Southern Dynasties literary fashion. Originally existing as disparate elements in varying literary sources stretching back over several centuries, they were welded together in the hands of later court poets into a unified, distinctive, well developed pattern of love poetry. The fascination of *New Songs from a Jade Terrace* lies

7

partly in the fact that the finest of these earlier love poems (excluding those of the two aforementioned collections) appear together with the later artefact. That the poems are arranged in the anthology in chronological order within metrical divisions heightens the reader's awareness of how the Southern Dynasties love poem developed from pastoral simplicity to courtly sophistication.

When the court poet composed a love poem, he would usually select as his subject a woman in love, rather than a man in love with a woman. When a man is featured in the poems, he is mostly portrayed as a homosexual love object akin to the way a woman is presented, or as a man mourning the death of his wife or mistress. The poet, usually male, takes on the literary persona of a woman in love, expressing in descriptive and lyrical terms her deep emotions. This literary pose had a long tradition before the Southern Dynasties era and derived mainly from the ballad, folk-song, and ancient style poem. What is significant in the new poetic vogue is that the female subject of the love poem conforms to a noble ideal of femininity. She would appear to be well-born and living in luxurious surroundings, preferably palatial. Even when the poet is clearly borrowing stock characters from the earlier tradition, such as a merchant's wife, a soldier's sweetheart, a courtesan, a country girl, or a barmaid, he gives them a courtly treatment insofar as their environment and appearance are concerned. His poetic portrait of a woman in love conveys impressions of noble breeding and pampered living through her physical appearance: she is slender, graceful, elegantly dressed, adorned with costly jewels, and heavily made up with cosmetics. This accent on glamour and wealth is a feature of the earlier ballad tradition, but in 'Palace Style Poetry' it is given a distinctly new emphasis.

Another obligatory convention of the love poem of this era is that the woman's lover must be absent from the love scenario. The court poet must depict her pining for him with unrelieved sadness. This melancholy mood pervades much of the ancient style poetic repertoire, and probably derives from the older poetic tradition of *The Songs of Ch'u*. This collection contains a pivotal poem dating from about the fourth century BC, 'Encountering Sorrow', and its later imitations, besides a suite of shamanistic songs. All these pieces are commonly characterised by the persona's pursuit of love – a mortal for a goddess, a shaman for his god or goddess, a courtier for his lord – and the ultimate frustration of such desire. Overshadowed by its literary precursor, the Southern Dynasties courtly love poem is imbued with a profound sense of obligatory melancholy. The woman portrayed therein should seem depressed but submissive in her acceptance of doomed love. Because of her literary role as a victim of love, she should strike a pose of appealing emotional vulnerability and pathetic physical weakness. Her time must be spent conventionally waiting in the palatial ambience of her boudoir or its environs for her absent lover. The poet should describe certain items there with sensuous and metaphorical detail. His portrait of a woman in love is usually framed in an interior setting where nature is not too far off. For the natural world outside and the interior world within are poetically deployed to contrast with the beauty and fate of a woman in love, to pinpoint the ephemeral aspect of time, and to underscore poetic statements on the meaning of love and of life. The general tenor of the court poet's portrait is one of touchingly pretty pathos.

Images of Woman

As this degree of conventionality suggests, woman is depicted by the court poet as a type rather than as a realistically observed individual. The poet does not seek to inject into the fictionalised image of a woman in love some semblance of his own personal experience. Courtly love was never intended to be autobiography, or biography in verse. Western readers who set a high premium on originality in poetic creation should resist the temptation to construct a consistent auto-biographical or biographical framework around these poems. One has only to compare a handful of poems with similar titles in the anthology, such as 'Green, green riverside grass', to realise that they share so many resemblances that the poets cannot be describing details drawn from the crucible of their own amatory agonies. On the other hand the 656 love poems of *New Songs from a Jade Terrace* do not by any means conform to an identical pattern of conventions in a narrow sense. That would be too monotonous, even for the most determined poetaster! One line of demarcation between the more loosely structured love poem and the stricter conventional love poem is temporal. About 150 poems dating from the second century BC to the late third century AD have a fairly flexible design, while the five hundred or so dating from the fourth to the early sixth century follow a recognisably conventional pattern.

This divergence between the old and new poetic styles is never more noticeable than in the physical portrait of a woman in love. In the older poems a woman is presented in an idealised way. Much of this mode of presentation derives from even earlier models in the literary tradition, such as the third century BC prose poem, *The Goddess*, attributed to Sung Yü, a courtier poet of Ch'u state. This image of divine femininity continues in an unbroken line up to the third-century AD poet Lu Chi, who gives this description of palace ladies:

> Sweet looks glister in white sun,
> Kind hearts soft and pure.

9

> Lovely eyes spread gleams of jade,
> Moth eyebrows like kingfisher plumes.
> Fresh skin, oh so smooth,
> Vivid bloom it seems one could nibble.
> Meek, mild, full of grace,
> Enchantingly clever wit.

This serene image of female beauty changes radically under the brush of later court poets. They prefer to show a woman not in terms of divinely perfect beauty but as the tarnished image of feminine loveliness. The flawless mask described in the earlier love poems surrenders to pathetic facial ruin. What has happened here is that the court poets have adopted the trend in earlier love poems toward expressing unhappy love and have extended it to its ultimate limits of personal neglect. A passage by Wu Chün (AD 469–520) illustrates this new mode of presentation :

> From grief green-glinting hair turns white,
> Pink cheeks from tears have paled.
> Tears not only form beads of pearl,
> But I see pearls change to drops of blood.

This change in perception marks a shift in sensibility from the earlier interest in woman as a divine image to the later preoccupation with woman as a victim of love's disease.

Furthermore, there is a marked contrast between the old and new love poetry in the manner of describing dress and adornments of a woman in love. In the older poems cosmetics, jewelry, and dress are described to be sure, but not to the same lavish degree as in the new style of love poetry. The court poets reveal a fascination for the opulent minutiae of feminine fashion. The typical portrait shows woman adorned with fine jewels, costly silk clothes, and elaborate make-up. She indicates her beauty and worth in a very material way through the sheer opulence of her personal decor. So closely and persistently is a woman's rich attire associated with her personal attractiveness that her portrayal as a desirable woman depends on the financial and status value of her costume. What this amounts to is an aesthetic convention of courtly love poetry : woman is adored when adorned. The effect of such an emphasis on material rather than personal, individual qualities is that human values seem to be less important than material values in the aesthetic consciousness of the court poets. A passage from a poem by Shen Yüeh (AD 441–512), one of the most popular poets of his day, typifies this way of presenting a woman in love :

10

She is lovely and pretty in face and figure,
Courteous and clever the way she talks.
Her waist and limbs are graceful,
Her clothes so sweet and fresh.
Her round red cape reflects early chill,
Her painted fan welcomes the first spell of heat.
On brocaded slippers is a pattern of like flowers,
On embroidered sash twin heart lettuce design.
Gold leaf brooches fasten her bodice edge,
Flower jewel pins hold up her cloudy hair.

Of the thirty-four lines of this poem only the second line here describes the woman's personality, whereas fifteen lines are devoted to her appearance. The female figure is redolent with sensuous luxury and an erotic, but impersonal, ornamentation.

A further distinction between the image of woman in old and new poetic styles is that earlier poetic settings of rustic simplicity were replaced by the new poetic charm of sophisticated urban life. It was inevitable that as life in the city, especially at the courts of the capital city and provinces, grew more genteel, affluent, and fashionable, it would become separate from the pastoral naivety of the countryside. The love poems of *The Book of Songs* have outdoor settings: rivers, mulberry patches, or city walls. The erotic poems of *The Songs of Ch'u* have settings that range from the terrestrial to the celestial and super-natural. The early folk-songs and ancient style poems continue this outdoor, mostly rural tradition, and such models are represented in this anthology. The courtly love poem, however, makes a significant break with this tradition: love moves indoors. The vertiginous, wild mountain bower of a goddess or the dusty, bustling corner of a city wall where a poor country girl waits for her lover become the polite boudoir of a court lady with nature domesticated in her cultivated garden. Hsü Ling set the tone for this shift of emphasis in his Preface. There he clearly established the boudoir of a woman in a palace harem as the typical setting of the new style of love poem:

And so,
Through labyrinthine spirals of pepper palaces,
Up mysterious elevations of thorn-tree halls,
Scarlet Crane keys impose privacy at dawn,
Bronze Clam knockers fall silent at noon.
Before the Three Stars twilight hour
The ladies are not summoned to bring their quilt.

Southern Dynasties poets depict the boudoir as a closed erotic world.

11

The normal elements of a lady's daily life, such as servants, children, friends, family, and, most important, her husband or lover, are pruned away from the scenario. In the full flowering of the love poetry of this era woman becomes confined to symbolic isolation in her luxury boudoir. This desolate, claustrophobic setting is an essential feature of the courtly love poem.

The most curious aspect of these love poems is the lack of physical contact between lovers. Superficially, this may be explained by the convention in love poetry that the male lover must be absent from the scene. At a deeper level, what informs this literary convention and court love poetry as a whole is a sense of decorum, or a taboo on explicit references to human sexuality. Birds mating tail to tail are the nearest the reader will approach to any form of sexual relations in the animal world. Comparisons are made between the inanimate and the animate to suggest intercourse. But in poetry lovers are only permitted to hold hands on the rare occasions when they are shown together. That the poets' literary evasion of carnal love was not due to personal bashfulness is indicated by the fact that in this period, and long before, there existed arcane erotic texts and illustrated sexual manuals, the function of which was to describe sexual intercourse in terms that the inexperienced would clearly understand. The omission of sexual references such as existed in these manuals from the love poetry of early China means that sex and human reproduction were considered unfit subjects for poetry. This erotic decorum accords with the general sense of refinement and restrained courtly grace that permeates even the most daring and avant-garde poems of that era.

Compulsorily deflected from the themes of procreation, reproduction, fertility, and virility which inform many occidental love poems, and Sanskrit love poetry in the Orient, the Southern Dynasties court poet had to modestly turn his attention away from related aspects of the female physique. Breasts, buttocks, hips, thighs, and genitalia are conspicuously absent from these poems. Instead the poet focuses his attention on key erogenous zones permissible within the bounds of poetic decorum. These might seem innocent at first glance, but in the absence of overt sexuality they act as compensatory erotic signals to the reader. Thus when the poet imagines a beautiful woman he sees her clothed outline, her face, waist, arms, sometimes her feet. Although the nude form is never described, the presence of flesh is suggested through diaphanous gowns. The bare waist is not seen, but is implied through a jewelled belt lovingly described. This is one of the more important of the various erotic signals the poet employs, for when the belt is unfastened, the woman's gown falls open. Such an act is a euphemism for sexual pleasure. Similarly, the arm is an erogenous zone, and is suggested often through descriptions of filmy sleeves. Since the sleeve is of a piece with the woman's dress, to describe a woman's sleeves and her arms suggests entrée to more intimate parts of her body. When a woman's foot is mentioned in these poems it is either bare or in an expensive shoe, and it has fetishistic overtones. The sexual appeal of a woman's foot has a long history in China. One example of it is an ancient dynastic myth which tells of the legendary ruler, Hou Chi, being conceived after his barren mother 'trod on the big toe of God's footprint'. More frequent in these poems is the description of a male lover's footprints leading up the path to a woman's boudoir. This is a negative image in the poems, for the woman in her boudoir usually keeps a lonely vigil and wishes she did see her lover's footprints. A good example of this occurs in lines of a poem by the third-century AD poet Chang Hua:

> My sweetheart roams, alive to me no more,
> Far, far, distantly sundered.
> Through bedroom lattice uninvited comes the wind.
> Doorway and garden bear no footprints.
> Reeds grow beneath my bed,
> Spiders spin round the four walls.

Much of the amorous intent and erotic appeal of these images of woman lies in the reader's ability to detect, analyse, and savour this kind of inverted, negative insinuation and innuendo.

Attitudes to Love

Courtly love poetry conveys indirectly through metaphorical language and directly through words voiced by the poet or his feminine persona various attitudes to love. Some of them are the universal and familiar expressions of lovers in any era or culture. Others are unfamiliar, the particular expressions of love which reflect currents of thought, cultural history, and literature in traditional China. One of the most frequent representations of a woman in these poems is as a divorced or deserted wife. When a Chinese girl married, she bound her hair, said goodbye to her parents, and entered her husband's parents' house. There she accepted the norms of fidelity, obedience, subordination, dignified respectability, and chastity in his absence. Though her husband might prefer one of his concubines, his wife was not in a position to complain. If he found fault with her on the grounds of childlessness or any other legal or trumped-up charge, she would be sent back home to her parents. They would not welcome the social stigma of her divorce, nor the economic burden of an extra mouth to feed. They would try to make her remarry. In poetic portraits such divorced wives always remain in love with their indifferent husbands.

13

Another recurring role is that of a discarded courtesan. Called a singing-girl, or dancer, or artiste, she is said euphemistically to live in a singing-house, and be visited by honoured guests. The typical situation is that a courtesan or singing-girl has been lavishly entertained and fêted by a wealthy merchant or honoured guest at the singing-house. After his sojourn at the brothel, the man continues on his way until his next tour in the area. The courtesan is left behind, hopelessly in love with him and desperate for his promised return.

There are many similar relationships in these poems : country girl and wayfarer, wife and wastrel husband, city mistress and casual lover or playboy, palace lady and lord, barmaid and page, grass widow and enlisted soldier. What they have in common is that the woman remains behind while the man moves on. The woman usually waits in hopeless longing within her boudoir; the man walks down the road of life often eager for his next amorous encounter. These love relationships not only conjure up polar images of female immobility and male mobility, but they also underscore woman's dependency on man. This is more than an emotional dependency, the poets seek to persuade. Without a man's saving love, it is implied, a woman will languish in emotional malaise to the extent that her health will suffer. Recurring images in the poems emphasise the frailty of a woman's emotional hold on her male lover. She is likened to alga clinging to the surface of water, to a plant reaching out for the sun, or to shadow pursuing form. Water, sun, and form are all images of male love. He is seen to confer love and life itself upon a woman. Many courtly love poems extend this kind of metaphor to its ultimate conclusion by depicting woman's malaise in images of surprising morbidity.

Love is not celebrated by the court poet. He is not usually in love, nor does his literary pose of a woman in love express love in the present tense of happy fulfilment. Rather the passing of love is mourned. The temporal sense is the past. Interwoven into this elegiac mood are several strands of thought and feeling which originated in miscellaneous philosophical works. One particularly prevalent idea deriving from *The Way and Its Power (Tao Te ching)* concerns the process of change. Like other phenomena, love inevitably progresses slowly and gradually to its peak of happiness and fulfilment, then lapses into swift, abrupt, ineluctable decline. This process is essentially linear, not cyclical. Love, once lost, can never be recaptured – this is the repeated refrain of the poems. Women cast their eyes backward and upward in longing to the ideal happy time of the past, and look down toward the present and future with pessimism and foreboding. Nostalgia reigns in boudoir poems.

The idea of natural determinism is another strand of thought that imparts a haunting mood of melancholy to the poems. The notion that the cycle of nature and the span of human life are linked already had a long tradition in ancient Chinese philosophy and literature. Human life is analogous to the seasons and subject to a similar pattern of transformation. It is a convention of Chinese poetry in general, and of love poetry in particular, that two seasons predominate in this type of analogy – spring and autumn. For these are seasons when nature is in the process of fundamental change and most clearly manifests its movements. The pathos of the human condition, these poems suggest, is not just that human life is finite, but that, whereas in nature life and beauty are reborn in an eternal cycle of return, human beauty and love terminate irrevocably long before the natural span of life ends. A woman is an object of desire mainly because of her physical attraction. In the poetic cameos of women poets do project some personal qualities, but these are idealised stereotypes and are subordinated to descriptions of appearance. Feminine beauty is often likened to a flower's bloom and scent, lovely in springtime, pathetic in autumn. According to the sentiment expressed in these poems, a girl is most desirable when she is between the ages of fifteen and twenty. Some poems mention girls of ten years as objects of desire and of pathos. So strong is the poetic convention of amorous melancholy that even this tender age engenders pathetic thoughts of how its beauty is neglected. These lines by Liu Hsiao-wei (d. AD 548) illustrate this feature :

> A lovely girl of ten or so
> Turns shyly smiling, smooths windblown skirts.
> He's off shooting pearl, can't be found.
> Left alone, who will comfort her, poor darling?

It is not surprising that when court poets elaborate the facets of natural determinism in poetic terms they depict women who are so anxious to keep the love of their wayward men that they become obsessed with their own physical appearance. Youth and age create a cruel dialectic. Vanity and day-dreams are major themes. The logical outcome of such an analogy between nature and human love is that unremitting pessimism penetrates the very fabric of the love poems.

Akin to these attitudes to love is the temporal concept of the brevity of life, and by extension of love. Life is likened to the evanescence of a fleet horse glimpsed through a crack in a wall, of a lightning flash, of evaporating dawn dew, of a traveller's sojourn, or of a flower's exquisite, ephemeral beauty. These similes and metaphors conventionally appear in the early Chinese literary and philosophical tradition. Such a sombre concept of the transience of life stands out stark and grim amid poems on love, for the bleak reminders of life's finite nature only serve to emphasise the fleeting nature of romance. These closing lines of a poem by Wu Man-yüan (*c.* AD 471) are a typical example of this attitude :

> Let us cling to our hundred year span,
> Let us pursue every moment of time,
> Like grass on a lonely hill
> Knowing it must soon wither and die.

Age, an aspect of time physically perceived, links the universal elements of beauty's bloom and decay, love's birth and death, the changes of which are wrought by the devastation of time.

Another characteristic of Southern Dynasties love poetry is the obsessiveness of a woman's love. Luxuriously immured in her claustrophobic boudoir and dependent emotionally on a lover who prefers to withhold his love, a woman's thoughts turn to amorous reverie, day-dreams, fantasy, and morbid brooding. It is the very intensity of this obsessiveness that makes many poems unique in the literature of love. Poets project into their portraits extremes of feeling based on idealistic concepts of love. A woman sees herself as pure, chaste, and faithful in her lover's absence. She demands that he observe her own rigid code of morality. When he fails to do so, by staying away, taking on a new love, or rejecting her, she is shown in these poems to be quite unprepared for such a catastrophe. She rails against his wrongs, his other women, and life's inequities in general. While there is a great deal of subjective introspection in the love poems, there is rather less self-perception. This is coupled with a reluctance to soften unrealistically strict moral codes and to accept life and love on their own terms. Such an inflexible attitude toward love brings in its wake a succession of pathetic reactions among women. Cast in the role of love's victim, a rejected woman responds by going into total seclusion, by ceasing all activity (including personal grooming), by weeping unquenchable tears, by litanising life's futilities and disappointments, and finally by letting health of mind and body deteriorate. The court poets are fascinated by unfulfilled love. With unerring vividness they picture the stages of a woman's psychological and physical disintegration when her relationship with her lover founders. Through the literary pose of a woman the court poet expresses love in terms of a malaise, describing in a unique way the pathology of love. Thus, while the poets of the anthology explore the light and dark sides of love, they prefer especially in the later court poems to describe lovingly the descent into the shadows.

Imagery

The structure of the poems is an interplay of lyrical expression and of imagery, which reinforces and develops the emotions of love. The logic of the poem progresses through the interpenetration of emotional statements and presentations of imagery. Individual images are rarely elaborated or sustained. Rather a series of images is presented. At first glance the sequence of images in a given poem might seem aimless and baffling. In fact the imagery is not a ragbag of word-pictures, but a finely spun thread of connections and suggestions. The imaginative pattern of the poet may sometimes seem to be roundabout, inconsequential, even abrupt. Yet his use of images is associative, not discursive. One image makes a subtle transition to the next. Fortunately, the poets use a shared repertoire of imagery and its associative meaning. This is particularly true of the later court poets. Theirs was not a private, subjective imaginative code, a 'miracle of unintelligibility', as Edmund Gosse called Stéphane Mallarmé's *L'Après-midi d'un faune*.

The main reason why the meaning of images in Chinese love poetry in this period is clearly intelligible is that they are drawn from a common repertoire of experience. The court poets did not pick randomly from any and every facet of experience. They were highly selective. They rigorously chose details to depict scenes, figures, and objects which would convey impressions and sensations agreeably recognisable to the cultural elite of their contemporary society. The imaginative world of their poems is courtly, palatial, and luxurious. It is infused, too, with images borrowed from earlier sources of love literature filtered through a courtly sensibility. Within the bounds of these two spheres of palatial reality and literary quotation, the poets created with their assemblage of details settings that are richly and vividly concrete. Their poems have an opulent aura in which luxury objects are lovingly displayed. The style of describing this interior decor is ornamental and sensuous. The impulse of the poet is decoratively artistic; hardly a surface exists that is not embellished with flourishes and curlicues. This kind of descriptive imagery operates at a simple, literal level. The most frequent is the visual and many poems have a pleasing pictorial quality.

On closer inspection, however, the majority of images in the poems prove to be not so much literal realism as figurative fantasy. Scenes, characters, and objects, while superficially appearing as sensitive vignettes of wealthy women in affluent surroundings, also create an emotional aura in the poems. In fact the framework of the poems is mainly analogical, either directly through simile, or obliquely through metaphor or symbol. States of mind, attributes, ideas, and feelings are conveyed through these vividly concrete images. A palatial boudoir with its ivory bed, silk bedcurtains, bronze lamps, and jade mirrorstand, occupied by an exotic, richly dressed beauty, evokes aesthetic besides erotic pleasure. A woman's finely carved ivory bed is pleasing to the eye of the

17

reader; but at the same time, when it is shown to be empty and covered with dust under rays of moonlight, this visual and tactile image also suggests the woman's sexual frustration due to her lover's conventional absence. Her bed so described also hints at sensuality – were it to be occupied. Thus the image of the bed acts as an emotive metaphor charged with aesthetic nuance. Similarly, an elaborately decorated bronze censer for perfuming clothes is pleasing to imagine with its flaring fire, coiling smoke, metallic sheen, and heavy scent; but it also serves as an analogy for the wanton destructiveness of passion's consuming fire and the volatile nature of love.

There are several complications about understanding some images and therefore the meaning of the poems where they occur. The first concerns the cultural response of the non-Chinese reader. If the average Englishman, for example comes across an image of two pheasants in a poem, he is likely to associate them with a brace to be bagged. In Chinese love poetry they in fact suggest marital devotion. Similarly, to the Western mind the image of a dragon is one of a virgin-devourer which needs to be slain by a hero on a white horse. In these love poems a dragon is an image of fertility and regeneration since it is the harbinger of fructifying water. A second difficulty the non-Chinese reader is likely to experience is the significance of images based on unfamiliar cultural objects. For example it was highly fashionable in the Southern Dynasties era for women to attach to their forehead a yellow beauty-spot in the shape of a flower, moon, or mountain. There was also the custom of giving one's beloved an incense candle marked with jewelled rings as a love-token. As the incense candle burned down the rings would slip and appear to sink, evoking images of time's passage and of ardent love that cannot be recaptured once it is consumed. The poets felt no need to explain such familiar items of fashion or custom in their poems. Often they referred to them in an elliptical way confusing to the uninitiated reader. A third complication is that many images have more than one meaning, some of them contradictory. The reader has to determine if all the meanings are valid in a given poem, and if not which of them is the valid one for this poem. The dragon image, for example has contradictory meanings: it can denote fructifying power, or the emperor, or celestial coursers of divinities. Another example of multiplicity occurs in the image of the jade terrace (*yü-t'ai*), which occurs in this anthology's title. It could mean concretely a platform for performances of dance, music, and song, or allusively the haunt of a seductive mountain goddess, or concretely a mirrorstand. Customary item of a woman's boudoir, the mirrorstand must have acquired fetishistic overtones. Like many courtly images, the jade terrace is no doubt an enigmatic pun combining all three complementary associations to create a unique erotic resonance.

One of the most fascinating aspects of imagery in the Southern Dynasties is the use of a string of images to form a cluster bound together by a single unifying theme. A complex and sophisticated example of this is what might be called the neglect-cluster. The poems generally suggest that when a woman is left alone for whatever reason by her lover she feels so emotionally neglected that she is driven to neglect her physical appearance and surroundings. Her hair grows matted, her face grimy with stale make-up, and her clothes drab. In sympathy with her predicament her jewels become lack-lustre, her gold objects tarnished, hairpins disconsolately drooping. Dust palls her bed and mirrorstand; cobwebs, lichen, and grass film the house and bedroom. She grows pale, sickens, and appears moribund. So many poets draw on this cluster of neglect images, each adding his own artistic detail, that the mode of presenting neglected love becomes stylised.

Many images go beyond immediate metaphorical association and shade off into symbols. The most central of these is the symbol of the boudoir with its counterpart of the road. A woman in love is typically shown to be in her boudoir not only isolated from her lover but also from all human contact. She waits for him with a deep sense of loss and despair. She spends her idle hours in luxury reminiscing about the past, dwelling on memories stimulated by certain boudoir objects. Her environment, her thoughts, and her activities are directed toward one goal: the pursuit of love. Cooped up in her magnificent boudoir she is not free to leave, nor free to love another man, nor free to rid her mind of obsessive love. Images of immobility, inactivity, and futility abound in this poetic atmosphere. The boudoir symbolises imprisonment. This enclosed setting is underscored by the poetic highlighting of certain architectural features, such as doors and windows which usually suggest access or egress. The lattice around a boudoir's outer wall is a pun for a cage (*lung*). A passage by Ho Sun (d. *c*. AD 517) illustrates this use of architectural features of a boudoir to suggest a physical and emotional prison:

> Fallen leaves cross the window sill,
> Beyond the blind flitting fireflies are trapped.
> Full of love she lowers kingfisher drapes,
> Tearful shuts the gold screen.

The boudoir is successful as a symbol of emotional withdrawal and imprisonment because it is so naturally wedded to the familiar world of the courtier and his cultivated audience.

Diametrically opposed to this symbol of the boudoir is the 'male' symbol of the road. The absent male who is the object of a woman's eternal longing is usually described as a wanderer on a road, either as a campaigner on the march, or an official on circuit, or a merchant, and so forth. His travels and destination are but vaguely mentioned in the poems. He figures as a shadow on the horizon. In contrast to the private, interior world of a woman's boudoir, the road is outdoors, connected with public life. Man is free to walk down the highways and byways of life while woman remains closeted. Just as a woman's world is full of architectural barriers, such as doors, windows, screens, and lattice, so the world of the male is inaccessible because of topological barriers, such as steep mountains, wide rivers without bridge or boat, and vast distances of ten thousand leagues. These two primary symbols play in ironic counterpoint throughout the love poems, evoking the emotional depths of discord and estrangement in woman's relationship with man.

The Hidden Witness

The most original feature of Southern Dynasties love poetry in the context of its tradition is the technique of erotic personification. Prohibited by taboo and poetic decorum from portraying sexual love, the court poets found an ingenious way to circumvent these restraints. If a man was forbidden to enter a woman's boudoir in a love poem, except in a dream sequence, then a permissible alternative was to animate boudoir objects with a male personality. The vehicle the court poets chose for this technique was the blandly named *yung-wu* poem, or composition on an object, which had probably evolved from the descriptive prose poem genre (*fu*) popular in the Han dynasty. The hand of the court poet exposed beneath this discreet title a whole new world of sighing bedcurtains, seductive lamps, flirtatious incense smoke, passionate beds, and jealous pillows. These animated objects speak in voices breathless with desire. An example of this type of erotic personification occurs in a poem by Liu Yün (AD 465–511) in which he allows a mattress made of fine blue-green rush to suggestively peep about a lady's bedroom and make lascivious comments :

> Island in a stream rimmed with light,
> Rippling breezes down green waters.
> Though not so light as a bed of one cocoon,
> I am happy with my blue robe colour.
> Specks of dust on my lady's silk sleeves,
> Rich tiaras over her ivory bed.
> Mistress, when you drink late at night
> Bring your lover here to feast awhile.

The curious aspect of these personifications is that the object personified as a male adopts a pleading, subordinate, cajoling tone that is quite

20

different from the absent male lover who features so dominantly, capriciously, even cruelly in the imagination of the woman in love. The voice of the personified lover finds its closest echo in the plaintive voice of the troubadour of medieval Europe who confesses hopeless love to an indifferent lady. Both are the voices of a vassal enthralled by a feudal sovereign, offering homage with no hope of requital. In the Chinese case the peculiarity is that the objects owned by a woman defer to her as their mistress, addressing her as a grovelling slave fawns on the mistress of the house who mistreats him.

The court poets devised other obviating methods to circumvent the rules of poetic decorum. The most popular was punning, together with the use of erotic emblems. The most common pun is on the word silk (*ssu*) which also means love. Lotus (*lien*) might just seem an exotic botanical image, but it is also a pun for passion. The willow tree (*liu*) is a pun for keeping someone, a lover, behind so that he will not leave on his journey. The word for the fulling tool used to pound silk fibres (love) was a complicated pun for a husband or lover. This hidden language is used with great finesse, such as in a poem about fulling cloth by Wang Seng-ju (465–522):

> I leave my loom, the slanting moon speeds west,
> Pound my block, the glowing sun hurries east.
> Sweet sweat like an orchid rinse.
> I avoid carved gilt dragon candles.

Since pounding has the erotic connotation of a lover and the woman in this poem is beating the silk/love all night, inevitably associations of lovemaking arise in the mind of the reader. The sweat is the link between the prosaic action of fulling and the suggested activity of love. It is not surprising that the fourth line here states that the image of fertility, the dragon, cannot be faced because of the (conventional) absence of the woman's lover.

Another device favoured by the court poets was that of the poet's roving eye peeping into bedrooms through curtains, under blinds, across silk window-panes, and even through chinks in the wall. To the poets these insinuating tactics were a great game, and some indulged in joyous elaborations and complications of the poetic sport. Many poems are, if read correctly, taut with a nervously negated eroticism. All is nuance, hint, suggestion. The reward of conventionally oblique expression and hidden meaning in the poetry of love was that they acted as a spur to the poets' fertile and fevered imagination. The dictum 'Let nothing remain unsaid' would have been anathema to these decorous, playful poets in the court of love.

Prosodic Features

The title of the anthology, *Yü-t'ai hsin-yung,* indicates that this is a collection of *yung,* a catch-all term for different kinds of poetry. If any definite meaning can be attached to this term it is that when used as a noun it vaguely means poetry which comes from the heart, and as a verb it means to compose. In fact it is generally true to say that with the exception of a few narrative pieces, ditties, punning songs, and so forth, *New Songs from a Jade Terrace* is a collection of lyrics. As Palgrave defines the term in his Preface to *The Golden Treasury,* 'Lyrical has here been held essentially to imply that each poem shall turn on some single thought, feeling, or situation'. It is also interesting to note in comparison that just as Palgrave restricts his anthology to shorter lyrical poems, so does Hsü Ling in the main. Of the 656 Chinese poems here, 515 are no more than twenty lines long. The majority of the poems has only four lines (157 poems), then eight lines (129 poems), then ten lines (85 poems).

A superficial survey of the poems suggests that there is great metrical and generic variety in the anthology, for there are five-word and seven-word *shih* or lyrics, five-word *chüeh-chü* or short pieces, five-word *yüeh-fu* or folk-songs and ballads, five-word ancient style poems, besides modern poems, *ch'ü*-songs, *sao*-songs, archaic tetrasyllabic *shih,* and poems of irregular metre. Despite this apparent diversity the anthology is metrically homogeneous. Of the ten volumes comprising the anthology, nine volumes (1–8, and 10) are in the five-word metre, and Volume 9 is in irregular metres. Volume 1 contains a good number of ancient style poems, and Volume 10 is entirely devoted to five-word, four-line poems. The principle operating in this context is that genre is not always tied up with metre. The typical *shih* or lyric form embraces such diverse themes as the didactic, martial, reclusive, and love poetry, and ranges from five- to seven-word metres of four to 355 lines in length. The *yüeh-fu* or folk-song form had originally been irregular in metre, simple and direct in expression, and anonymous; it varied in theme from protest poem to love poem and in form from narrative to lyric. In the later years of the Han Dynasty named poets began to imitate this humble poetic form, transforming it into polished, metrically regular pieces. By the date this anthology was compiled, it became increasingly harder to distinguish between poems entitled *shih, yüeh-fu,* or *ch'ü* in terms of metre and style, at least when they dealt with the same theme of love. To sum up the metrical categories, there are 569 poems in the anthology in the five-word metre (from four to 355 lines long), fifty in the seven-word metre (from two to twenty lines), one in the archaic four-word metre (sixteen lines long), four poems in the six-word or *sao*-song metre (from six to sixty lines), and thirty-two poems of mixed metres (from four to fifty lines), making 656 poems in all.

22

It is clear from the different types of literature prevalent in the sixth century AD that writers conformed to miscellaneous literary conventions. The prose style was markedly different from the poetic, and both these written styles were divorced from colloquial speech. Classical Chinese poetry has many unique prosodic features which partly arise from the special nature of the literary language, and partly from consciously observed poetic conventions. The classical language is monosyllabic, that is words have only one syllable, except for descriptive binomes similar to ding-dong or pell-mell. There are no grammatical inflections of declension, conjugation, case, number, or gender : the monosyllabic word remains unchanged in the syntax of the sentence. A word can have different syntactical functions; it can act as a verb, noun, adjective, adverb, or predicate. Verbs, being uninflected, can carry no idea of tense. Occasionally in poetry a particle acting as an adverb of time is inserted into the line. Also the subject or object of a verb are often omitted from poetry, especially when these are pronouns. A poem can quite happily exist in the Chinese without any indication of subject, tense, object, verbal mood, number, gender, definite or indefinite article, and so forth. To compensate for the phonetic limitations of the mono-syllabic language, words are further differentiated in meaning by tones, four in the classical system (different from the four of modern Mandarin). These impart a quality of lilting euphony to the verse.

As such a prosodic system suggests, there tends to be a great deal of ambiguity in the poems, especially for the untutored reader. Some types of ambiguity are deliberately employed by the poet. Others occur when the reader is unable because of cultural differences to infer correctly what the poet intends. The usual ambiguities arise in cases such as the number of noun – is it a lone bird (pathetic) or a flock (felicitous)? Or gender – is it a male or female I-persona? Or tense – when the poetic stream of consciousness shifts, is it to the subjunctive mood from the past tense or to the future tense from the present? Or subject – when the speaker seems to change in the poem, from which persona is there a change and to which persona? This elliptical style brings to the poetry the advantages of verbal compression, linguistic versatility, universality, and artistic ambiguity. Against the disadvantages of such a style, particularly a certain confusion of meaning, several prosodic elements operate to hold the poem together. First, in most cases each line is an independent unit in terms of sense; it is called an end-stopped line. Then each last word of a couplet, or every even line, has either verbal or tonal rhyme; often the same class of rhyme continues through-out the poem. Furthermore, parallel couplets are frequent; one line compares or contrasts with the next in terms of sense or syntax, or both. The metre, usually the five-word line, is uniform throughout the poem, with rare exceptions. To this regular metrical scaffolding is welded the image, or series of images, unifying the poem in terms of sense and mood. Thus metre, rhyme, parallelism, and imagery form the basic structure of the poem, carrying the burden of meaning.

Of these prosodic features parallelism and imagery translate best from the Chinese into English. It is fortunate, therefore, that they are both fundamental pivots of the poem. It is also fortunate that the Chinese word order is similar to the English. The metre is more of a problem in translation. Where the lapidary Chinese original maintains a staccato rhythm of five syllables per line for, say, twenty end-stopped lines stripped of non-functional words, the result when translated word for word degenerates into a weird telegram or list of headlines at best, and into pidgin English at worst. The literary idiom of classical Chinese poetry cannot be left to flounder in a literal *reductio ad absurdum*. Since in English poetry conventional grammar and syntax are the nuts and bolts, things have to be spelled out in translation in order that the sense is not obfuscated. Sometimes, however, the density and ambiguity of the Chinese original may be retained in English, especially where a litany of epithets and nouns is used. In general, what all this means is that by adding so much in translation the unique stringent metre of the Chinese original is lost.

A further problem arising from rendering into English such a style of linguistic compression and consciously artistic ambiguity is that multiple meanings rarely survive the process of translation. Like all poetic language, some words are culturally bound and have resonances not shared by other countries. 'To return' (*kuei*) in Chinese not only means to go back, go home, retire, and rotate cyclically, but also to die, to return to one's source of origin, and for a woman to be divorced. In many poems such an evocative word conveys some of the multiple meanings simultaneously. Then again in a culture where certain objects such as chopsticks are a special indigenous invention, the image of jade chopsticks for tears will not seem totally odd. Chopsticks, like streams of tears, come in pairs and are translucent when made of jade. In such cases of cultural specialities it is wrong for the translator to paraphrase such an image in the misguided notion that the reader will not understand what is going on in the poem, or will be aesthetically offended. By such criteria translations would be more emasculated than they are. The image being the soul of poetry is sacrosanct.

A more complex problem is one of interpretation. This is not necessarily limited of course to the foreign translator who is forced to select one of many possible interpretations of a poem, or line of a poem, or word. For Chinese scholars and readers themselves argue about meaning and write extensive commentaries proving their version is the right one. But, as a translator, I acknowledge that the mere act of translation means interpretation and that further down the line of communication the individual reader may have his fancy stimulated by certain images to interpretations never entertained by me, or perhaps the poet himself. It is comforting to recall in this respect the wisdom of T. S. Eliot on the subject of a production of *Sweeney Agonistes*, the interpretation of which differed fundamentally from his own original intent. He was asked, 'But if the two meanings are contradictory, is not one right and the other wrong? Must not the author be right?' To which Eliot ambiguously replied, 'Not necessarily, do you think? Why is either wrong?'

Finally, how will the translator differentiate the styles of various writers? Obviously the conventional system of the love poem as a genre and the linguistic conformity inherent in classical Chinese poetry mean that the style of many poets in this anthology, especially those dating from between AD 400 and AD 545, bears several resemblances. It has been possible to keep a good number of stylistic techniques in my translation, whether they are inversions, novel placements of words, bizarre appositions, or padding. The more general stylistic question of who the finer poets are is partially solved, in Hsü Ling's view, by the proportion of their poems in the anthology. Thus his patron, Hsiao Kang, reigns supreme among the 105 known poets there with seventy-six poems, followed by his father and emperor at the time of the compilation, Hsiao Yen, with forty-one poems, then Shen Yüeh with thirty, Wu Chün with twenty-six, Wang Seng-ju with nineteen, Pao Chao with seventeen, Ho Sun and Hsieh T'iao with sixteen each. To Hsü Ling's list, with which I concur, I would add Wang Yün and Fei Ch'ang. These ten poets are the major poets of China in the Southern Dynasties era of the fifth and early sixth centuries. Tastes vary. The placement of poets, their rank in order of merit, has been a favourite literary game in China. The sixth-century AD critic, Chung Hung, ranked 122 poets in three classes of excellence in his book, *The Classification of Poets (Shih p'in)*. He marked down Shen Yüeh, Hsü Ling's favourite non-royal poet, besides Pao Chao and Hsieh T'iao, as poets of the second rank. Subjective though he was, even Chung Hung had to grudgingly admit that Shen Yüeh's poetry was popular in his own day. Today Pao Chao is the darling of the literary critics in Mainland China because his poetry is deemed to voice the protests of the people and to monitor their hardships. In the West Pao Chao is admired for quite different, artistic reasons. But the question of who sits higher at the table remains with the final arbiter, the reader.

The Courtly Love Poem as Artefact

Compared with other collections of love poetry in world literature *New Songs from a Jade Terrace* has suffered a curious fate. Chinese down through the centuries have tended to look askance at it, dismissing much

25

of it as 'all flowers and moonlight', or hiding it from public view as a delectable object of shame. Had it not been commissioned by a crown prince who later became an emperor, it might well have been consigned to oblivion. For in the succeeding era of the Sui Dynasty (AD 589–618) there began a barrage of abuse against the anthology, echoes of which reverberate still today. Furthermore, had it not been read and enjoyed by the Japanese, and in more recent years studied by the great sinologist, the late Suzuki Torao, this anthology would still be languishing under the dust of time.

Southern Dynasties love poetry seems to me remarkable, but it has been made the target of a great deal of undeserved criticism. The usual accusations against it include mannerism, shallow conventionality, tedious cleverness, excessive allusion, pretension, and ornateness. It is charged with being poetry of the head, not of the heart. All this is very strange when one thinks of poetry of different countries and eras which is prized while being mannered, or allusive, or clever, or ornate. *New Songs from a Jade Terrace* has also borne the dubious distinction for centuries of being regarded as morally decadent. 'Not for gentlemen!' was the verdict of Hsiao Kang's biographer. 'The sound of a state in collapse!' was the opinion of a later historian. 'A poetic disgrace!' is the view of critics in Mainland China, who argue that courtly love poetry is worthless because it was the product of an aristocratic society. Through this roar of prudery and polemic Hsü Ling's invitation to his reader echoes with urbane charm : 'For long hours be diverted'.

One major difficulty the Western reader may have in getting through to certain poets and poems is that our criterion of 'real' poetry is that it must be an intensely personal thing and the creative poet must write from individual experience. The love poems of *New Songs from a Jade Terrace* were never intended to be autobiographical. Court poets wrote within a well-defined system of conventions in which subject, theme, mood, and diction were already established. Their poems were meant to be finely wrought professional artefacts, embodying rhetorical techniques and distilled emotion. It would be entirely wrong, therefore, to judge them by mistaken critical standards. When the poets appraised the poems of their own era their criteria were fine craftsmanship, verbal ingenuity, apt allusion, delicate imagery, and harmonious rhyme and rhythm. The poems they admired were consciously artistic, sophisticated, subtly ambiguous creations, evincing a trained poetic imagination and technical virtuosity.

The Southern Dynasties was an exciting period for Chinese poetry. A new style was being developed, and poets were eager to show their mastery of it. That this meant observing certain rules of composition was immaterial. Most forms of Chinese literature had long been full of conventions. That it also meant employing an extended set of allusions was

26

likewise no handicap. Poetry had long been allusive and full of quotations. What had changed so radically was the concept of what were legitimate subjects for poetry. Court poets certainly reaped a rich harvest here. Going far beyond the traditional repertoire, they now wrote love poems which mentioned all sorts of private details hitherto forbidden. Tinted notepaper, a coiffure net, ladies' slippers, a camisole, a powder-puff, all became fit for poetic parlance. Although these were items drawn from daily life in noble circles, it did not mean that anything and everything was suitable subject matter for poetry. It was all right to mention eyebrows, wine-cups, and silkworms, but indecorous to mention the nose, a carving knife, and a cat. A strict system of high and low diction was in effect. On the other hand the language of love experienced an enrichment of vocabulary. Just in the category of words for a lover, male and female, there were seventy-four possibilities, ranging from 'mop-and-broom', 'idol', 'quilt sharer', 'lovely date', to 'my delight', slightly more than the list in Roget's *Thesaurus.*

In addition the technique of the court poets rested on selecting and arranging words expressively within each line. This involved sound and sense. In the fifth century AD the Chinese poet's latent interest in euphony was awakened to a new consciousness. While euphonic effects had appeared in earlier poetry, it was random and unconscious. Now poets elaborated patterns of sound and tonal harmony to create a pleasing play of music in the poem. Like the originator of the new wave of 'Palace Style Poetry', the inventor of the new tonal principles is not properly known. Liu Yün and Shen Yüeh are usually said to be their inventors. As Shen Yüeh puts it, egotistically thrilled with their novelty: 'Only the men of my generation who can appreciate music properly are able to understand – I do not exaggerate! If you don't believe me, wait for the verdict of future sages.' Some of his contemporaries claimed to be mystified by Shen Yüeh's comments on euphony, such as his reigning monarch, Kao-tsu, who asked haughtily, 'What *are* these four tones?' Still, a number of poets began to apply his rules in a rudimentary way. Coupled with a sense of the right word and the right placement of the word this musicality resulted in lines of haunting beauty.

Another technical development was the great artistry with which court poets described ways of seeing things in the world around them. Their sensuous, aristocratic imagination revelled in descriptions of fashionable luxury. Images appealing to the five senses suffuse their poetry with richly decorative and voluptuous detail. Their poems have bejewelled surfaces. Yet it was not simply the furnishings and objects of palatial interiors, the erotic decor, that caught the eye of the court poets. Their artistic imagination was also stimulated by the way these objects looked in a certain light, or in movement, or in reflection. The oblique presentation of reality became a fascinating new game. They described not a crowd of people by a river, but the shadows of their hats on the river's surface; not just rouge on a woman's cheek, but sunset red deepening her rouge; not just dust shifting, but dust changing colour as it moves from surface to surface; and not just a silk scarf, but a woman's made-up face reflected on a silk scarf. The impulse of the poet was decorative and painterly. It is probably no coincidence that at the same time as Southern Dynasties poets became interested in the architectonic qualities of poetic composition, such as tonal musicality, they also became fascinated with aspects of design, such as colour, shape, and patterns of light and shade.

The courtly love poem of the Southern Dynasties has a distinctively elaborate, formal, and rhetorical style. Rich in evocative imagery, symbolism, decorative pathos, and verbal virtuosity, the poems open a new world of amatory art. They reveal an unusual interpenetration of the material and the emotional, of the natural and the human spheres of experience – a literary phenomenon taken to even greater heights by poets of the T'ang Dynasty, acknowledged as the Golden Age of Chinese poetry. The court poets of the Southern Dynasties enriched the framework of love poetry by dint of embellishing their borrowings from the literary heritage and weaving new imaginative material into their artefacts. In subject, setting, and diction, they extended the repertoire of love. Until now, the legacy of these court poets has by no means been fully appreciated or acknowledged. When their poems have been read, much of what seemed original in later poetry will be recognised as derivative. Many claims for the creativity of later poets will have to be pruned back to allow the full flowering of Southern Dynasties love poetry to be admired in its own rightful setting. If today there is a quickening of the pulse, a frisson when these love poems of erotic decor, decorously erotic, are read, then Hsü Ling's purpose, 'For long hours be diverted', will have been fulfilled.

ANNE BIRRELL
Guildford, 1981

CHAPTER ONE

Early Folk-songs and Ballads

(first and second centuries AD)

Anon. Eight Old Poems

Bittersweet

Uphill I picked sweet herbs,
Downhill I met my former husband.
Kneeling I asked my former husband,
'Your new one, what is she like?'
'My new one is good, I suppose,
But not as fine as my old one.
In looks they are like each other,
But their hands are not the same.
My new one comes in through the main gates,
My old one would leave by the back door.
My new one is skilled at weaving finespun,
My old one was skilled at weaving homespun.
Finespun is one yard a day,
Homespun over a yard.
Comparing fineweave and plainweave,
My new one won't match the old!'

Cold winds

Chill, chill, the year now fades.
Mole-crickets at dusk sadly chant.
Cold winds suddenly blow fierce,
The traveller feels chill with no cloak.

A brocade quilt he sent to Lo shore,
My bed-sharer has betrayed me.
Alone I sleep endless long nights.
In my dreams I see his bright face:
My darling remembers past rapture,
Drives toward me, offers his coach strap.
I long for eternal charmed laughter,
Holding hands share his carriage home.
He did come, but for a moment,
Not to live within my many doors.

Clearly without the wings of Dawn Wind
How can I soar on the wind?
I glance sidelong to send my thoughts,

30

Lean forward staring far after him.
Uncertain, I nurse wounded feelings,
Trickling tears soak twin door-leaves.

There is a time
Bit by bit the orphan growing bamboo
Marries its roots to Mount T'ai's flank.
To you am I newly wed,
Dodder attached to creeping vine.
There is a time for dodder to grow,
There is a time for man and wife to join.
A thousand leagues far we are married,
Wide, wide by mountain slopes divided.

Longing for you makes me grow old,
Your high carriage comes so slow.
I'm wounded by the rich orchid bloom,
Full glory brandishes brilliant gleams.
It lives its season, but is not plucked,
With weeds of autumn to wither.
If you hold true to your chaste vows,
What would be better for me?

Fierce winter's cold air
Fierce winter's cold air has come,
North winds so bitter and cruel.
Sorrow keener knows long night.
I gaze up at hosts of serried stars.
The fifteenth's bright moon is full,
The twentieth's toad and hare are waning.

A traveller came from faraway,
He brought me a letter.
Above it says 'I'll always love you'.
Below it says 'Long must we part'.

I put the letter in my bosom sleeve.
Three years no word has faded.
My single heart keeps true, true.
I fear you'll never know.

31

Joy of Love quilt

A traveller came from faraway,
He brought me a length of silk.
Gone from me more than ten thousand leagues,
My old love's heart is still the same.

Its pattern of a pair of lovebirds
I make into a joy of love quilt,
Stuff it with always love you padding,
Bind it tight, never to sunder.
Throw glue into lacquer –
Who could ever break them apart?

The bronze censer

Gentlemen, not so loud!
Please hear me sing a song,
Let me tell of a bronze censer.
Craggy like Mount Chungnan,
Summit boughs are of pine and cypress,
Roots overspread its brazen dish.

Carved patterns of all different kinds,
Convolutions interwoven.
Who could create such a vessel?
Kung Shu and Lu Pan.

Scarlet flames flicker within,
Black smoke billows around,
Borne on a breeze it slips inside your breast.

Of her audience there was none but sighed.
Perfumed breeze does not stay long,
Only makes the orchid waste away.

Come back home

Sad to part from a dear friend,
Distraught, I cannot speak.
I would give myself to you in love,
The road is far, we cannot meet.

Man's life lasts no time at all,
Trouble reigns throughout its course.
I remember you cast me off,
New love now holds you enchanted.
Your mind is set on blue clouds up above,
When will you come back home?

32

My vow

Soft, soft the pure breeze comes
Blowing my silken skirt.
His green shirt is like spring grass,
Long blades with the wind a'waving.

At dawn I climb the ford bridge,
Lift my hem, watch the one I love.
How to be true unto 'clasping the bridgepost'?
By the white sun I make my vow.

Anon.　Six Old Folk-songs

Mulberry up the lane

Sunrise at the southeast corner
Shines on our Ch'in clan house.
The Ch'in clan has a fair daughter,
She is called Lofu.

Lofu is good at silkworm mulberry,
She picks mulberry at the wall's south corner.
Green silk is her basket strap,
Cassia her basket and pole.

On her head a twisting-fall hairdo,
At her ears bright moon pearls.
Green silk is her lower skirt,
Purple silk is her upper shirt.

Passersby see Lofu,
Drop their load, stroke their beard.
Young men see Lofu,
Take off caps, put on headbands.
The ploughman forgets his plough,
The hoer forgets his hoe.
They come home cross and happy –
All from seeing Lofu.

A prefect from the south is here,
His five horses stand pawing the ground.
The prefect sends his servant forward

33

To ask, 'Whose is the pretty girl?'
'The Ch'in clan has a fair daughter,
Her name is Lofu'.
'Lofu, how old is she?'
'Not yet quite twenty,
A bit more than fifteen'.

The prefect invites Lofu,
'Wouldn't you like a ride with me?'
Lofu steps forward and refuses:
'You are so silly, Prefect!
You have your own wife, Prefect,
Lofu has her own husband!
In the east more than a thousand horsemen,
My husband is in the lead.
How would you recognise my husband?
His white horse follows black colts,
Green silk plaits his horse's tail,
Yellow gold braids his horse's head.
At his waist a Lulu dagger –
Worth maybe more than ten million cash.

'At fifteen he was a county clerk,
At twenty a court official,
At thirty a chancellor,
At forty lord of his own city.

'As a man he has a pure white complexion,
Bushy whiskers on both cheeks.
Majestic he steps into his office,
Dignified he strides to the courtroom,
Where several thousand in audience
All say my husband has no rival!'

A grand house

We met in a narrow alley,
A path so tight would not take carriages.
Well, the two boys,
Hubs aligned, asked 'What about your house?'

'Your house is so easy to recognise,
Easy to recognise, hard to forget.
Yellow gold are your gates,
White jade your hall.

34

'Up in the hall stand flagons of wine
Served by Hantan singers.
In the garden grow cassia trees,
Flowery lamps how they blaze!

'Brothers you have, two or three.
The middle one is a chancellor.
One in five days he comes home.
On his way he creates a bright light.
Yellow gold braids his horse's head.
Spectators crowd the roadsides.

'You enter the gates and always look left,
All you see are pairs of mandarin ducks,
Mandarin ducks seventy-two,
Lined up in formation.
Their song how murmurous!
Storks chant on east and west houses.

'The eldest wife weaves fine silk,
The middle wife weaves flowing yellow,
The youngest wife has nothing to do,
She hugs her lute, goes up the high hall:
"Kind sirs, please sit quiet,
My tuneful strings are not midway!"'

The perfect wife

What's up there in the sky?
Twinkle, twinkle stands White Elm star,
Cassia trees starrily grow along the way,
Green dragons face across road corners,
Male and female phoenix sing lullabies,
A hen leads her nine chicks.
And as I look back upon the world of men
There's a scene of joy quite unique.

A fair wife goes out to greet her guests,
Her face happy and cheerful.
Bending low, she kneels twice,
Asks the guests, 'Was your journey pleasant?'
She invites the guests up the north hall,
Seats the guests on woollen cushions.
Of clear white wine each his own tankard,
Beaded bubbles full at the brim.
She pours wine, hands it to her guests,

The guests say, 'Hostess, you have some!'
She declines, kneels down twice,
Then accepts one cup.
Before talk and laughter are ended,
She looks back to the left, gives orders in the kitchen:
'Hurry up and make a fine meal,
Mind you don't dilly-dally!'

Cordially she shows her guests out,
Majestic they stride into the office.
In showing the guests out she doesn't go too far,
Her foot won't cross the gate-pivot!

Taking a wife might be like this,
But even Ch'i Chiang was not so good.
A hearty wife who keeps a good house and home
Is worth more than one fine husband.

Don't make eyes at me!
Flit, flit swallows by the hall
Show winter hides, summer is here.
Of my brothers, two or three
Rove and roam in another part.
Old clothes who must mend?
New clothes who must sew?
I'm lucky to have a just master,
He makes sure they are sewn for me.

The man of the house through the gates comes,
Leers across at my northwest room.
Don't make eyes at me, sir!
Water runs clear, pebbles show,
Pebbles show in heaps and heaps.
Going far is not as good as going home!

Today a keg of wine
White as mountaintop snow,
White as the moon between clouds.
I hear you have two loves,
That's why you broke from me so long.
Today a keg of wine at a party,
Tomorrow dawn the top of the canal.
I trudge along the royal canal,
Canal water east then westward flows.

36

Bleak, so bleak!
A bride at her wedding must not weep,
She longs for a man of one heart,
Till white-haired time he would not leave her.
Fishing rod supple!
Fishtail so glossy!
When a man prizes the spirit of love,
What need has he of dagger-coins?

Two white geese
Flying this way two white geese
Are from the northwest come,
In ten tens and five fives,
Uneven, straggling formation.

Suddenly one falls ill,
Cannot fly with the other.
Five leagues and one looks back,
Six leagues and one has faltered.
'I would carry you away in my beak,
But my beak is sealed and will not open.
I would carry you away on my back,
But my feathers and tail each day would be crushed'.

How happy they were to fall in love!
Sadness comes with lifetime separation.
Pausing, it looks back on its old flock mate,
Tears drop trickling criss-cross.
Today we delight in our mutual love,
Ten thousand years we promise.

Anon.   Nine Miscellaneous Poems

The sound of strings and song
Northwest there is a tall house,
Above level with floating clouds.
Delicate tracery set in silken windows,
Roofs in three tiered storeys.
Above there is the sound of strings and song,

A melody so sad.
Who could compose such a tune?
No one but Ch'i Liang's wife.

Autumn's pure note carries on the breeze,
Halfway her tune falters.
One chord, two or three sighs,
Yearning grief has a deeper sorrow.
I don't pity the singer's bitterness,
I'm only wounded so few will understand.
I wish we were a pair of wild geese
With rushing wings to soar up in the sky.

A melody so sad

East city wall high and long
Twists and turns in never-ending line.
Whirlwinds whip the earth,
Autumn grass lush and green.
The four seasons in succession change,
The year fades all too swift.
Dawn Wind nurses a bitter heart,
Crickets pine in prison pent.
Immaculate, absolved of passion,
What need have I of self-control?

Yen and Chao are full of lovely women,
Beauties with faces like jade,
Wearing silken filmy clothes,
They face the doorway, practising clear tunes.
A melody so sad!
Strings quicken, sensing tightened frets,
Exciting my passion. I straighten my robe,
Hum low, hesitate a while.
Imagine we are two flying swallows
With mud in our beaks to nest in your home.

On, on, ever on and on

On, on, ever on and on,
From you a lifetime separation,
Away from one another ten thousand leagues,
Each lives on each horizon.
Ways, paths steep and long,
Who can tell if we will meet again?

38

The Hu horse neighs into the north wind,
The Yüeh bird nests in southern boughs.
Away from one another each day ever further,
Robe and belt each day ever looser.
Floating clouds screen the white sun,
The wanderer never looks back.

Longing for you makes one grow old,
Years, months are suddenly grown late.
Rejected, I'll say no more,
Try hard to eat and stay alive.

Despair will make me old

Wading the river I pluck hibiscus,
Orchid marsh full of sweet grass.
I pick hoping to send them to someone.
The one I love lives down a far road.
I look back and stare at our old village,
The long path stretches vast and wide.
Sweethearts, yet we live apart,
The pain of despair will make me old.

Green, green riverside grass

Green, green riverside grass,
Lush, lush willow in the garden,
Sleek, sleek a girl upstairs,
White, white faces her window.
Fair, fair her rouge and powder face,
Slim, slim she shows her white hand.

Once I was a singing-house girl,
Now I am a playboy's wife.
A playboy roves, never comes home,
My empty bed is hard to keep alone.

Stored memories

Orchid, flag-iris grow in spring glory,
Broaching winter still they sleekly bloom.
Wistful I seek past love,
My faithful heart moved by the four seasons.
My lovely one lives on the cloudy horizon,

A skypath remote, no promise.
Night's glimmer shines through dark shadow,
Long sighs desire the one I love.
Who says I feel no despair?
Stored memories bring on madness!

How time passed
In the garden front there is a wondrous tree,
Green leaves burgeon with blossoms moist.
Pulling a twig I break off its glory
To send the one I love.
Sweet perfume fills my bosom sleeve,
The road is far, it will not reach him.
This thing of nature – why is it worth sending?
Just that I'm moved how parting time passed.

Without a word
Faraway Herdboy star,
White, white girl of River Han,
Slim, slim lift white hands,
Click, clack ply her loom's shuttle.
All day long she never ends her pattern,
Tears she sheds fall like rain.
River Han clear and shallow,
Away from each other how much longer?
In spate the whole river widens.
She stares and stares without a word.

Bright moon white
Bright moon white, so white
Shines on my silk bedcurtains.
In sad despair I cannot sleep,
I take my robe, get up and pace.
To travel, they say, is pleasant,
But not as good as coming back home.
I go outside, stroll in solitude.
My sad longing to whom can I tell?
I lean forward, go back to my room,
Tears fall soaking my robe.

Li Yen-nien

A song
In the north there is a lovely woman,
Beyond compare, unique.
One glance destroys a man's city,
A second glance destroys a man's kingdom.
Would you rather not know a city and kingdom destroyer?
Such beauty you won't find twice!

?Su Wu

If I die
We bind our hair, become man and wife,
True love sundered we never suspect.
Pleasure is ours tonight,
Happiness lasts the good times.

A campaigner yearns for the distant road,
Gets up to view how fares the night.
Antares and Orion both now sinking,
Away, away from here they depart.

The campaigner on the battlefield
Never promises to meet.
With clenched fists he sighs one long sigh,
Tears glisten from lifetime separation.

Try hard to cherish spring flowers,
Don't forget our hour of rapture.
If I survive, I'll come back to you again,
If I die, I'll love you for eternity.

?Hsin Yen-nien

The Imperial Guards officer
Once there was a slave in Huo's household,
Surnamed Feng, his name was Tzu-tu.
Exploiting General Huo's power,
He flirted with a Tartar winemaid.
The Tartar girl, aged fifteen,
One spring day keeps shop all alone.
Her long skirt with embracing boughs belt,
Her wide sleeves with joy of love bolero.
In her hair jade from Indigo Field,
Behind her ears pearls from Greater Ch'in.
Two coils of hair so dainty,
In all the world none so fine.
One coil over five million cash,
Two coils over ten million!

By chance this guardsman
Suave, sleek, passes by the wineshop.
His silver saddle so dazzling,
Kingfisher canopy lazily dawdling.
He comes up to me, asks for clear wine.
By its silk cord I lift the jade jug.
He comes up to me, asks for delicacies.
On a gold plate I slice carp.
He gives me a green bronze mirror,
Fastens my red silk waistband.

I don't mind red silk torn,
Why bother if he scorns my poor body?
A man loves his new wife,
A woman always thinks of her former husband.
In life there's the new and the old,
Lowly have no chance against noble.
With respect, Mr Guardsman,
Selfish love is just a bore!

?Lady Pan

Regret
Newly torn off fine Ch'i silk
Fresh, pure as frosted snow,
I cut into a joy of love fan,
Round round like the bright moon,
To go in and out of your sleeve
Stirring a gentle breeze.
I always fear when autumn's season comes
And cold winds plunder flaming heat,
It will be cast aside in a box,
Sweet love severed midway.

Sung Tzu-hou

Flowers fall
Down Loyang's east city road
Peach and plum grow by the wayside,
Flower and flower face each other,
Leaf and leaf each turn to the other.
Spring winds from the northeast rise,
Flowers, leaves fall and lift.

I don't know whose daughter
Carries her basket off to pick mulberry.
Her slim hands break twigs of blossom,
Flowers fall, whirling and swirling.

May I ask this pretty maid,
'Why are they being damaged?
In high autumn's eighth and ninth months
White dew will turn to frost.
At year's end they'll come whirling down,
How will their sweet scent last?'

'In autumn time it's theirs to shed and fall,
In spring months there's fragrance renewed.
Is that better than beauty's season passing,
Love's rapture forgotten eternally?'

I want to end this song,
This song that saddens a man's loins.
Let me go home and pour fine wine,
Hug my lute and go up the high hall.

Anon.   A Ditty of the Han Era

Half across her forehead!
In the city she likes a tall coiffure –
The country girl goes one foot high!
In the city she likes long eyebrows –
The country girl goes half across her forehead!
In the city she likes wide sleeves –
The country girl goes the whole bolt!

Chang Heng

Like sounds
By chance I met you, my lord,
Favoured to serve in your harem.
When we fell in love, first came together,
I trembled as if I held boiling water.
I tried my sorry best
To do what I ought as your spouse.
I tuck my sleeves up, order your kitchen,
Attend with reverence winter and autumn sacrifice.

44

I long to be a rush mat
Underneath covering your square bed.
I wish I were a silk canopy and quilt
Up above warding off windy frost.
I sprinkle and sweep, cleanse your pillow and mat,
Perfume slippers with savage scents.
The doors I lock with golden bars,
High and low I light flowery lamps.
I slip off my robe, put on net and powder,
Lay out pictures, draw our pillows close.
White Girl is my teacher
For doing the myriad positions!
What every husband hopes to see
Old Man of Heaven taught the Yellow Emperor.
No rapture was sweeter than the rapture of this night,
To the end of my days I will never forget!

Ch'in Chia

To my wife, three poems

I

Man's life is like the morning dew,
Existence full of trouble.
Hardship that ever comes too soon,
Happiness ever sadly late.
I remember when I took my present post
Leaving you further each day.
I sent a carriage to welcome you home,
Empty it went, and empty it returned.
I study your letter, feel disheartened,
At meals I cannot eat,
Sit alone in our empty bedroom.
Who will give me good cheer?
Long nights I cannot sleep,
Lean on my pillow, toss and turn alone.
Despair comes like a circling ring,
My 'not a mat' heart can't be rolled away.

45

2

Sacred gods feel no selfish love,
The good they do is bearing Heaven's blessings.
Pity yourself and me!
When we were very small we suffered desolation.
Then we came to be joined in marriage,
Love's rapture was sadly unfulfilled.
I remember I had to go far from you,
Fondly remember I told you my heart was true.
The river is wide without boat or bridge,
The path is near but cut off by hills.
I look down the road, disappointed,
Drive halfway, then halt undecided.
Drifting clouds rise from tall mountains,
Doleful winds fret in deep vales.
My good horse won't be saddled for home,
My light coach won't wheel its hubs round.
Though needle and drugs can often help,
Sad love unending is hard to bear.
This faithful man is steady from first to last,
Love and marriage cannot fail.

3

Briskly the drivers set out,
Jingle-jangle sound the merry bells.
At daybreak I must start off.
I fasten my belt, wait for cockcrow.
I look back in our empty room,
Dim, dark, I imagine your face and form.
Once parted I nursed ten thousand regrets.
I get up, sit down, cannot settle.
How shall I describe my heart?
I send my love, pledge fidelity.
The jewelled pin can sparkle in your hair,
The bright mirror can reflect your image.
The sweet scent will banish stale aromas,
The plain lute has clear tones.
A poet once moved by his lady's quince token
Wanted to respond with jasper.
I'm ashamed at your generous gifts to me,
Embarrassed these my presents are so slight.
Though I know they are inadequate gifts,
Their value lies in the message of my love.

Hsü Shu

Response to my husband, Ch'in Chia
My poor body felt so unwell,
Weighed down with illness I came home.
I lie limp indoors,
Seasons pass, I don't improve.
I am remiss not being at your side,
Neglectful in love and respect.

You have now received your commission,
Gone far away to the capital.
A vast gulf divides us,
There is no way to tell you my feelings.
Hoping to see you I dance for joy,
Then stand still, perplexed.
I long for you, my feelings tangle,
I dream I see your radiant face.

You set out on your journey
From me more remote each day.
I hate not having feather wings
To fly up high in pursuit of you.
I moan for ever, sigh long sighs,
Tears fall and soak my blouse.

?Ts'ai Yung

Watering horses at a Long Wall hole
Green, green riverside grass.
Skeins, skeins of longing for the far road,
The far road I cannot bear to long for.
In bed at night I see him in dreams,
Dream I see him by my side.
Suddenly I wake in another town,

Another town, each in different parts.
I toss and turn, see him no more.

Withered mulberry knows wind from the skies,
Ocean waters know chill from the skies.
I go indoors, everyone self-absorbed,
Who wants to speak for me?

A traveller came from far away,
He brought me a double-carp.
I call my children and cook the carp.
Inside there is a white silk letter.
I kneel down and read the white silk letter.
What does it say in the letter, then?
Above it has, 'Try and eat!'
Below it has, 'I'll always love you'.

Ch'en Lin

Watering horses at a Long Wall hole
I water my horse at a Long Wall hole,
The water's chill hurts my horse's bones.
I go and tell the Long Wall officer,
'Mind you don't keep us T'aiyüan men for good!'
'Corvée has a set time to run!
Swing your sledge! lend your voice!'
'We men would rather die fighting!
Why be bored to death building the Long Wall?'

The Long Wall how it winds and winds,
Winds and winds three thousand leagues.
Border towns full of strong young men,
Homesteads full of widowed wives.

I write a letter to my wife at home:
'Better remarry, don't stay on at my home.
Better to serve new in-laws.
From time to time think of your old husband'.
Her reply reached the border:

'What you came up with is so silly!
You are in the thick of disaster –
How could I stay in another man's house?'

'If a son is born, mind you don't raise him!
If a girl is born, feed her dried meat.
Don't you just see below the Long Wall
Dead men's skeletons prop each other up?'

'With bound hair I went to serve you,
My aching heart sealed with care.
I know full well your border grief –
How can your wife survive for long?'

Hsü Kan

Bedroom longing

Deep shadow grips sorrow's despair,
Sorrow's despair, for whom will it lift?
I brood on a lifetime parting from you,
Each living on another horizon.
Happy reunion will never have its day,
Deep my heart within is crushed and wounded.
It's not anxiety for an evening meal,
But I feel hopeless craving.
I sit straight, practise Inaction,
Faint is the light of your face.

Sheer, sheer mountain peaks high,
Vast, vast ten thousand league road.
You left, each day ever further,
The grip of despair makes one grow old.
Man's life, his whole existence,
Is swift as spring grass dying.
Time cannot be had again,
So why do we fret and fume?
Whenever I repeat your past kind vows,
How will my poor self repay you?

Drifting clouds remote,
I long to confide my message.
Whirling, swirling they can bear none.
Hesitant, I long in vain for you.
When people part they always meet again,
You alone give no promise of return.
Ever since you went away
My bright mirror darkens neglected.
Thoughts of you are like a flowing river,
When will they ever cease?

Cruel, cruel the season dies away,
Orchid blooms shed and fall.
I gasp and sigh long sighs,
Your promise soothes my passion.
I toss and turn sleepless,
Long nights are skeins and skeins.
I put on slippers, rise, go outside,
Look up at Three Stars.
Hating myself for desire unfulfilled,
I weep tears like a gushing stream.

Longing to see your turban and comb
Increases my weary burden.
How will I get huge phoenix wings
To see this man of my heart?
True love will clearly not be won.
I scratch my head, stand dismayed.
How to admit I won't see him even once,
And to meet again there is no way?
Long ago we were like fish eye to eye,
Now we're divorced like Antares from Orion.

'There is no one who has no beginning',
I dream you can make this last.
Since parting years have passed,
Old kindness how can you promise?
Favour the new, forget the old!
That's my lover's wrongful way.
I trust myself to him though far,
How to forget you one moment?
Since you are generous, not mean,
I dream I am sometimes in your thoughts.

Lack-lustre

The high palace looms sheer, sheer,
Broad roofs freeze chill, chill.
Faint winds stir by a boudoir door,
The setting sun shines on steps and garden.
I linger beneath cloudy roofs,
Whistle and sing against flowery pillars.
You set out, not yet returning.
Why bother to adorn myself?

Censer incense lies closed, unused,
On my mirrorcase dust is spreading.
Silks fine have lost their colour,
Gold, kingfisher are dull, lack-lustre,
Choice foods I've long forgotten to taste,
Fine wines also foregone.

I look back and stare: empty, hushed,
All I hear is swallow and sparrow noise.
Despairing thoughts linked in a chain,
My heart within is like a hangover.

Fan Ch'in

We pledged our love

I left the east gate to roam
And chanced to receive your bright dust.
I long for you to come to my hidden room,
I would help you to bed, take your robe and turban.
Nowadays no courting in mulberry,
But seduced by this passerby!
I fell in love with your figure,
And you are charmed by my face.

How does he convey doting affection?
He clasps my arm with twin gold bands.
How does he convey deep devotion?
He slips on my fingers a double ring.
How does he convey touching care?

51

At my ears twin bright pearls.
How does he convey firm fidelity?
A scent pouch he ties at my elbow.
How does he convey courteous warmth?
He encircles my wrists with twin bangles.

How does he seal loving passion?
Jade pendants stitched to my silk belt fringe.
How does he seal deep love?
Pure white thread joins twin needles.
How does he seal mutual intimacy?
A gold leaf painted head-scratcher.

How does he comfort me in separation?
Behind my ears tortoiseshell pins.
How does he respond to pleasure?
Of pure white silk three skirts.
How does he seal sorrow's comfort?
White silk twin under-robes.

He promised to meet me where?
He promised by the east hill nook.
It was sunrise! he didn't come.
East vale breezes blew my jacket,
I stared far, saw nothing,
Shed tears, got up in reluctance.

He promised to meet me where?
He promised in the hill's south sunshine.
It was noon! he didn't come.
South winds soft blew my blouse.
I wandered, glimpsed nothing.
Hoping for you saddens my loins.

He promised to meet me where?
He promised by the west hill slope.
It was dusk! he didn't come.
I dawdled, sighed long sighs.
I stared far, chill winds came.
I looked up and down, tidied my clothes.

He promised to meet me where?
He promised on the hill's north ridge.
It was sunset! he didn't come.
Bitter winds blew my collar.
I hoped for him, could not sit still.
Despair, anguish made my heart grieve.

52

I kept myself for him – why?
I regret my flowered season.
Our deep passion had been true, true,
Then we made our pledge.
I lifted my hem, trod mown grass,
Saying you'd never deceive me.
Now I mix with the depraved kind,
Here and there, nowhere to go.
Wounded for loss of my heart's desire,
Tears fall like twin silk threads.

Anon.　A peacock southeast flew

Preface. At the close of the Han Dynasty, during the years 196–220 AD, the wife of Chiao Chung-ch'ing, the magistrate of Luchiang prefecture, whose maiden name was Liu, was dismissed from home by her husband's mother. She swore to herself that she would never remarry, but her own parents and family brought a great deal of pressure to bear on her. So she committed suicide by drowning herself. When her husband, Chung-ch'ing, learned of this, he also committed suicide by hanging himself from a tree in the garden. A contemporary poet felt deep sympathy for these two and composed a poem about them. It goes as follows:

A peacock southeast flew,
After five leagues it faltered.

'At thirteen I could weave white silk,
At fourteen I learned to make clothes.
At fifteen I played the many-stringed lute,
At sixteen recited *Songs* and *History*.
At seventeen I became your wife
And my heart was full of constant pain and sorrow.

'You became a government clerk,
I kept chaste, my love never straying.
At cockcrow I went in to weave at the loom,
Night after night found no rest.
In three days I cut five lengths of cloth,
Mother-in-law still nagged at my sloth.
It wasn't my weaving that was too slow,

53

But it's hard to be a wife in your home.
I don't want to be driven out,
But there's no way I can stay on here.
So please speak with your mother
To let me be sent home in good time'.

The clerk heard these words
And up in the hall spoke with his mother.
'As a boy my physiognomy chart was unlucky,
I was fortunate to get such a wife as she.
We bound our hair, shared pillow and mat,
Vowed to be lovers till Yellow Springs.
We both have served you two years or three,
From the start not so long a time,
Yet the girl's conduct is not remiss,
Why do you treat her so unkindly?'

His mother said to the clerk,
'How can you be so soft!
This wife has no sense of decorum,
Whatever she does she goes her own way.
I've borne my anger for a long time now,
You must not just suit yourself!
Our east neighbours have a good daughter,
Her name is Ch'in Lofu.
So pretty her body, beyond compare,
Your mother will seek her for your wife.
It's best to dismiss this one as soon as we can,
Dismiss her, we won't let her stay!'

The government clerk knelt down in reply,
'Now I only have this to say, Mother.
If you dismiss this wife today,
For the rest of my life I will not remarry!'
His mother heard these words,
Thumped her bed, then in a fierce rage:
'My son, have you no respect?
How dare you speak in your wife's defence!
I have lost all feeling for you,
On no account will I let you disobey me!'

The government clerk silent, without a word,
Bowed twice and went back within their doors.
He started to speak to his new wife,
Stammered, unable to talk.
'I myself would not drive you away,

But there's my mother, scolding and nagging.
You just go home for a little while,
Today I must report to the office.
It won't be for long, I'll soon be coming home,
And when I come back I'll be sure to fetch you.
So let this put your mind at rest.
Please don't contradict me!'

His new wife said to the clerk:
'No more of this nonsense!
Long ago in early springtime
I left home to come to your gates.
Whatever I did I obeyed your mother,
In my behaviour never dared do as I pleased.
Day and night I tried hard at my work.
Brought low I am caught in a vice of misery.
My words have been blameless,
I fulfilled my duties diligently.
Why then, as I'm being summarily dismissed,
Do you still talk of my coming back here?
I have embroidered tunics,
Gorgeous they shine with a light of their own;
Red silk funnel bedcurtains,
At the four corners hang scent sachets;
Dressing cases sixty or seventy,
Green jasper, green silk cord;
Many, many things, each of them different,
All sorts of things in these boxes.
I am despised, and my things also worthless,
Not worth offering your next wife,
But I'll leave them here as gifts.
From now on we'll never meet again,
From time to time please bring me some comfort,
And never, never forget me!'

The cock crew, outside it was getting light.
The new wife got up and carefully dressed.
She puts on her broidered lined gown
And four or five different things.
On her feet she slips silk shoes;
On her head tortoiseshell combs gleam;
Round her waist she wears flowing silk white,
On her ears wears bright moon pendants.
Her hands are like pared onion stems,

Her mouth seems rich scarlet cinnabar.
Svelte, svelte she walks with tiny steps,
Perfect, matchless in all the world.

She went up the high hall, bowed to Mother.
The mother heard she was leaving, didn't stop her.
'Long ago when I was a child,
I grew up in the countryside.
I had no schooling from the start,
On both counts would shame the man of a great house.
I received from you, Mother, much money and silk,
I do not want to be summarily dismissed;
Today, though, I am going back home.
I am afraid I have brought trouble to your house'.

She withdrew and took leave of her sister-in-law.
Tears fell, beads of pearl.
'When I first came as a bride
You were beginning to lean on the bed.
Now as I am being dismissed,
You are as tall as I, sister.
Care for Mother with all your heart,
Be nice and help all you can.
On the first seventh and last ninth of the month,
When you're enjoying yourself, don't forget me!'

She left the gates, climbed the coach, departed,
Tears fell in more than a hundred streams.
The clerk's horse was in front,
The new wife's coach behind.
Clatter-clatter, how it rumbled, rumbled!
They met at the mouth of the main road,
He dismounted, got into her coach.
With bowed head he whispered these words in her ear:
'I swear I won't be parted from you,
Just go home for a little while.
Today I am going to the office,
Not for long, I'll be back home.
I swear by Heaven I'll not betray you!'

His new wife said to the clerk:
'I feel you love me fondly,
And you seem to hold me in high esteem.
Before long I hope you will come for me.
You must be rock firm,

'I must be a pliant reed.
The pliant reed is supple as silk,
The firm rock will not be rolled away.
I have my father and brothers,
Their temper is wild as thunder;
I fear they will not abide by my wishes,
But oppose me, destroy my hopes'.
They raised their hands in a long, long farewell,
For both loves the same wistful longing.

She entered the gates, went up the family hall,
Approaching, withdrawing with expressionless face.
Her mother beat her fist loud :
'We didn't plan for you to return on your own !
At thirteen I taught you to weave,
At fourteen you could make clothes,
At fifteen you played the many-stringed lute,
At sixteen you knew ceremonial rites,
At seventeen I sent you off in marriage,
Telling you to swear not to give offence.
What have you done wrong now that
Uninvited you come home yourself !'
'I, Lanchih, have brought shame on my mother,
But your child has truly done no wrong'.
Her mother's heart was broken with deep sorrow.

She had been home more than ten days
When the district magistrate sent a matchmaker.
He said, 'We have a third young master,
Charming beyond compare in all the world !
He is barely eighteen or nineteen,
Eloquent, very talented he is !'

Mother said to daughter :
'Go, you may answer yes'.
Her daughter choked back the tears :
'When I, Lanchih, first came home,
The clerk showed me great kindness,
Swore on oath he'd never desert me.
If I were now to betray our love,
I fear this act would be wrong.
Let's break off the betrothal talks.
In good time we'll discuss the matter again'.

Her mother explained to the matchmaker :
'In all humility, I do have such a daughter,

57

'She went away in marriage, but is returned to our gates.
She was reluctant to be an official's wife,
How would she please a fine gentleman's son?
I hope you will be successful with other inquiries.
We cannot at present give permission'.

The matchmaker was gone many days,
Then a deputy was sent for, asked to reconsider.
'They say they have a daughter, Lanchih,
Whose forefathers for generations have held office.
Say, "My master says he has a fifth son,
Elegant, refined, not yet married.
My deputy I've sent as matchmaker,
And a secretary to bring his message" '.

Immediately they put their case: 'The prefect's family
Has such a fine son,
He wishes to take solemn vows of marriage
And so we are sent to your house'.

The mother refused the matchmaker:
'My daughter has already sworn an oath.
What dare a mother say?'
When her brother learned of this
He was disappointed and furious in his heart.
He broached the matter, telling his sister:
'In these arrangements, why are you so unreasonable?
First you married a government clerk,
Later you might marry a squire.
Fortune is like Heaven and Earth,
It can bring glory to your person.
Not to wed this lord now,
What will happen in the future?'

Lanchih looked up and replied:
'In fact what my brother says is right.
I left home to serve my bridegroom.
Midway I returned to my brother's gates.
It's my place to follow my brother's wishes,
Why would I do as I please?
Though I made a vow with the government clerk,
I may never chance to meet him again.
Tell them straight away I agree to marry,
They may arrange a betrothal'.

The matchmaker got down down from the ritual couch:
'Yes, yes!' and 'Quite, quite!'

58

He went back to the office and explained to the prefect :
'Your servant has carried out your command.
Our discussion has met with great success !'
When the prefect heard this
He rejoiced in his heart.
He scanned the calendar, opened the almanac :
'It will be auspicious this month,
The Six Cardinal Points are in conjunction.
The luckiest day is the thirtieth,
Today it's now the twenty-seventh,
You may go and conclude the nuptials'.

Discussions on both sides hastened the wedding gifts,
In succession like floating clouds.
A green sparrow and white swan boat,
At the four corners were dragon banners
Softly curling in the wind.
A gold coach of jade its wheels,
Prancing piebald horses,
Coloured silk threads and gold stitched saddles.
A wedding gift of three million cash,
All strung on green cord.
Assorted silks, three hundred bolts,
From Chiaokuang a purchase of fine fish.
A retinue of four or five hundred men
Densely massed set out to the palace.

Mother said to daughter :
'I have just received a letter from the prefect,
Tomorrow he will come to invite you in marriage.
Why aren't you making your clothes?
Don't fail to start now !'
Her daughter, silent, without a word,
Sobbed with her kerchief stifling her mouth.
Tears fell as if poured.
She moved her seat of lapis lazuli,
Set it near the window.
Her left hand held shears and rule,
Her right hand took the sheer silk.
By morning she finished an embroidered robe,
Later she finished an unlined dress of silk.
Dim, dim, the sun was about to darken,
With sad thoughts she left the gates and wept.

When the government clerk heard of this affair
He asked for furlough to go home a while.

59

Before he had come two or three leagues
His wearisome horse sadly whinnied.
His new wife recognised his horse's whinny,
Slipped on her shoes and met him.
Sadly from a distance they gazed at each other,
She knew it was her long lost one coming.
She raised her hand, patted his horse's saddle,
Her loud sighs tore his heart.
'Since you parted from me
Unimaginable things have happened!
Things have turned out not as we once wished,
Nor could I make you understand.
I have had my parents – father and mother,
Bringing pressure to bear joined by my brother,
To make me consent to marry another man.
You have come back, what do you hope for?'

The government clerk said to his new wife:
'Congratulations for winning such high promotion!
The firm rock square and strong
Could have endured a thousand years.
The pliant reed, once so supple,
Is reduced to this in the space of dawn to dusk!
You may reign supreme like the sun,
I will face Yellow Springs alone'.

His new wife said to the government clerk:
'What do you mean by such words?
Together we have suffered this great crisis,
First you, and then your wife.
Down in Yellow Springs we will meet,
Don't betray our vow made this day!'
They held hands, then went their separate ways,
Each returning to their different gates.
For the living to make a parting unto death
Is more hateful than words can tell.
They think of their farewell from this world,
Never in a million years to be brought back to life.

The government clerk went back home,
Up in the hall he bowed to his mother:
'Today the great wind is cold,
Cold winds have crushed a tree,
Harsh frosts grip the garden orchid.
Your son today goes to darkness,

Leaving Mother to survive alone.
For I must carry out a most unhappy plan,
Torment our souls no more!
May your life be like South Mountain's rock,
Your four limbs healthy and strong!'

When his mother heard these words
Teardrops fell with each word:
'You are the son of a great family,
With official position at galleried courts.
Don't die for the sake of that wife!
About noble and base are you so naive?
Our east neighbour has a good daughter,
Meek and mild, the loveliest in town.
Your mother will seek her for your wife,
All will be arranged between dawn and dusk'.

The government clerk bowed twice and went back
Sighing long sighs in his empty rooms.
The plan he made was fixed as ever.
He turned his head toward the door,
Slowly he watched, grief's oppressive rage.

That day horses and cattle lowed,
His new wife goes into her green hut.
After dusk had fallen
A quiet hush, people start to settle down.
'My life will end today,
My soul will vanish, my corpse will linger a while'.
She lifts her skirt, removes her silk shoes,
Stands up and goes toward the clear lake.

When the government clerk hears of this act,
His heart knows it is the long separation.
He hesitates under a garden tree,
Hangs himself from a southeast branch.

The two families asked for a joint burial,
A joint burial on the side of Mount Hua.
East and west were planted pine and cypress,
Left and right catalpa were set.
Branch with branch joins to form a canopy,
Leaf with leaf meets in wedlock.
Among them are a pair of flying birds,
Called mandarin ducks, drake and hen,

61

Lifting their heads they call to each other,
Night after night until the fifth watch.
Passersby stay their steps to listen,
Widows get out of bed and pace to and fro.
Be warned, men of the future,
Learn this lesson and never forget!

CHAPTER TWO

Poets of the
Wei and Chin Dynasties
(third and fourth centuries)

Ts'ao P'ei

A newly wed knight parts from his bride
Newly wed to you
We had to part overnight.
Cool winds stir autumn grass,
Crickets moan in trailing choir.
Chill, chill a cold cicada chirps,
Cicada chirps, hugs a dead twig.
The dead twig swings, a moment's flight,
A bodily form is suddenly moved away.

I am not sad your body moved away,
Only regret years and months have raced,
Years and months unending.
To meet, how can we foretell?
I wish we were two brown geese
Wing to wing playing by crystal pools.

A dull ache
A double boat basks on the long river,
Calm, soft it sways and rocks.
Strings, song carry midstream,
Sad echoes leave trailing music.
The sound of music pierces the breast,
A dull ache wounds the human heart.
Heart's wound, what does it remember?
Only desires fond love deeper felt.
I long to be the Dawn Wind,
Fly double over north woods gliding.

Empress Chen
Rushes grow in my pool
Their leaves so thick and lush.
A perfect, dutiful marriage
None knows so well as your wife.
Common gossip that melts yellow gold
Has forced you to live apart.

I remember when you left me,
Alone I grieve, ever keen my sorrow.
I imagine I see your face,
Feelings tangle, bruise my heart.
I remember you, ever keen my sorrow,
Night after night unable to sleep.

Don't through glory and renown
Reject one you loved before.
Don't because fish and meat are cheap
Reject the leek and shallot.
Don't because hemp and jute are cheap
Reject straw and rushes.

Outdoors I feel a deeper grief,
Indoors I feel a keener grief.
Many the sad border winds,
Trees how they rush and roar.
May army life though lonely make you happy!
May your years last one thousand autumns!

?Wang Sung

Bedcurtains, two poems

Preface. Wang Sung was the wife of the commander-in-chief, Liu Hsün.
She married him at the age of twenty or so. Later Hsün fell in love with
a daughter of the Ssu-ma clan from Shanyang and because Wang Sung
was childless he divorced her. On her way back to her parents she
composed these two poems:

I

Billow, billow bedcurtains,
Flare out to hide the shining lamp.
Once I went away with you,
Now I have come back with you.
Locked up in your case
When will you lie open once more?

Who says a divorced wife is mean?
A divorced wife's love grows kinder.
From a thousand leagues you come, don't spit in my well!
No more than you'd defile bedcurtains you once used.
Faraway gazing does not take me far,
Hesitant doubt won't move me forward.

Ts'ao Chih

A wanderer's wife
Bright the moon shines on a tall house,
Flooding light now ebbs, now flows.
Upstairs there is a sad wife in love,
Her mournful sighs brim with grief.
'I beg you, who is sighing?'
She says, 'I am a wanderer's wife.
You journey more than ten years,
Bereaved your wife still nests alone.
You are like clear highway dust,
I am like thick river mud.
To float, to sink, each a different impulse.
To meet, when will we agree?

'I long to be the southwest wind
Coursing far to enter your breast.
If your breast never lies open
What will my own love trust?'

A weaving wife
Northwest there is a weaving wife,
Fine flowered silk so tangled.
At bright dawn she plies loom and shuttle,
By sundown her pattern lies unfinished.

Great sighs last the long night,
Sad whistling pierces dark blue clouds.
My body keeps to our empty room,

My lover marches on campaign.
He promised in three years to return,
Now nine springs have passed.

Bereaved a bird circles a tree and hovers,
Sobs and cries, calls to its lost flock.
I long to be a south streaming sunbeam –
I'd race light to see the man I love.

A hint of shadow

A hint of shadow screens the sunshine,
Pure winds ruffle my gown.
Darting fish hide in emerald waters.
Soaring birds cleave to skies in flight.

Lost to sight is the wanderer,
Faraway wars won't bring him home.
When first he left harsh frost gripped,
By now white dew has dried.

The traveller sighs the song of *Millet thick*,
The wife at home sings *How few!*
Depressed I face my honoured guest,
Downcast I ache with inner grief.

Solitude

I take my coat, leave my inner room,
Aimlessly pace between two pillars.
Idle bedroom how hushed and still,
Green grass carpets steps and garden.

The empty house gives birth to winds,
All the birds glide southward bound.
Spring love how can I forget?
Despair is my companion.

My handsome man stays on the far road,
I am alone in solitude.
Blissful meetings cannot happen twice,
Sweet iris will glory no more.

Men always cast off old love,
Will you be true all your life?
Cleaving to pine I become dodder,
Clinging to water I am like floating alga.

I tidy myself, fix belt and collar,
Dawn to dusk they won't slip awry.
If only you'd take one last backward glance
To help me ever in my deepest love.

In a land south

In a land south there is a lovely girl,
A glorious bloom like peach or plum.
Dawn she roams the river's northern shore,
Dusk she rests on Hsiang river isle.

Modern fashion spurns her rosy cheeks.
For whom will she flash white teeth?
She looks up and down, the year about to fade,
Glorious light is not a lasting hope.

A beautiful woman

A beautiful woman charming and graceful
Picks mulberry between forked paths.
Long twigs gaily stretch and stretch,
Tumbling leaves flurry and flurry.

She tucks up her sleeves, reveals white arms,
White wrists clasped by golden bands.
On her head gold sparrow pins,
Her waist is strung with kingfisher jade.
Bright pearls lace her jade body,
Coral interweaves with green pearl.
Her silken clothes swirl and swirl,
Light collar twirls with the breeze.

Her backward glance bequeaths spangled light,
She whistles long, the air seems orchid.
Passersby halt their coach,
Those who rest forget their meal.

May I ask, 'Where does the girl live?'
'She dwells by the city wall south.
Her green house overlooks the highway,
Tall gates are bolted by heavy bars.
Image of a bloom glistening in dawn sun,
Who would not desire her sweet face!'
'The matchmakers, what are their plans?'
'Jade and silk were importunate betrothal gifts'.
The lovely one admires lofty virtue,

Her search for a worthy man is very hard.
All men clamour for her in vain,
How can they know what will make her happy?
Through the flowering years she dwells in her house,
At midnight she rises with long sighs.

Sharing a quilt
I plant beans below the south hill,
Bean creepers form their own shade.
When first I married you,
We bound our hair, our wedded love was deep,
Love's pleasure reigned on pillow and mat,
We slept nights sharing a quilt.
I secretly burned for the *Cherry tree* lyric,
Sweet joy, harmony of lute and harp.

The year moves into darkness late,
My handsome man loves another heart.
Fondness severed joins with me no more,
My love has foundered and sunk.

I go outdoors, what to look back on?
Hesitant I walk through northern woods.
Below are cattle nuzzling their necks,
Looking up I see two nesting birds.
I hold a branch, heave long sighs,
Tears fall and soak my silk collar.
A kind bird knows my sorrow,
Stretches its neck trilling to me.

Once we were fish of the same pool,
Now we're like Antares and Orion.
In days long past all I met was joy,
Now in the present I suffer loneliness.
Divorce offends the will of Heaven,
Sad heart, how will this be borne?

Floating alga
Floating alga clings to clear water,
Windblown east and west it flows.
With bound hair I took leave of stern parents,

Coming to be a mate for you.
Polite, busy I lived dawn till dusk,
Then for no reason incurred your blame.

In the past you covered me with fond love,
Joy harmonious like harp and lute.
Why am I now rejected?
Estranged like Antares from Orion?
Dogwood has its own scent,
But not as sweet as cassia and orchid.
New love may be lovable
But not as dear as past love.
Sailing clouds have a time to return,
Your kindness still may turn midway.

Dejected I gaze up at heaven and sigh,
Where will my sad heart appeal?
Sun and moon do not stay fixed for ever,
Life is as brief as a sojourn.
Sad winds come into my breast,
Tears fall like trembling dew.
I take out a box, make you a robe,
Cut and stitch silks fine and white.

The deserted wife

A pomegranate planted in the forecourt,
Green leaves toss celadon tints,
Cinnabar blooms blaze with fiery flames,
Dazzling tones of bright glory,
Bright glory the sheen of rare turquoise
Where blessed spirits might flit.
There birds flock and fly,
Beat their wings in mournful choir.
In mournful choir, but why?
Cinnabar blooms have not borne fruit.

She strokes her heart, sighs long sighs,
The childless wife must be sent home.
With child she is the moon that sails the skies,
Childless she's like a falling star.
Skies and moon each wax and wane,
A falling star dies without a glimmer.
She lodged a while, failed in her duty,
Now she will fall among tiles and stones.

Despair and longing surge within me,
My sighs go on till cockcrow.
I toss and turn unable to sleep,
Wander through the forecourt.
I pause in doubt, go back to my room,
Wistful bedcurtains rustle.
I roll up the drapes, tidy my dress,
Stroke the strings and play my plain lute.
Anguish carries on echoing notes,
Haunting, sad and clear.

I hold back the tears, sighing long.
How did I offend the sacred Gods?
The Troubled Star waits for frost and dew.
Must spring and summer alone bring ripeness?
Late harvests make for fine fruits –
Please, my lord, don't be impatient!

Ts'ao Jui

Dull nights
Shine, shine white moon bright,
Let gleaming rays lighten my bed.
One in despair cannot sleep,
Dull, dull nights so long.
Soft breezes blow the bedroom door,
Silk curtains unmoved flare and drift.

I take my robe trailing its long sash,
Put on slippers, leave the high hall.
East, west, which way to turn?
I hesitate and falter.

A spring bird southward flies,
Soars and soars fluttering alone.
Sad its voice calling to its mate,
Mournful cries that wound my breast.
Moved by nature I long for my lover,
Sudden spilling tears drench my coat.

In close embrace
I planted melons by the east well,
Bit by bit they creep over the wall.
When I first married you,
Melon tendrils were locked in close embrace.

I lean my poor body against you
As if clinging to Mount T'ai.
Stemless, rootless dodder
Spreads out and upward clambers.
Alga leans on clear currents
Ever fearing bodily harm.

Covered by hillock favours
My humble self holds true, true,
The sun in the sky shining knows,
I dream that you will ever be the same.

Juan Chi

We'll never forget
Two fairies play by the river bank,
Float aimless with the breeze.
Chiao-fu treasures their rings and pendants,
Seductive, full of fragrance,
Soft, tender, passionate with love's rapture :
'We'll never forget you for a thousand years'.
They ruin cities, bewitch Hsiats'ai.
Their fair charms entangle his loins.

Emotions excited breed despairing thoughts.
The flower of oblivion they plant by orchid rooms.
Hair glossed and rinsed, for whom are they groomed?
'Let it rain! We hate the dawn glow!'
Why do bonds of metal and rock
In one morning change to parting's wound?

Gay boys

In olden times the gay boys,
Anling and Lungyang,
Fresh, fresh blossom of peach and plum,
Glowing, glowing with a brilliant sheen,
Happy as nine springs,
Pliant as if bowed by autumn frost.

Melting glances soften pretty faces,
Words and laughter release sweet scent.
Holding hands they share love's rapture,
Spend nights sharing a fitted quilt.

We long to be birds flying double,
Wing to wing we'll both soar and glide.
Cinnabar and green paint inscribe their clear vow:
'To eternity I'll never forget you!'

Fu Hsüan

Green, green riverside grass

Green, green riverside grass.
Long, long ten thousand league road.
'When grass grows in spring'
He vowed to return from the far road.
Spring came, grass no longer grows,
For vows broken I sigh voiceless sighs.

Moved by nature my loving heart yearns,
Dreaming rouses deep passion.
I dream we are like mandarin ducks
Wing to wing gliding through the clouds;
When I wake, silence, I see your face no more,
Remote as Antares and Orion.

The Lo and Yellow rivers are safe enough,
But not as sure as Mount Sung.
Incoming tides never reach home,
Floating clouds pass and then come back.

73

Sad winds trouble my loving heart,
Far away, who will ever know?
Suspended planets neither stop nor stay,
Swift as a team of racehorses.

I bend my ear to listen for your echo,
Avert my gaze, tears double spill.
In our lifetime there is no hope of meeting,
I'll see you down in Yellow Springs!

Pity me!

Pity me! my body is female,
My lowly state is hard to describe.
A boy faces door and gate,
Comes down on earth with a natural birthright,
His manly heart burns for the four seas,
Ten thousand leagues he yearns for windy dust.

A girl is born, there is no celebration,
She is not her family's prized jewel.
Grown up she is hidden in private rooms,
Veils her head, too shy to look on others.

Shedding tears she marries in another village,
Sudden like a cloudburst of rain.
With bowed head she calms her features,
White teeth clenched beneath red lips.
She kneels down countless times
To maids and concubines like grim guests.
Happy love is like Cloudy Han,
Like mallow or bean that lean toward spring sun.
Loving hearts in conflict are worse than water on fire,
One hundred wrongs are heaped upon the girl.

Her jade face with the years alters,
Her husband takes many new loves.
Once they were form and shadow,
Now they are Hun and Chinese.
Hun and Chinese sometimes see each other.
Love once severed is remote as Antares and Orion.

There's a girl

There's a girl enshrined in sweet scent,
Fair, fair she walks through eastern rooms.
Moth eyebrows part in kingfisher wings,
Bright eyes illumine her clear brow.
Cinnabar lips screen white teeth,
Delicate her face like sceptre jade.
Ravishing smiles reveal her dimples,
The host of her charms can't be litanised.
Such a beauty rarely appears in this world,
She's the Mao Ch'iang of olden days.

On her head is set a gold tiara,
From her ears hang bright moon orbs.
Pearl bangles clasp white wrists,
Kingfisher bird pins cascade pure gleams.
Her patterned coat is broidered with reed and axe,
Her jade body shimmers under a blouse of silk.

Besides the present glamour of her beauty,
Her chaste air is like the autumn frost.
Sweet music skims blue clouds,
Sound and echo flood the four points.
How rare her flower of virtue!
Worthy consort of a duke or king.

Sacred matches are made each myriad epoch,
Sun and moon now and then conjoin.
Matchmakers display betrothal rolls of silk,
Lamb and goose shriek in the front hall.
A hundred coaches crowd the main road,
She rises like phoenix in paired flight.
Ordinary men just stamp and strut,
She fades from view remote as Antares from Orion.

Dawn song

Shine, shine dawn hour sun,
White, white bright morn moon.
At fifteen I entered your gate,
Once we parted my hair turned hoary white,
Sweethearts suddenly became strangers,
Estranged like Hu from Yüeh.
Yet Hu and Yüeh will meet;
Antares and Orion are far and aloof.
Of form and shadow no faint image,
Sound and echo are mute, indistinct.

75

Delicate strings excited on taut stops,
Touch them, sad music escapes.
Passionate thoughts like a ring full circle,
Despair visits, won't be repulsed.

T'u-shan was full of remorse.
A poet sang *Picking beans.*
Crickets moan near my bed,
Eddying winds stir by the dark door.
Spring glory falls with the dew,
Hibiscus blooms at the tip of the tree.

Sad am I with my unhappy life,
From fine dawn parted for ever.
How can I bear things as they are?
Like fine white silk torn,
Like the lone hen hovering over its old nest,
Like a falling star's extinguished gleam,
My soul races ten thousand leagues,
My willing heart seeks our shared grave.

Bright moon

White, white the bright moon glistens,
Flame, flame the dawn sun glows.
Once I was spring cocoon silk,
Now I am an autumn girl's dress.

Scarlet lips line white teeth,
Kingfisher glints dart from moth eyebrows.
A charming child, full of sweet talk,
The joy of love plays around her features.

The jade face flower has its season,
Delicate skin through the years will wither.
She ever fears new love supplanting old,
Disaster that stems from nothing.

Floating alga has no root or stalk,
What will it lean on, if not water?
Sorrow and joy usurp each other,
The peak of joy must revert to sorrow.

Autumn orchid

Autumn orchid shades a jade pool,
Pool water clear and fragrant.
Lotus blooms to the wind unfold,
Among them are a pair of mandarin ducks.
And paired fish impulsive leap and dart,
And two birds capricious wheel and glide.
You promised nine autumns past
To share with me your robe in bed.

How does he ask after me?

My beloved, where is he?
He's in west Ch'angan.
How does he ask after me?
An incense candle's double rings of pearl.
How does he ask after me again?
Plumed pins and kingfisher jade.

Now, oh! now I hear that you
Once more, oh! once more have changed heart.
So incense won't be burned,
Nor rings sunk.
For incense burning daily is consumed,
Rings sinking each day fall the deeper.

A pure wife

Ch'iu Hu brought his fair wife home,
In three days he was detailed to another town.
White, white his pure wife's face,
Cold, cold she keeps to her empty room.
Pleasure was not to last the evening,
They parted like Antares and Orion.
Despair comes deeper than four seas.
It's easy to be moved, hard to guard one's feelings.
People say life's day is brief,
The mourner hates the long hours of the night.

When all plants wave their springtime glory,
She tucks up her cuffs to pick soft mulberry.
White hands search for thick boughs,
Falling leaves don't fill her basket.
Silk clothes film her jade body,
Roving eyes float iridescent.

77

Her lord work-weary comes home,
His carriage and horse prance like dragons.
Their souls race ten thousand leagues,
Man and wife meet, neither recognises the other.
The traveller in love with her sweet face
Begs, 'Rest awhile beside this tree'.
He tempts her with the 'meet a minister' ploy,
Then tosses down a bag of yellow gold.
Fierce, fierce the chaste girl's anger,
Her refusal harsh as autumn frost.

A long gallop brings him to house and home,
He takes his gold, goes up the north hall.
His mother stands and calls his wife to come.
Before their joyful reunion gets halfway,
Ch'iu Hu sees the other woman!
Nervous as one carrying hot water is he.
'To betray love, surely that's no disgrace?
Lasting vows aren't meant to be kept!'

Clear and cloudy always rise from different springs,
Duck and phoenix never glide together.
She withdraws, goes to the long flow.
The outcome? A chaste wife's pluck.
That man was none too moral,
Yet this wife was rather too severe!

Chang Hua

Tour of duty
In the north there is a lovely woman,
Grave she sits drumming her tuneful guitar.
All morn she strokes her flute and strings,
By twilight has not made music.

Despair comes, ties knots that won't unfasten.
My thoughts dwell on my idol.
My lord has gone on a tour of duty,

His secluded wife nurses a bitter heart.
First it was a three year parting,
Till now he has tarried longer.

Lichen grows over door and window.
The garden bower has become a jungle.
Gliding birds sing escorting their mates,
Grass insects hum harmonious chant.

My saddened heart is easily aroused.
I look up and down, tears stream on my collar.
I long to take wing with the Dawn Wind
And neatly sashed serve beside your quilt.

Vigil

The bright moon shimmers with clear rays,
Soaring light shines on a dark porch.
A secluded person keeps still night vigil,
Turns and enters empty bedcurtains.
His sash tied, he waits for dawn,
Sprinkled morning stars grow sparse.

As sleep embraces our kindred souls
I gaze on my lovely one's face :
Charming smiles with pretty dimples,
Twin graces her eyes and brow.
As I waken my long sighs grow keener,
Dejected my heart is lonely and sad.

Vacant shadow

Clear winds stir curtains and blind,
A dawn moon brightens a dark boudoir.
Her handsome one lives far away,
From orchid rooms his radiant face is absent.
Her breast collar hugs his vacant shadow,
His light quilt drapes an empty bed.

When we live in joy we mourn the speed of night,
In sorrow we resent the dim night's tedium.
She strokes her pillow, heaves lonesome sighs,
Endless skeins the wound within her heart.

My tiny heart

You live in north seas sunshine,
I dwell in south river shadow.
Far-flung the distant route remote,
Mountains, rivers sheer and deep.
Favoured with love, drenched with lavish care,
I bound my life to serve him I adore.
I cherish your kindness, keep my marriage vows,
To ten thousand leagues entrust my tiny heart.

Marsh orchid

I let my eyes roam beyond the four wilds,
I wander and pause in solitude.
Marsh orchid rims a clear brook,
Rich blooms shade green banks.

My handsome one is not here.
If I pick, who would I give them to?
Nesting creatures sense the winds whirl,
Burrowing beasts know of dark rains.
If you have never lived far apart,
How can you know desire for your mate?

Last sweetness

Idly I wander through the springtime palace,
Enjoy a rest by the green lake bend.
White lemna with matching white leaves,
Scarlet plants lush with cinnabar blooms.
Gentle winds shake flag iris,
Rippling waves rock sweet lotus.
Glorious glints shimmer in the woods,
Drifting scents invade silky gauze.

A prince wanders without return,
Distant his road, far beyond reach.
With whom will I savour last sweetness?
I stand still alone and sigh.

He keeps away

Gradual sun and moon revolve,
Cold and heat abruptly fluctuate.
My sweetheart roams, alive to me no more,

Far, far, distantly sundered.
Through bedroom lattice uninvited comes the wind.
Doorway and garden bear no footprints.
Reeds grow beneath my bed,
Spiders spin round the four walls.

Heartfelt longings surely won't breed more?
Moved by nature they teem and hatch anew.
Roving geese wing to wing are gliding,
Homing swans know they are of a feather.
Come to me, oh man of mine!
Careless, idle, he keeps away.

P'an Yüeh

Homebound

I live in quiet, longing for my delight;
I climb the city wall and gaze on the four marshes.
Spring grass is lush green, green,
Mulberry and thorn dense, dense,
Fragrant forests shake scarlet splendour,
Green water hits white rocks.

When I first travelled, ice had not thawed.
Suddenly I'm shaking out summer clothes.
Wide, wide three thousand leagues,
Far, far recedes the distant traveller.

Racing passion desires her scarlet cheeks.
The inch of shadow extends beyond one foot.
Night grief lasts until clear dawn,
Morning sorrow abides into the dusk.

Mountains, rivers truly never-ending,
Desire clearly unattainable.
I lean forward, ask a homebound cloud.
Sinking thoughts find no comfort.

Homeward

Alone I pine. Where is the one I desire?
Man's life is like the morning dew.
Through boundless space I cleave to my severed land,
With tender passion I remember the way we were.
Your love pursues me even here,
And my heart looks homeward to you.
Our bodies parted cannot touch,
Our souls embrace midway.

Don't you see the hilltop pine?
In dead of winter it never changes from old.
Don't you see the cypress in the glen?
In yearend chill it keeps the same appearance.
Don't say I sought this separation,
From far away the bonds of love grow firmer.

I mourn her passing

Sluggish winter bows out to spring,
Cold and heat suddenly fluctuate.
This child returns to Eternal Springs,
Heavy earth seals her lasting darkness.

Who can control private feelings?
And what is the good of lingering on?
I try hard to perform court duties,
Turn my mind back to former tasks.

I stare at the hearth, thinking of that person,
Enter her room remembering the past.
Curtains, screen hold no fleeting image,
Pen and ink bear her last trace.
Drifting fragrance still not faded,
Her clothes are left hanging on the wall.
Ghostly faint, she seems to live on.
I feel nervous, uneasy, afraid.

Like those feathered birds of the woods,
Nesting mates bereaved one dawn.
Like those roving fish of the stream,
Eye to eye, then sundered midway.

Spring breezes through a crack visit,
Dawn moisture trickles down the eaves.
Asleep, rising, when will I forget?
Deep despair weighs heavier each day.
I crave the hour of my fading.
Chuang Chou's pot can still be drummed!

Bereavement

White, white moon through a window
Shines on my room's south end.
Clear-tone winds usher autumn in,
Sultry heat ebbs with the season.
Bleak, bleak cold winds rise,
I begin to feel my summer quilt too flimsy.
I wouldn't say I have no thick clothes,
But with whom will I share year's end cold?

The year's end cold no one to share with.
Lustrous moon so glistening!
I toss and turn, stare at pillow and mat.
The long mattress lies empty on the bed,
The bed lies empty, lost to clear dust.
To my vacant room mournful comes the wind.

I'm alone, have no vision of Lady Li.
Vague, faint, I glimpse your face.
I stroke my collar, sigh long sighs,
Tears unawares soak my breast,
Soak my breast, how can I stop them?
Sad longing wells deep inside me.

Asleep, awake, in my eyes your image lives on.
Your last words still echo in my ear.
First I'm shamed by Tung-men Wu the stoic,
Last I'm disgraced by Chuang Tzu of Meng.
I compose poems, try to tell of my feelings,
In bereavement it's hard to set them down.
How can fate be borne?
Prolonged grief brings ruin in its wake.

Shih Ch'ung

Wang Chao-chün's Farewell

Preface. Originally, Wang Ming-chün's name was Wang Chao-chün, but because it violated the taboo name of Emperor Wen of the Chin Dynasty, Ssu-ma Chao, she had to be called Ming-chün. When the Huns were becoming more powerful, they demanded a Chinese bride. Emperor Yüan of the Han ordered Ming-chün, daughter of a good family and one of the ladies of the imperial harem, to become the Hun consort. Many years previously when a Chinese princess married into the Wusun tribe, the Han court arranged for music to be played on the balloon guitar while she rode away, in order to comfort her as she pined on the path from China. The escort for Ming-chün was exactly the same. The new song composed on that occasion was so full of sad regret that I set it down on paper. It goes like this :

> Once I was the daughter of a Han family,
> Now I go in marriage to the Shanyü court.
> Before my farewell had ended,
> Front riders were raising the banners.
> The coachman's tears spilled down,
> Shaft horses neighed with grief.
> Oppressive sorrow hurt my whole body,
> Falling tears soaked my pearl pomander.
>
> On, on, each day we travelled further
> Till we reached the Hsiungnu capital.
> They drew me to a round tent,
> Gave me the title of 'Princess'.
> Their foreign race offered me no comfort,
> Even their honours afforded me no glory.
> By father and son I was cruelly defiled,
> I felt shame and terror toward them.
> Suicide would not be easy.
> In silence I lived my mean life.
>
> In my mean life what refuge had I ?
> Heavy thoughts always overwhelmed me.
> I longed for the wings of a flying goose
> To ride far away.
> The flying goose would not look back.
> I stood still, breathless and anxious.

Once I was jade in a jewel box,
Now I am a flower on a dungheap.
The blossom of dawn isn't worth its pleasure –
Better to lie alongside autumn grass!
These words I bequeath to men of the future :
Marriage far from home is hard on the heart.

Tso Ssu

A dainty girl
In my house there is a dainty girl,
Fair, fair, she glistens so very white,
Her nursery name is Silk Blanche.
Her mouth and teeth are finely chiselled,
Sidecurls sweep across her wide brow,
Twin ears are like the linked planets.

At daybreak she toys with cosmetic trays,
Kohl eyebrows look daubed and streaked,
Thick scarlet smears cinnabar lips,
Yellow beak is smudged with crimson gloss.

Dainty words like fine links in a chain,
She flies into a rage, then her words come clipped and clear.
Holding a pen she favours the cinnabar holder,
But her seal-script expects no prize!
Taking a book out, she admires its thick pure silk,
And in recitation she brags of what she's conned.

Her young sister's name is Orchid Sweet,
Her face and eyes glisten as if in a portrait.
Lightly dressed she frolics near the house,
Leaning near the mirror she forgets to reel thread.
She lifts a jar, copying Chang of the capital,
She applies beauty-spots, then changes them round,
Plays at sticking them between her eyebrows.

She rushes madly to work at loom and shuttle,
Calm and composed she loves the Chao dance,
Stretching out sleeves, image of wings in flight.
Whenever the string stops are raised or lowered,

Literature and history books are tucked away.
Coyly she eyes the painting on a screen,
As if she's seen something remarkable.
Cinnabar and green darken each day with dust,
Clear inscriptions become indecipherable.

They bolt and scuttle into the orchard,
Under fruit trees pick all the raw ones :
From red corollas tear purple calyx,
Alga blebs they quickly throw away.
Greedy for blossom even in a storm,
They hurtle outdoors hundreds of times.
They stamp hard, frisky in frosty snow,
Shoelaces in perpetual tangled heaps.

Twin hearts dote on choice morsels,
They sit straight and arrange tidbits on a dish.
Pen and ink gather in a box,
Often kept far out of sight.

They constantly rush out to the pedlar's gong,
Slippered feet go helter-skelter.
Impatient for tea leaves to brew,
They huff and they puff at his kettle.
Greasy fat smears white sleeves,
Soot stains fine silk.
Their clothes all a puddle of blots
Can't be scrubbed clean in water green as jade.

I'd let these kids do as they please,
They blush at adults' scolding.
But aware that a caning is due,
They swallow tears, both turned to the wall.

CHAPTER THREE

Poets of the Chin Dynasty

(third and fourth centuries)

Lu Chi

Sad echoes sweet
A tall house so sheer all round,
Remote, sheer, and calm.
Silken windows vault the dust beneath,
Flying stairs scale the cloudy horizon.

A lovely woman strokes her jasper lute
With slim fingers pure and soft.
Fragrant breath laces the breeze,
Sad echoes sweet as orchid.

Her jade face who dares to watch?
She ruins cities with one chord.
I stand and stare at sunset,
Hesitate with one or two sighs.
I wouldn't mind standing here longer,
I only want the singer's happiness.
I long to ride homing goose plumes,
Wing to wing we'd soar in shared flight.

Harmonies clear and sad
West hills how sheer!
Layered folds loom rough and rugged.
Showering dew drops thickly from skies,
Orchid leaves fade, wilting in the woods.
Heat and cold interplay,
Seasons vanish swift as ruins.

Ch'ü Yüan hitched flying reins.
In old age we mourn the sinking rays.
Why be lured by worldly matters?
The heart within grieves at self-betrayal.

Ch'angan and Loyang are full of beauties,
Jade faces like jasper tendrils.
In hushed night they stroke plaintive lutes,
Harmonies clear and sad.
Crooning moves to a faster beat,
Sad notes follow heightened string-stops;

One song, ten thousand men sigh,
Two songs, rafter dust flies.
I dream we are birds of a river bend,
Roving mates along the fertile strand.

I dream

The fine tree grows in dawn light,
Stiff frost enchains its boughs.
Steadfast its heart, faithful through the seasons,
The year grows cold, it will not wither.
A lovely woman, so remote is she,
Scintillates in cloudy mist.
Many a time I dream as years and months pass,
Whistle long to pierce the whirlwinds.
I crane my neck to stare at land's end,
Like a flower that craves the sun.

River without a bridge

Bright, bright Han of the sky sparkles.
Radiant, radiant glitter her steps in the sky.
Herdboy turns northwest,
Weaver looks back southeast.
How silky her dainty face!
Her waving arms sway like white threads.

She hates that River without a bridge,
Mourns this year drawing to its close.
She stands on tiptoe, despairs of wedded bliss.
Bright he shines, but cannot ford the River,
She cranes her neck, stares at its great flow.
Twin streams of tears like soaking dew.

Soft, soft, sweet river grass

Soft, soft, sweet river grass
Vivid spangles grow beside the river.
White, white the pretty girl
Gracefully weaves at the eaves.
Dazzling her charming form,
Radiant her lovely face.

Her lover wanders with no return.
She nests apart, a lonely widowed wing.
Into her empty room come mournful winds.
At midnight she gets up with a sigh.

At orchid time departed

My darling friend at orchid time departed,
Faraway words are muffled.
Yü Gulf drags down dying rays,
Four seasons pass as if in flight,
Sweet grass long since mown.
My lovely one has not returned.

I walk in doubt by woods and shores,
Kind winds creep into my breast.
Moved by nature I desire my darling.
I pick, but who will have my gift?

Deep longing

Uphill I pick jasper buds.
The hollow valley teems with sweet orchis.
I pick and pick, but don't have one handful,
Faraway dreaming of him I adore.

So remote our old village!
Mountains, rivers perilous and sheer.
Deep longing mantles ten thousand leagues.
Doubtful, alone, I breathe a sigh.

Farewell to home!

Farewell to home! I'm going far away,
Far and wide three thousand leagues.
Ch'angan and Loyang full of windy dust,
White clothes turn black.

I soothe my body's pain of bitter grief,
Moved by memories of my sweetheart.
Great longing troubles a corner of my heart,
Sunken desires slumber unwaking.

Desires sunken, never to revive,
My heart troubled, never to heal.
I long to borrow homing goose wings
To circle the streams of Chekiang.

Estranged

In the southeast there is a pining woman,
Long sighs fill her hidden bedroom.
May I ask, 'For whom do you sigh?'
'My lover is lost to the far horizon,
A circuit official long not returning.
Mountains and rivers far and wide,
Form and shadow, estranged Antares and Orion.
News from afar never comes through,
Parting, meeting have no fixed pattern,
Like arrowhead and bowstring.
I long to keep my body gold or rock firm,
To relieve my constant hunger and thirst'.

Broken threads

From broken threads I weave sheer silk
To make you a single tunic.
You journey, won't you look back?
She longs for you, this woman her man.
Some time ago I got your letter,
Heard you lived in Grand Plains.
Today I get your letter,
Hear you live in the capital.

The capital is the place for flowery beauty,
Dazzling – it's a very different part.
Men usually long to wander afar . . .
Don't you know I'm thinking of you?

Some time ago when I parted from you
The year was fading, soon to fail.
Days, months all too swift!
White autumn sheds drenching dew.

Drenching dew steady, how steady!
Thoughts of you drag the year late.
I face my food, but cannot eat,
Lean over my winecup, but cannot drink.

Palace ladies

From Leaning Mulberry a dawn glow risen
Shines on the brink of this high terrace.
The high terrace has many charming beauties,
From secret rooms peep bright faces.
Sweet looks glister in white sun,
Kind hearts, soft and pure.
Lovely eyes spread gleams of jade,
Moth eyebrows like kingfisher plumes.
Fresh skin, oh so smooth,
Vivid bloom it seems one could nibble.
Meek, mild, full of grace,
Enchantingly clever wit.

In late spring their spring clothes are made,
Scintillating silks and satins.
From gold sparrows hang wispy plumes,
Jasper pendants laced with fine jade.
A line of coaches raises clear dust.
They rinse their feet in Lo river ripples.
Hazy, hazy windblown clouds gather,
What a gay crowd of beauties!
South shore full of gauze veils,
North bank thick with carriages.

The clear river drinks in reed shadows,
High slopes carpeted with flower's cinnabar.
Sweet, sweet scented sleeves flutter,
Plink! plink! slim fingers strum.
Sad song breathes pure music,
Elegant dance sways to *Secret orchid,*
Cinnabar lips hum *Nine autumns,*
Delicate steps trace *Seven spirals.*
Overture tunes quicken like startled swans,
Finale rhythms are like flocking phoenix.
Exquisite poses change with their expressions,
A fathomless fountain of limpid shapes.
Up and down they look, all soft and tender,
Backward glancing steps are delightful.
Last scents blend with whirling winds,
Floating shadows mirrored in clear streams.
Their charms I have no power to praise.
For such pleasure I might well sigh!

Magic haunts

Flitting sprites cluster in magic haunts,
Meet on high in layered mountain nooks.
Long winds lift ten thousand leagues,
Balmy clouds hover in sheer peaks.

Fufei appears from Lo river bank.
Wang and Han scale great Mount Hua.
The North summons the girl of Jasper Terrace,
The South demands Fairy Radiance of Hsiang river.

Swift, swift sky carriage moves,
Twirl, whirl kingfisher canopy plumes.
On feather pennants perch magic bird bells,
Jade axles murmur sonorously.

T'ai Yung plucks strings shrill,
Hung Yai bursts into clear song.
Pledgecups now pass round,
Light wheels mount purple haze.

They hitch reins on Leaning Mulberry boughs,
Rinse their feet in Bright Valley waves.
Pure rays flood the Gates of Heaven,
Blessings pour down on the royal house.

Along the bank

Sweet river grass grows on hidden isles,
Faint scent barely spreading.
A happy marriage of wind and rain
Has moved you to a lake's flowered bank.
Blades sprout near a jade terrace,
Cast shadows on blue grotto depths.
Now sleek with moisture rich
Your roots entwine deep and firm.

The four seasons course unresting,
Glorious blooms cannot stay fresh long.
Fair weather fails with the season,
Last scents fade with the wind.

Natural law has its shifts and turns,
Moral law lacks saving constancy.
When men seek pleasure, the smart defeat the dull;
Of women in love the withered avoid the sleek.

93

I do not pity my poor rejected body,
But fear the blueflies' gossip.
I long for your last broad wave of light
To shine on my sparse fading years.

Lu Yün

Four letter-poems between husband and wife

1

I live in Three Rivers sunshine,
You live in Five Lakes shade.
Mountains, seas, a gulf so vast,
Like the gulf between fliers and divers.

My eyes imagine your clear kind face,
My ears hold echoes of your good sweet voice.
I sleep alone with many distant dreams,
Then waken, caressing your empty collar.
Oh beautiful heart of my heart!
My love is only for you.   (from the husband)

2

Far, far away you journey on,
Alone, all alone I stay still.
How to cross mountains and rivers?
Forever cut off, road of ten thousand leagues.

Mansions in the capital are full of pretty charms,
Brilliant, brilliant city women.
Elegant footsteps, soft waists slender,
Bewitching smiles show white teeth.
Their loveliness is so enviable,
My ugliness hardly worth a mention.
I received your fond words from a distance,
I cherish the kind thought unexpected.   (from the wife)

3

Flurry, flurry windblown tumbleweed travels,
Lovely, lovely cold tree glorious.
Wandering, resting, to each his own nature.
To float, to sink, no two natures are alike.

Great love wed us in the past,
Vows of fidelity bound us to the Three Gods.
I keep my heart metal and rock firm –
How would I be lured by mere fashion?
Lovely eyes may pass, I don't look!
Slender waists are nubile in vain!
How shall I pledge my deep affection?
I look up and point at that pole-star!   (from the husband)

4

He who sails the ocean finds rivers dull.
He who roams forests finds other scenes pall.
Beauty at its peak more precious grows,
The flower of dawn mourns the passing day.

White, white those pretty girls,
Bright, bright kissed by springtime splendour.
The west side is skilled at courtly dance,
Concert halls resound with clear strumming.
Tuneful pipes ring out from cinnabar lips,
Scarlet strings vibrate beneath white wrists.
Light skirts quiver like lightning,
Twin sleeves streak like mist.
Flower faces suffuse spangled curtains,
Sad echoes pierce Cloudy Han.

Few in the world appreciate such music,
Except you, who could appraise them?
Forget your pole-star!
Solicit these Dark Dragon starlets.
Time grows late, no more words.
A wilting flower reason makes a reject.   (from the wife)

Chang Hsieh

No passing footsteps
Autumn night. Cold winds stir.
Pure air exiles torpid heat.
Crickets chirp beneath the steps,
Flying moths brush candles bright.

A lord serves in distant campaign,
His lovely lady keeps to solitude.
Living apart, how much longer?
The fire-drill soon changes kindling.

Bedroom lattice, no passing footsteps,
Garden grass a wilderness of green.
Emerald moss clings to the lonely fence,
Spiders weave webs around four walls.
Troubled by nature, keen her many longings,
Sinking despair ensnares her innermost heart.

Yang Fang

By your side
Tigers roar, valley winds rise,
Dragons leap, iridescent clouds scud.
Like sounds accord with each other,
Like souls seek each other out.

My love is close to you
As shadow follows form.
For food we share grain from the same root,
For drink we share a kissing bough cup.
The clothes we wear are double thread silk,
In bed we share a seamless quilt.

At home I long to kneel by your side,
On the road hasten to hold your hand.
You rest, I do not move,
You journey, I will not stay behind.
Like those birds of one heart,
Like the fish that swim eye to eye.

My passion aroused splits metal or rock,
Is stronger than glue mixed with lacquer.
My one desire is never to part,
That we'll make our bodies one.
In life we'll be the double-body thing,
In death we'll be dust in the same grave.
The girl of Ch'in bragged of high ideals,
My love for you can find no rival.

Cling close together
Magnet attracts long needle,
Speculum pours down fiery smoke,
Do and *re* notes harmonise with each other,
Sweethearts cling close together.

My love is married to you
As shadow pursues body.
In bed we share a close-weave quilt,
Padded with floss of clustered cocoons.

In the heat we flutter fans wing to wing,
In the cold we sit on rugs side by side.
You laugh, I'm sure to smile,
You're sad, I feel no joy.

Coming I tread in your footprints,
Going I walk in your dust.
We are like the fabled double creature,
No matter what, we'll never lose each other.

All I desire is never to part,
That our bodies will become one.
In life we'll share a happy home,
In death be joint grave dwellers.
Lady Hsü bragged of high ideals,
My love can find no words.

An empty room
I sit alone in an empty room.
Sorrow has many thousand beginnings.
Sad echoes answer sorrowful sighs,
Unhappy tears respond to bitter words.

I wander and gaze all around,
The white sun enters western hills.
My mistress I do not see coming,
I only see birds flying home.
Flying birds so joyful,
At dusk they rest, each to his own flock.

Crystalline
Flying Chestnut champs long reins,
Winging, winging turns the light wheels.
My lover looks down as he fords green flowing torrents,
Looks up as he crosses the hill's nine folds.
The long path is winding and perilous,
Autumn plants grow on both sides.

Yellow blooms like heaps of gold,
White flowers like scattered silver,
Green buds shoot kingfisher tints,
Crimson corollas image red clouds.

And in their midst dew-laden boughs,
Purple blossoms enshrining plain scent
Hang luxurious in patterns crystalline,
Wafting fragrance and freshness.

My eyes grow dizzy with glorious designs,
My mind whirls with wondrous colours.
I soothe my heart, mourn the lone traveller,
Look down and up, feel self-pity.
I pause with a sigh by the garden wall,
Take my pen and compose this verse.

Fine tree
My south neighbour has a fine tree,
It greets the sun, stretches white blooms,
Sleek fronds sheathe long boughs,

Green leaves screen red stems.
With the wind it breathes faint whispers,
Perfumed air pierces purple mist.

My heart burns for this tree,
I long to move it near my home.
At dusk I would stroll underneath,
At dawn caress its corollas.

How deep and firm the roots!
So mean and low my home!
To transplant it is a hopeless dream,
The sighs I sigh, what good are they?

Wang Chien

Seventh Night

Herdboy is sad in his alien lodge,
Weaver mourns in her exiled home.
Once a year the promise of one night,
This promise of true pleasure.

Majestic the Dark Gates open
To flying arcades massed in crested peaks.
Rumble, rumble a thousand coaches coursing,
Rattle, rattle across the starry stream.
Six dragons strain at jasper reins,
Streaked serpents bear her jade carriage.

Flaming Cinnabar raises her jasper torch,
White Girl holds nephrite blooms.
Crimson banners seem to shoot lightning,
Scarlet canopies appear like swaying mist.
Cloud gate, Nine chord, how the fanfare roars!
Drums of the gods beat measured rhythms.

She stops her coach, turns her gaze on high,
Looks back for me on sheer cliffs.
Soaked in sweet dew moist

99

His favour, enriched with orchid breezes.
Till daybreak they pleasure together,
Phoenixes fluttering circle round.

We pleasure as one in joy not ours to share,
Memories of you deepen sorrow's pain.
Humbly I implore through the Trinity Prayer,
That you may join Consort O.

Li Ch'ung

Parody of a lover
Sweethearts, we felt the same pleasure,
So deeply were we involved.
You sensed my desire,
And I guessed your heart.

Serene years went by
Harmonious as lute and harp.
Good times did not keep me company,
Midway we grew distant like Antares and Orion.
You separated south of northern hills,
I separated south of south river.
Happy joy no longer sought,
Heavy thoughts, how to bear them?

My eyes carry the charm of your image fair,
My ears hold the beauty of your clear voice.
Through the day endless memories surge,
Far into night I sigh in lonely grief.

When you departed on circuit
And said we must part, tears soaked my collar.
Please honour me with your jade footsteps,
One look is more than a thousand in gold.

Ts'ao P'i

In the night I hear fulling
Cold begins. Preparing white silk
Lovely women make robes and quilts ready
On wintry nights clear and long
When the white moon shines in dark halls.

Slim hands fold light silks,
Staccato pounders strike ringing blocks,
Pure winds waft complex rhythms,
Gusts sprinkle faint humming.

I sigh for time's swift flow,
Mourn for the heart's dark tedium.
Pounder and block trouble my breast –
Are these things mere sound and noise?

T'ao Ch'ien

She drinks deep and sings
Sunset, cloudless skies,
Spring breezes fan faint warmth.
A beauty, lovely in clear night,
Till dawn she drinks deep and sings.
Her singing ends, she sighs long sighs,
For these disturb her more.
Bright, bright moon between clouds,
Sparkling, sparkling flowers among leaves.
Don't the best things come but once?
They don't last, what can we do?

Hsün Ch'ang

A grand house

Dawn stirs Hantan city.
Dusk brings quiet to Wellpath.
Wellpath so narrow,
Horse and coach cannot move.

Suddenly I happen to meet you,
We exchange a word on the rough track,
A word, no room for more.
I lean on the rail, ask about your house.

Your house is easy to recognise,
Easy to recognise and easy to find.
South it fronts onto Lord P'ingyüan's residence,
North it runs to Lin Hsiang-ju's pavilion.

Flying storeys overlook the famed city,
Avenue gates lean over flowery suburbs.
You enter the gates, not a soul to be seen,
All you see are pairs of roosting storks.
Roosting storks in several tens
And mandarin ducks flocked in rows.

Your oldest brother wears gold earrings,
Your middle brother flaunts capstring tassels.
Summer and winter feastdays they come home
And neighbouring hamlets grow in splendour.
Your youngest brother has nothing to do
But go to cockfights at east lane crossroads.

The eldest's wife weaves fine silks,
The next wife sews sheer robes,
The youngest wife has nothing to do
But hug her lute and play sonorous stops.
'Kind sirs, don't leave your seats,
Rafter dust is going to fly!'

Green, green riverside grass
Glow, glow fires on the hill.
Faraway Lung East remote.
Lung East is out of reach,
Our souls become one as we sleep.

As we sleep we share quilt and bedcurtain,
Suddenly I wake in another land.
Another land, each in a strange city.
I seek but never find you.
Lost in a wilderness I stand and stare through smoke.
Trees have shed, I sense the ice is hard.

Up at court each man is bent on self-advancement.
Who will want to promote you?
A traveller came from the north,
He brought me a piece of thick black silk.
I asked my maid to open the black silk,
Inside was an embossed cryptic jade disc.
I bowed low and read the cryptic disc,
The words were bitter, the tone painful.
At the top it said, 'Let's both try to cheer up'.
Underneath it said, 'I'll always love you'.

Wang Wei

What do I desire?
A lone mulberry girl, what do I desire?
In my tilted basket not yet one handful.
I confess my sorrows are many,
I brush them aside, they won't go away.

Mine is a sorrow that cannot be told,
My burden of grief will not disappear.
A cold goose migrates where I would follow,
Midway has lost her helpmate.

Impetuous he clapped and galloped off,
Wildly in defence of court and altar.
He ever yearned to cleanse the Han shame,
Ever wished to restore Chou glory.
Prizing fame he sought his memorial,
Scorning life he desired a hero's epitaph.
Ten thousand leagues he crossed through desert,
With far-flung troops trod the northern wastes.

I heard tell of troops defeated,
Saw no one come back home.
Where did they bury the flags?
Where were horse and chariot interred?

I soothe my heart, mourn my honest man,
Falling tears mask my face.
I only thought we would be parted long,
Never dreamed of lasting widowhood.
Soft, soft I shut the tall gates;
Alone, alone, empty wide eaves.
I waited for you, you did not come home,
Serene I go now to my coffin.

Who will know?

A pining woman leans from a tall terrace,
Distant dreams yearn from flowery eaves.
She strums strings, her tune not finished,
Sad songs bid goodbye to wounding words.

His dust-and-mop deserted by the river,
Her lover living at Goose Gate Pass.
Why dwell on his robeless misery?
All she knows is white fox-fur warmth.

Day darkens, cattle and sheep move down,
Birds of the wild fill the empty orchard.
Fierce winter's cold winds stir,
East Wall star appears due south in dusk.

Scarlet flame, shine on a lonely one,
Embrace my shadow's sad regret.
Who will know the tempest deep in my heart?
With my beloved I cannot speak.

104

Hsieh Hui-lien

The Seventh

The sinking sun hides behind eaves and pillars,
The soaring moon illumines bedroom lattice.
Drip, drop, dew on leaves,
Creak, creak wind tossing boughs.

I stamp my feet down the wide courtyard,
Blink as I gaze at the serried dome.
In Cloudy Han there's the divine couple,
They pass the year waning in pursuit.

The distant river thwarts their passionate love,
The long shore dims his clear image.
She works her shuttle, never ends her pattern,
She tugs the reins, gallops swiftly forward.

They parted long ago, two autumns now,
They meet tonight, a night that won't be double.
The sloping river she easily circles,
The face of desire not long enjoyed.

Glossy her coach divine glides round,
Soft veils of cloud form a void.
Forlorn love looks back to flowery sleep,
His faraway heart follows her racing dragons.
I sigh, deeply moved by you,
Profound feeling makes my love the keener.

Fulling cloth

Scales' cycle does not stay its course,
Time's motion suddenly seems to hasten.
White dew soaks orchard chrysanthemum,
Autumn winds make garden locust trees shed.
Twitch, twitch grasshopper wings,
Chill, chill cold cicada cry.
Darkness of dusk wreathes empty curtains,
Gloaming moon whitens an inner bedroom.

105

A lovely woman prepares clothes,
Neatly groomed she holds her friend's hand.
Hairpin jade leaves the north room,
Tinkling gold treads down south stairs.

Verandahs tall with fulling-block echoes ring,
Pillars long with pounder thuds moan.
Faint perfume lifts from two sleeves,
Light sweat glistens on twin brows.

Fine white silk is now ready,
Her lord journeys, not yet home.
For cutting she uses cabinet scissors,
Sewing she makes his ten thousand league robe.
Snugly encased with her own hands,
Tightly sealed, patient for her lord to open.
'My waist sash measures the same as long ago –
I don't know today if that is good or bad'.

A gown near my body
A traveller came from far away,
He brought me goose-pattern damask,
Stored in a loving you case
Tied with sweetheart string.

I cut it into a gown near my body,
Stuffed it with sleeping together floss.
Since you left years have passed,
My passion can journey no further.

Sprinkle some wine in a well –
Who can tell water from wine?
Mix water from two rivers in a cup –
Who can judge Tzu river from the Sheng?

Liu Shuo

On, on, ever on and on
On, on, brave the long road.
Far, far, travel further on.
He turns his coach away from the capital,
Waves farewell to all that.

In the hall shifting dust will spread,
In the garden green grass will flourish.
Cold cicadas flit across the river bend,
Autumn hares hug the foothills.

The fragrant season has a flowery moon.
My lovely one gives no promise of return.
Twilight's cool wind stirs,
I face wine in love with you for ever.
Sorrow pours forth in *Chiangnan song*,
Despair is banished by *Your collar* poem.

Lying down I watch the bright lamp dimming,
Sitting up I see my light silk is dingy.
Tearful face long unadorned,
Darkened mirror I can no longer polish.
Please send down last wan rays
To brighten my Mulberry-Elm time.

Bright moon white
Sinking stars halfway over far walls,
Floating clouds veil serried turrets.
From the jade vault come pure winds,
Silk curtains reach out to the autumn moon.

Wrapped in thought she dreams of that man,
Sunk in despair she longs for day to break.
Who'd have thought a man would travel so long?
Many a time she sees flowing fragrance fade.
Waters wide, river without a bridge,
Mountains high, paths denying passage.

107

Fierce winter's cold air comes
White dew, autumn winds start,
Autumn winds, the bright moon is new,
Bright moon shining on tall storeys,
White dew blanching dark porches.
Now is the time cold clouds rise.
As I walk I see chill woods bare.

A traveller came from far away,
He brought me a thousand league letter.
First it said, 'I long for my old love'.
Last it stated, 'Long must we live apart'.
The first time its meaning was not quite clear,
The third time my heart was overflowing.
Please grant me a life of fond regard,
Don't let your sweet words prove hollow!

Green, green riverside grass
Bleak, bleak Sip Dew Terrace,
Brisk, brisk Welcome Breeze Lodge.
A pining girl goes out to curved eaves,
Her sad heart transfixes Cloudy Han.
She strokes sad strings and weeps,
Lone she faces bright lamps and sighs.
Her beloved has been on campaign long,
Virginal pure she passes dusk to dawn.
Sharp and clear her *Autumn river* song,
Wistful, wistful *Picking caltrop* strumming.

Herdboy and Weaver stars
Autumn surges, clear winds fan,
Fire star veers, fiery air subsides.
Wide lattice sips shadows of night,
Tall eaves touch the evening moon.

Gentle she steps, circling scented woods,
Upward she stares beyond cloudy turrets.
Fringed drapes rimming Han unfold,
Her dragon coach crowning the skies emerges.

Who says Long river is distant?
It's just as soon crossed as a mat!
Before their deep love has been told,
Fleeting light suddenly flickers.
Tomorrow's meeting is remote, hopeless.
Today's joy from this hour is dead.

CHAPTER FOUR

Poets of the Southern Dynasties
(early fifth century)

Wang Seng-ta

Beneath the moon on Seventh Night
Over faraway hills swirling mist thickens,
On a broad garden rippling moonlight streams.
Summer air subsides, winds press through cracks,
Autumn returns, dew glistens on the bough.
Now the hot season is fading
She shakes out sheer silk mid-heaven.
The joy to come only lasts one night,
Gathering tears spill on the River that divides.

Yen Yen-chih

Weaver's poem to Herdboy
Wunü couples with Warp stars,
Ch'ang O nestles on the gliding moon.
I'm ashamed not to have the power of these beauties
To change shape and serve by Heaven's towers.
The Gates of Heaven are not shining yet,
How can I wash my hair in Hsien pool?
On Han's dark south night curtains are not drawn,
For whom will I cross Long River?
Though there's promise of a feast soon,
I must wait for cold winds to blow.
I count in vain the Two Discs' revolutions,
Idly languish while Three Stars fade.
I don't resent shuttle and spindle labours,
I just think how flowery fragrance fades.

A pure wife

Catalpa lean toward lofty phoenix,
Cold Valley waits for singing pipes.
Shadow and echo, don't they fall in love?
All mates love, distant though they are.
Lovely the girl in her hidden room
When she became wife in her lord's home.
Strict her virtue, taut with autumn frost,
Radiant her beauty, like the morning sun.
'Good fortune is with us now,
We dearly hope it lasts to the end of our days'.

They lived in bliss, but before each knew the other well
Her beloved had to go on a journey long.
He removed his headband to go beyond ten thousand leagues,
Tied on official ribbons to go up to the royal domain.
He ordered his servants to come at break of dawn,
His followers all came to his side.
Driven in his coach he left the suburbs,
His path slow and winding.
If he lived, they would be parted long,
If he died, he would nevermore return.

Oh I hate official travel!
Three hills I suffer from dawn to dark.
Hitching coaches tight we trek through winds chill,
Unsaddling we brave frosty dew.
High plains, wet lowlands redouble our misery,
Whirlwinds roll tall trees.
Scattered beasts appear in wild trails,
Frightened birds flee in panic.
Wretched the man on official circuit,
As he struggles along paths of crag and creek.

Far away the traveller grows distant,
Smoothly roll the years away.
Happy hours turned to such a parting,
Days and months are drawing close to summer.
Who knows how many seasons hot and cold?
In a glance I see nature bloom and wither.
The year ends, I go toward my empty room,
Cold winds stir from the corners.
In bed or rising I feel the days grow colder,
White frost spreads over garden weeds.

113

I worked hard, but gave in to homeward thoughts,
The road back skirts hills and rivers.
Long ago I said goodbye before autumn whitened,
Now is the season of flowers.
In silkworm months I see a time of rest,
In mulberry fields all is busy movement.
A lovely girl doing her work,
Graceful she draws high branches down.
Who would not look back at her city-razing beauty?
I slow my pace, pause halfway up the ridge.

Years have passed. Such pining they had suffered!
His work was distant, word and image remote.
Though it was a five-year separation,
Each was a stranger to the other's normal life.
He leaves his coach, treads his old path,
A duck among waterplants he gives a quick wink.
Southern gold he by no means undervalues,
But at such a time he counts it as little!
Married love brings many sorrows.
He whispers words of gold and jade.

Her high principles forbid him to dally.
At long last he leaves her, nothing won.
Slow, slow he covers the old path,
Eager, eager he reaches his gate-post.
Going up the hall he offers respectful greetings,
Entering his room he asks, 'Where's my wife?'
'At sunset she comes home from picking,
At nature's Mulberry-Elm time'.
A beautiful woman arrives toward dusk.
He gasps with shock – he'd been with her before!

Who can stop love once love happens?
Let's tell of this wife's own hardship.
We lived apart year in, year out.
Once parted, river and pass blocked our way.
Spring comes, perhaps he no longer enjoys it?
Autumn falls, he must feel cold sooner?
Till daybreak I fret my sad heart away,
In my room I rise with long sighs.
The year is dark in my bitter anguish,
The sun has set upon my wanderer's face.

Playing high notes causes broken strings,
Intense music comes from high-pitched chords.
Long ago when I enjoyed your bright dust
We vowed to be true from first to last.
Aren't you who made our parting so long
To blame for all that's gone wrong?
Since you betrayed our pure marriage,
With whom will I end my days?
Disgraced like the *Dewdrops* woman
I'd better drown myself in the long river.

Pao Chao

Admiring the moon from the west city gate
First seen over southwest houses,
Fine, fine as a jade hook;
Later reflected on a northeast porch,
Soft, soft like a moth eyebrow.
Moth eyebrows screened by pearl grilles,
Jade hooks set apart by silken windows.
At the time of the fifteenth and sixteenth
It shines one thousand leagues on you and me alike.
Night moves on, Scales and Han stars set,
It shimmers still through curtained doors.
Fallen flowers early destroyed by dew,
Loosened leaves soon dismissed by winds.

A man on travels hates the hardship, and
This official is weary of windblown dust.
Happily today I'm free from work,
A time for feasting at my own pleasure.
Shu lutes play *White snow*,
Ying melodies render *Sunny spring*.
Fine food has been eaten, wine not run out,
The gold clock-jar starts its evening trickle.
I turn my coach, fix its light canopy,
Linger over drinks and wait for my darling.

Loyang capital

Phoenix houses twelve deep
With four doors and eight silk windows,
Broidered rafters with golden lotus,
Cassia pillars with jade coiling dragons,
Pearl blinds that don't keep out the dew,
Sheer drapes that don't ward off the wind,
Exquisite curtains in thirty million rooms –
All for your face one morning!

You spread fragrance upon purple smoke,
Drop bright colour through its green clouds.
Spring piping turns the white sun back,
Frost-time singing makes rampart geese fly down.
All I fear is autumn dust will rise,
Love's bloom will follow withered tumbleweed.
When I sit up I see green lichen's rank fullness,
When I lie down I face mattress brocade emptiness.
Lutes, guitars jumbled in heaps,
Dance robes hanging unsewn.
Since time began love always withers,
How will your love alone thrive?
Just watch that pair of brown geese
Follow each other a thousand leagues.

Jealous hate

Straight as silk of scarlet strings,
Pure as ice in a jade jar,
Why should I be ashamed of past love?
Jealous hate wells up inside me.
People in love despise favours grown old,
Public opinion shuns failure, courts success.
Once a flaw minute as a hair appears
Even mountains won't fail to crumble.

The seedling gobbler is the big rat,
The whiteness smircher is the bluebottle.
Ducks and geese from afar become prized,
Firewood and feed are valued out of all proportion.
Queen Shen was deposed when Paossu was promoted.
Lady Pan retired when Chao Feiyen was in ascendance.
Each day the king of Chou sank deeper in obsession.
The Han emperor sang her praises ever louder.
Their doting admiration was unreliable,

A courteous veneer is not something to trust.
Since time began it has been like this,
You aren't the only one beating your breast!

Picking mulberry

Late spring plum starts falling,
Women's work turns to silkworm care.
They pick mulberry between Ch'i and Wei rivers,
Or play near Upper Palace pavilion.
Early reedmace weaves timely shade,
Late bamboo begins to shed bark.
Hazy, hazy mists fill boudoirs,
Soft, soft sunlight floods curtains.
Nursing swallows hunt for insects,
Bees harvest petals for their hives.
This is the season of warmest charms,
Once again beauty's dress is dazzling fresh.

I silence my sighs, face the distant road,
Pour out my song, play *Beanleaves in my patch*,
Pluck my lute, try to soothe my pining.
I offer you my girdle, trust myself to you.
Please praise my song like the man from Ying!
In my faithful heart I'm thankful for your favour.
Wei songs have always been thought depraved,
Cheng morals long considered debauched.
I'm saddened by Ch'ü Yüan's empty dream of crossing the Hsiang,
I smile at Ts'ao Chih's futile poem on fording Lo river.
The season of blooms never comes twice;
Deepest love no one can exhaust.
You, my lord, strum the strings
While I pour you cassia wine!

Dreaming of home

Biting back tears I leave the suburb gate,
Stroke my sword at deserted crossroads.
Sandy winds rise dark along the border,
My exiled heart stares to my village and realm.
Midnight. I go to my empty pillow,
Dream of going home for an instant.
My widowed wife sighs at the door,

117

Unwinding silk she makes the loom hum again.
We talk happily of our long separation,
Return together to silk bedcurtains.
Faint, faint chill beneath the eaves,
Dim, dim gleam in the window.
Cut orchids compete with her fragrance,
Plucked chrysanthemum contends with her bloom.
From opened boxes she gathers sweet herbs,
Feels inside her sleeve, unties sachet strings.
In my sleep the long road grew nearer,
After I woke the great river cut me off.
I got up afraid, sighed futile sighs,
My fevered soul flew forward.
White river in spate menaced, menaced,
High mountains grim loomed large.
Billowing tides change from flux to ebb,
Windy frost turns bloom to decay.
This land is not my land,
No one to tell of my despair.

One she knew long ago
Riverside grass has not yellowed,
Hun geese are spreading their wings,
Autumn crickets moan huddled against the door,
A chill wife weaves from dawn to dusk.
Last year a serviceman came home,
Bringing news of one she knew long ago.
I hear when you climbed Lung range
You looked east with long sighs,
Overnight your clothes and belt hung looser,
Dawn to dusk your appearance changed.
Imagine how anxious this makes me
As nights lengthen, anxiety grows sharper.
My bright mirror lies in its dusty case,
My precious lute is overspread with cobwebs.

Swallows
A pair of swallows plays near cloudy cliffs
Till wings bob up and down.
In and out of the south boudoir they come,
Through the north hall they go,
Longing to nest in your curtains,

118

But a tall pillar they cannot spy.
Panting while the scented season grows late,
Hesitant as spring glory departs,
With sad song they leave their old love,
Beaks full of mud they seek a new friend.

To my former love, two poems

I

Cold ash dies, flares once more,
Evening flowers freshen at dawn once more.
Spring ice though thawed for a while,
Hardens once again into winter ice.
My lover cast me off,
Bonds of love true broken for ever.
Happiness comes, but never stays,
Each time I'm moved it's end of year sadness.

2

A pair of swords about to part
First cried out in their case.
In night smoky rain they became one,
Then they took different forms.
The female sank in Wu river water,
The male flew into Ch'u city.
Wu river is deep, fathomless,
Ch'u city has forbidding portals.
Once Heaven parted from Earth
Wasn't that worse than Light gone from Dark?
Magic things do not part for ever,
One thousand years and they come back together.

Wang·Su

Love's favour
Deep love arouses distant longing,
Rings of obsession bring dreams of my love.
Muffled notes I hear of bamboo flutes,
A singing phoenix welcomes Lady Ying.
They leave together on cloudy wings,

Joyfully happy, holding hands.
I say to those in the flush of beauty :
Love's favour, good fortune won't last for ever !
Ching and Wei are known as muddy and clear,
Read that in the *Valley wind* poem !

Wu Man-yüan

Two white geese
A pretty pair of white geese
Double, double, far from dusty chaos;
Wings embracing, they play in bright sunlight,
Necks caressing roam the blue clouds.
Trapped by nets or felled by corded arrow
Hen and cock are parted one dawn.
Sad echoes drift down river bends,
Lonesome cries ring out from river banks.
'It's not that I don't long for my former mate,
But because of you I won't reach my flock'.
Drop by drop she sheds a tear.
'A thousand leagues I'll wait for you !'
How happy to fall in love,
So sad a lifetime parting.
Let us cling to our hundred year span,
Let us pursue every moment of time,
Like grass on a lonely hill
Knowing it must soon wither and die.

Sunny Spring Tune
I stare at Hsienyang one hundred leagues away,
I can tell it's the imperial capital.
Green trees sway with cloud and light,
The spring city stirs with billowing colour.
A beauty loves its sparkling flowers,

Dappled shimmers beside her garden bank.
Her charming face is the gorgeous moon's image,
Her silk clothes cicada wings ruffled.
Though Sung Yü sang *Sunny spring,*
Man of Pa brought the deepest sighs.
Odes and love-songs aren't valued alike,
Don't these last make your heart ache?
All my life I will treasure your kind love,
For my single self, is there an end to pity?

Long separation
I cannot bear to hear of lifetime parting,
Much less long separation between us.
Why be apart from you
When at the peak of beauty?
Each time the orchid bloom trembles
My heart seeks comfort in vain.
My bloom lacks the rapture of plants and trees,
My wilting surpasses the gloom of frosty dew.
Wealth and status slow down the body's ageing,
Poverty and misery hurry on the year's waning.
To rely on that would break my heart,
As you might guess yourself.

In Huaiyin there was a famous general
Who broke his wings rather than soar.
And in Ch'u a warrior who lifted heavy cauldrons
Left his gates never to return.
Just for the sake of a Duke Highnose
You grip your sword, enter Tzu-wei galaxy.
Maybe your talent is like these men?
But the white sun falls with struggling gleams.

I'll always love you
At dawn there was a traveller on the road.
Wistful, wistful he neared our gateway,
Man and horse the colour of windy dust,
I knew they were from the river border.
Once I had a fellow nestler,
He joined up, wandered to Hantan,
No different from this traveller,
Same hunger, same cold.

121

May I trouble you with my silk letter?
My heart is bared in it.
I've said, 'I'm always tired and thin,
I sing no more with a smiling face.
Eaves shadowed by trees of a thousand frosts,
Garden orchids countless decades have died.
Passing spring never lifts my sleeves,
Autumn's fall I prefer to watch no more'.
Once you see him, please tell of my love:
'Your gates are locked ninefold.
Yü Ch'ing set aside his minister's seal,
Carried an umbrella for his sweetheart.
My room's shadows early frost will touch.
Why waste time tarrying?'

Pao Ling-hui

Green, green riverside grass
Svelte, svelte bamboo peeps through my window,
Thick, thick catalpa leans over the gate.
Glowing, glowing a girl by green eaves,
Icy, icy in her tall terrace.
Her bright ideals beggar autumn frost,
Her jade face enriches spring pink.
In life who does not part?
I hate you for enlisting so fast!
Tinkling strings disgrace me by the night moon,
Indigo kohl shames me in autumn winds.

In the key of farewell
A traveller came from far away,
He brought me a lacquer singing lute.
On its wood a loving you design,
Its strings were set in the key of farewell.
All my life I will keep this chord,
The year grown cold will not change my heart.
I long to compose a *Sunny spring* tune
With *do* and *re* for ever in pursuit.

Poem sent to a traveller
Ever since you went away
My tense face near the porch won't soften,
Pounder and block no longer sound at night,
Tall gates at noon stay locked.
Into my bedcurtains drift fireflies,
In front of the garden purple orchids bloom.
Nature withers, sensing the change of season,
Swans arrive telling of travellers cold.
Your journey may end at winter's close,
I'll wait till late spring for your return.

An old theme addressed to a modern person
Cold lands have no season's change of clothes,
Wool is worn instead of patterned silks.
Month after month I hope for your return,
Year after year you never untie your capstring.
In Ching and Yang spring is early and mild,
Yu and Chi still have frost and hail.
Your northern cold I already know,
My southern heart you will never see.
Who will tell of my unhappiness?
I'll send my love through two flying swallows.
My figure is gaunt, silk consumed in a shuttle,
My face has withered, lightning chased by winds.
Lovely looks vanish one morning,
But to the end my heart will never change.

Bright moon white
Bright moon white, so white
Through hanging curtains shines on a silk bed,
Appearing to join our night of love,
Seeming to share my dawn of despair.
Fragrant flowers, please pity my beauty!
Frosty dew, you spare no one!
My love, you aren't a blue cloud drifting,
Yet you hover around Hsien-Ch'in.
I will have a lifetime of tears
As autumn comes and springtime goes.

123

His pillow makes me dream
About to go on distant campaign
My lover sent me twin inscribed brocades.
Toward the time of departure
He also left me his loving you pillow.
His inscription I always press to my heart,
His pillow makes me dream we sleep together.
On, on, each day further on,
The more I feel my pining keen.

Ch'iu Chü-yüan

The seven-jewel fan
For exquisite silk Tunghsia is prized,
The best artists come from Wu cities.
Cut like a white jade disc,
Sewn like the bright moon's wheel.
Its face inlaid with seven jewels,
Its heart filled with rare rhino horn.
Painting creates trees on grand mountains,
Sketching evokes Lo river goddess.
A welcome toy for the hand
It enters home, an intimate of rings and bangles,
To create a breeze by long sleeve cuffs,
To cool the bloom of rouge and powder sheen,
Brush near bright eyes flirting nuance,
Reflect by stealth a humming singer.
Time moves on, a man is quick to forget old love;
Seasons change, he tirelessly courts new love.
With tender affection he takes her to his ivory bed,
With an easy mind he discards his quilted mat.
Dislike, rejection – what can I say?
Respect? that lasts the span of heat!

Rapturous song

I loosen my robe, weary of circuit debates,
Lean on the coach-rail, tired of literary wit.
Tumbleweed gates have long been still,
Empty seats show signs of dust.
A luxury beauty parlour overlooks my house,
My east neighbour has a drum and pipe stage.
Through the clouds rapturous song soars,
In the wake of winds floats sultry music,
Making blossoms fly on jade kingfisher curtains,
Fragrance drift from gold and jasper cups.
Long since dead, beauty of Central Plains.
So too the memories, ashes of Huhsiang.
My legacy of feeling is grief for life today.
The grandeur of Chungshan, where is it now?

Wang Yüan-chang

The hour of return

Birds of the air know dusk is the hour of return,
Only the wanderer fails to come home.
I waste unawares the flower's fragrant breath,
Pass futile time with the splendour of the moon.
A frowning face appears in my morning mirror,
Pining tears stain my springtime dress.
On Mount Wu sunrise mists are fading,
Along Ch'i river green boughs grow bare.
I wait for you, you never come.
Autumn geese fly double, double.

Numb

Frosty air falls on Meng ford,
Autumn winds blow through Hanku Pass.
I think of you shivering with early cold
As I stand on the porch wrapped in silk.
My frail hands put aside cutting and sewing,

On straggling hair I stop using gloss.
One thousand leagues, no news of you,
My inch of heart feels stifled, numb.
Especially on nights when fireflies flit
Or leaves from trees scatter in jumbled heaps.

The balloon guitar
This cradled moon seems to glimmer,
Caressed its breeze is still purer.
To its strings I tell my feelings,
To its flowers I confide spring passion.
Depressed, it has a rare timbre,
Melancholy, it resounds with lovely music.
Scented sleeves happily brush it sometimes,
Otherwise what a waste of Dragon Gate trees!

The curtain
Lucky to be sewn with pearls,
Wispy, wispy round your pillars.
No need to roll me up in moonlight,
Light am I when breezes blow.
Always gathering gold censer breath,
Ever catching jade lute whispers,
All I ask is lay out casks of wine,
Let light orchid oil jars face the glow of night!

Mount Wu high
I dream of Mount Wu high,
Dim twilight, Sunny Terrace nooks,
Smoky mists first spread, then furl,
Herb scents now snap, now thread.
Perhaps that lovely girl will promise me?
I wake, just see a dim vision.
Disappointed, yet I love her.
Autumn winds fall on my garden green.

Hsieh T'iao

In love for ever
Sunset, she sits at the window
Rouged, her face beautiful.
Dance clothes are pleated, not sewn,
Flowing yellow silk lies covered, unwoven.
Dragonflies on tips of grass hover,
Roving bees from flowertops sip.
Once they met, fell in love for ever,
She longs for wings to soar with him.

As the spring scene fades
For fluting clear he asks for Green Jade,
For strings strumming he orders Green Pearl.
Light songs disturb silk belts,
Gurgling laughter loosens silk gowns.
The rest of their tunes, about how many?
Tall carriage, won't you linger?
For dawdling as the spring scene fades
They just have the corner of Loyang city wall.

Resentment
She was summoned from the harem to a remote land.
At Eternal Gate Palace she missed happy feasts.
Her meeting him is sung in *Sweet herbs.*
Removed from favour she grieved in the *Round fan.*

On flowery tufts scatter swarming butterflies,
Through windblown blinds come two swallows.
Wasted, my spring sash gets looser,
Helpless, I mourn my pink face changing.
Nowadays I'd treasure his one glance,
Long ago a thousand gold was thought cheap.
My old love's heart may still be true,
But my old sweetheart I never meet.

127

Singer in the night, two poems

1

In a jasper boudoir I hear bracelets tinkling,
Jade mats fill with fragrant dust.
I order a Loyang girl,
Ask for Chiangnan flutes.
Full of love their languid dance movements,
Their passionate singing so tender.
You'll know if you're my secret love –
Jade bracelets declare my inch of heart.

2

Honoured guests lend brilliance to the four seats,
Lovely beauties are worth a thousand gold.
Dangling hairpin pledges ripped capstring,
Dropped earring answers lutenist passion.
Moth eyebrows laugh now with everyone,
Piquant scent clings to a guest's lapel.
Happy joy grows calm into night,
Kingfisher curtains hang hushed and still.

A former palace lady marries a supplies sergeant
All her life she lived in galleried halls,
Constantly attended cinnabar court.
In opened wardrobes her sheer dresses outshone all,
Her face in the mirror rivalled all moth eyebrows.
When first she went away her feelings lay suppressed.
Years later sorrow deepened with each dawn.
She grew imperceptibly thin and pale,
But a trace of flirting beauty still remained.
Faint images of the past flickered in her dreams
Murmuring yet : 'At royal feasts I won high favour!'

Autumn nights
Autumn nights when urgent looms hum,
South neighbour's fulling hurries,
I think of you nine heavens distant,
Night after night I stand still, helpless.
From north windows light curtains hang down,

Through the west door moonlight comes in.
How do I know white dew has fallen?
From where I sit I see front steps moist.
Who can long endure separation?
Autumn ends, winter is here once more.

The lamp

Flashing kingfisher tints in Han river slanting,
Hoarded treasure on Mount T'ang peaks,
It throws stem silhouettes like a god's palm,
Breathes flares like Torch Dragon.
Flitting moths make two or three circles,
Light blooms grow four or five petals.
Alone I face this night of loving you
That shines in vain on dance gown stitching.

The candle

Under apricot rafters guests have not dispersed,
Cassia Lodge brilliance is about to fade.
Blurred colours on flimsy curtains,
Lowered lights brighten a jewelled lute.
Flickers of cloudy chignon shadow,
Glitters of silk lattice gilt.
I hate you on moonlit autumn nights
For leaving my quiet room to darkness.

The bed

My first home was a tidal pool,
Falling shadows reflected in flickers,
Shallows screened by iris,
Secret isles conquered by sweet river plants.
Once you chanced to gather me,
A jade couch to offer gold cups.
All I desire is silken dress caresses,
Nor would I mind a powdering of white dust!

The mirrorstand

Reticulated like scarlet lattice,
Vertiginous as Dark Tower,
Facing phoenixes overhang clear ice,

129

Suspended dragons dangle above a bright moon.
Reflected powder is brushed with rouge,
Flowers inserted are fixed in cloudy hair.
A jade face vacantly stares at itself,
Forever dreading his love might fade.

Falling plum blossom

New leaves freshly uncurl, uncurl,
Fresh blossom's newly fallen snowdrift.
I met you at a rear garden party,
Close together we went home in charmed laughter.
Since you troubled with your own jade fingers
To pick some for your Nanwei,
I pinned it in my cloudy chignon
To enhance kingfisher plume sheen.
At sunset its petals dropped for ever,
Your gift of love I never can regain.

Lu Chüeh

I will end like them!

Lady Ju slept in a royal bedroom,
Lady Pan sat in the imperial coach.
At Vast Wave they shared drink and bedcurtains.
At Forest Gleam, spoils of Ch'in, they feasted.
The year darkens, chill gales come.
Autumn floods, hibiscus blooms fall.
Mi Tzu-hsia presumed upon his lord's coach,
Lord Lungyang wept for the first fish.
I will end like them!
And you? I'm not sure how you'll behave!

Shih Jung-t'ai

Playful laughter

Chao women groom their lovely faces,
Yen girls perfect their cosmetics.
Make-up done, peach is ashamed of its pink!
Kohl applied, grass is disgraced for its colour!
Silk skirts, several tens of layers,
Yet lighter than one cicada wing.
I won't describe her gauze sleeve light,
Just sigh for winds too strong.
Tinkling pendants near a jade pool,
Playful laughter by a silv'ry terrace.
She breaks willow for the delight of her eyes,
Picks cat-tail for one known to her heart.
When she came, her glamour had not faded,
When she goes, what of her glamour then?

CHAPTER FIVE

Poets of the Southern Dynasties
(the decades AD 490–510)

Chiang Yen

Separation
Faraway places keeping you from me
Are as far as Goose Gate Pass
Where yellow clouds pall a thousand leagues.
Traveller, when will you come home?
Seeing you off seems like yesterday,
Dew by the eaves already forms beads.
I don't regret orchids late,
What I mourn is the road chill.

You live on the horizon
Long sundered from my body.
My longing to see your face just once
Is not unlike desire for the Jade Tree branch.
What dodder and waterplant
Rely on never moves away.

Lady Pan's 'Poem on the Fan'
White silk fan like a round moon
Appearing from the loom's white silk.
Its picture shows the king of Ch'in's daughter
Riding a lovebird toward smoky mists.
Vivid colour is what the world prefers,
Yet the new will never replace the old.
In secret I fear cold winds coming
To blow on my jade steps tree
And, before your sweet love has ended,
Make it shed midway.

Parted love
Autumn moon reflected on eaves and lattice,
Cascading light enters cinnabar court.
A beauty strums her lilting lute,
Clear night, she stays by empty curtains.
On the orchid path few passing footprints,
The jade mirrorstand cobwebs overspread.
Garden trees vaunt a vivid red,

Bedroom plants enshrine a green moisture.
Fine silks I prepare for you,
To give my love ten thousand leagues away.
Please pour down your favour's drenching dew,
Swear to keep your white sun vow.

Unhappy parting

Northwest autumn winds come.
Traveller of Ch'u, how far away your heart!
Sunset, blue clouds gather.
His love has not yet come.

Dewy spangles splash riches,
The moon's flower starts to shimmer.
Precious books because of you are closed,
My jade lute how could I bear to uncase?

I pine for you on Mount Wu's lea,
Stare jealous at Bright Cloud Terrace.
The gold censer's sinking gleams die,
Silk mats' shifting dust spreads.
Cassia river rolling one thousand leagues a day
Follows familiar longings in my heart.

Ch'iu Ch'ih

Nostalgia on campaign

Her clear song I think charming,
Simply graceful her elegant dance.
From her ears she removes bright moons,
Down her hair slip golden pins.

Sparrows at dawn fly round about,
At dusk coming through the silk window.
Fish sport north and south, yet
Home in the end near lotus leaves.
All I see is your travel long,
New Year is not ours of last year.

Bitter warfare?
Her husband shouts, 'Yes, I'll go!'
Takes his commission, neglects his family.
The dregs and a reject,
His wife's hair tangled grows like matted hemp.

Indirectly, she hears from a Loyang traveller
That escorted in gold canopied coaches
He has audience, occasional royal visits,
His splendour beggars description.

When his private rooms open wide,
Twice eight girls, all fragrant flowers,
In silk skirts some long, some short,
With kingfisher sidecurls not too low, nor too wavy,
Long eyebrows sweeping over jade faces,
White arms filmed in sheer gossamer,
Idly watch butterflies alight on the well,
All gather blooms from the eaves fallen.
How can he complain of bitter warfare?
She hugs her knees, sighing empty sighs.

Shen Yüeh

I climb high to look at spring
I climb high to look at Loyang city,
Streets and lanes criss-cross far and wide.
I turn my head to view Ch'angan,
City turrets bristle zigzag.
Sunrise glints on jewel pins and kohl,
Passing winds ruffle sheer silks.
Ch'i boys stamp their red boots.
Chao girls smooth of kingfisher plume brow.

The spring breeze sways dappled trees,
Rich blooms emerald and cinnabar.
Jewelled lutes, ruby stops,

136

Gold harness, tortoiseshell saddles.
Youth loiters, sleeps at Hsiats'ai,
Pours wine on the way through Shanglan.
Relaxed eyebrows pucker again
Showing it's hard to keep a dazzling smile.
Lovers linger and dawdle,
Tearful from bliss unfulfilled.
'My honoured guest is now out of sight,
Through you I send him long sighs'.

Wang Chao-chün's Farewell
At dawn she leaves Spreading Scent Hall,
By dusk she ferries the river at Fenyin.
From here she feels the nine death sorrow,
From then she puckers her twin moths.
Her damp make-up is like soaking dew,
Tears wreathe her breast like eddying waves.

Each day she sees swirling sands rise,
Gradually senses tumbleweed grows rank.
Hun gales assault her flesh and bones,
Besides damaging her silk so fine.

She chokes back tears, hazards a southward glance :
Passes, mountains tower menacing.
First she composes a *Sunny spring* tune,
Last she makes a *Bitter cold* lyric.
Only on nights of the fifteenth
Is there the clear moon's brief passing.

For a young bridegroom
The daughter of the Shanyin Liu family,
Don't say she's from the country !
She is lovely and pretty in face and figure,
Courteous and clever the way she talks.
Her waist and limbs are graceful,
Her clothes so sweet and fresh.
Her round red cape reflects early chill,
Her painted fan welcomes the first spell of heat.
On brocaded slippers is a pattern of like flowers,
On embroidered sash twin heart lettuce design.
Gold leaf brooches fasten her bodice edge,
Flower jewel pins hold up her cloudy hair.

137

My heart is full of rapture,
How will I express my excitement?
I offer my love to her eyebrow kohl,
Whisper my passion to lipstick on her mouth.
Defenceless before her precious three springtimes
I die for her thousand gold coin body.
A full-length green bronze mirror,
A one-inch diameter Hop'u pearl,
These would I give, but have no way.
I long to take wing with two flying ducks.

Her skirt opens, showing her jade foot,
Her blouse sheer reveals gleaming marbrous skin.
I'm ashamed to talk of Chao Feiyen,
Quite scorn Ch'in Lofu.

I check my looks. Though wretchedly thin,
Capped and canopied I'll brighten the city corner!
Her tall gates lined with coach and driver,
Broad avenues a parade of black horses.

Why blush for my Lulu dagger?
Why belittle my office swagger?
Back home let her ask in the village,
'Who's good enough to be my husband?'

Holding hands

Reins tossed aside, he leaves his carved coach.
I help him change, serve by his jade bed.
Slanting hairpins in autumn water reflected,
In an opened mirror spring make-up appraised.

My fear is red cheeks will fast fade,
Your favours cannot last long.
Pheasant-cap, make yourself comfortable!
Who cares if cassia sprays die?

The one I love

Marching west I scale Lung summit,
Look east, cannot see my home.
Trees of the pass push out purple leaves,
Frontier plants sprout green shoots.
K'unming lake must be nearly brimming,

Grapevines should be bursting into bloom.
Streaming with tears I go before the Han envoy,
Trust him with my letter to her narrow lane.

Night after night

River Han long and wide,
Northern Dipper wide and straight,
Starry Han void like this
How can you know of love?

The lone lamp dims, bright no more,
The cold loom at dawn still weaves.
I shed tears. To whom will I speak?
At cockcrow I just heave a sigh.

Spring

Willows tangle like silk threads,
Sheer silk I cannot bear.
Spring grass green and emerald,
The wanderer's heart aches at such an hour.
Kingfisher lichen binds Wei river now,
Jade water brims in the Ch'i once more.
Sunny florescence brightens Chao lutes,
Breezy flickers ruffle Yen skirts.
On my collar ten thousand trickling tears
Are because I long only for him.

Peach

Winds come blowing leaves astir,
Winds go, and I fear for flowers wounded.
Red blooms shining now in splendour
Shine richer in sunlight caress.

Singing boys at dusk rehearse their tunes,
Roving girls by night sew their coats.
How will I lessen the tears of spring
That could break a lover's heart?

139

The moon
The moon's florescence looks on silent night,
Night silent, stilled the thick dust.
Jagged rays across a doorway enter,
Curving shadows through a gap visit.
In her tall house a pining woman suffers,
In West Park learned men stroll.
Webbed eaves gleam with pearl strands,
Ying Gate glimmers with emerald green.
In cloistral rooms still no hint of dawn.
How far away those pure beams are!

Willow
Light shade sweeping Chienchang Palace,
Fringing the road that leads to Weiyang,
In the breeze knots and unravels,
Soaked with dew grows softer and longer.
The lady of Ch'u seems consumed with love,
Lady Pan's tears turn to streamlets.
The wanderer may not have set out . . .
For its sake, come back to your old town!

The flute
In Chiangnan, the land of flutes,
Sublime echoes pour from young shoots.
Her interest she conveys through jade fingers,
Playing high and low full of love.
Notes circle carved rafters twice, thrice,
Light dust moves four or five times.
In her tune there is profound emotion.
What do you know of cinnabar fidelity?

I remember when she came
I remember when she came,
Fair, fair up the court steps,
Excited, excited to meet after parting,
Eager, eager to say she loved me.
I'd look at her and never grow bored,
Watch her and forget to eat.

I remember when she sat
I remember when she sat,
Prim, prim before the silk bedcurtain.
Either she'd sing four or five songs,
Or she'd play two or three chords.
When she laughed there was no one like her,
When she sulked she was even more adorable.

I remember when she ate
I remember when she ate,
Leaning toward the dish, her face bashful,
Ready to sit, but too shy to sit,
Ready to eat, but too shy to eat.
She'd keep the food in her mouth as if not hungry,
Lift her plate as if so weak.

I remember when she slept
I remember when she slept,
Though one slept she struggled to stay awake.
To undress she never needed coaxing,
Moving to the pillow she'd wait to be drawn close.
Then nervous one might see,
All coy charm before the candle.

Embroidery on her collar
Slender hands fashion a novelty
Into an adorable embroidered shape.
From cross-stitching fly phoenixboys,
From double needle-weave flowerboys spring,
All seeming to stir and breathe, noiseless,
To hover with grace in windless air.
If her beauty were never to fade
This collar would hold her cloudy locks of hair.

Slippers on her feet
Up cinnabar court fluttering,
Down jade halls swiftly tapping,
They pirouette and her pearl belt tinkles,
Early scent creeps from her broidered coat.
Skirts open near the dance floor,

141

Sleeves brush round the song hall.
They sigh for their indifferent mistress :
'We're tossed aside when she enters silk curtains'.

Green, green riverside grass
Dense, dense dust on the bed,
My inner heart remembers past love.
Past love I cannot bear to remember,
Midnight's endless sighing.
Sighing I imagine his face
Who did not want this long parting.
Separation slowly grown prolonged.
My empty bed. I give in to cups of wine.

Three wives
The eldest's wife dusts her jade jewel box,
The middle wife ties silk bed drapes.
The youngest wife alone has nothing to do,
She faces the mirror painting moth eyebrows.
'Darling come and lie down,
All night long I'm left to myself'.

For nothing
She hugs her lute near Shrub Terrace,
Lingers to cherish fair beauty,
Stands still for the setting of the sun,
Sad, sad her embittered human heart.

Dewy mallows are now fully gathered,
Ch'i river has not wet the awning.
My brocade quilt lonely will not be warm,
My silk dress for nothing is perfumed.
The bright moon though it shines outside
Can hardly know the pain in my heart.

I dream of a lovely woman
At night I hear long sighs
And I know your heart remembers,
Then the Gates of Heaven open wide,
Our souls kiss, I gaze on your face.
You offer me your Mount Wu pillow,

142

Humbly serve me food.
We stand and stare, lie across the bed.
Suddenly I wake, you are gone from my side.
Do you know if my spirit is wounded?
Welling tears soak my breast.

My inch of heart

Lovely cassia spray!
A lone drake longs for its old mate.
The year fades, he changes his nest;
Spring comes, still they are parted.

Mountains, rivers block the long road,
The road far eclipses her face.
I won't say there's no other mate for me,
But my inch of heart will never stray.

Early spring

For signs of spring down the road they search,
Pretty women all holding hands.
Grass still a faded colour,
Woods all bare.
Useless to seek plum blossom,
Silly to think there'll be willow!
So . . . I might as well go home
And whisper my passion to a cup of wine!

Bereavement

Last autumn's moon of the fifteenth
This autumn too lights her room.
This spring's orchid plant
Next spring will exhale more perfume.
Sad how different this is from human life –
Once we depart, we are for ever gone.

Screens, cushions in vain laid out,
Drapes, bed arranged just as before.
Drifting dust shrouds her empty seat,
Bereaved curtains hang from the empty bed.
Of all creatures none escapes death.
Still, this wounds us who survive.

143

Liu Yün

Fulling cloth
The waif quilt tugs pining heartstrings,
The lone pillow hurts limits of despair.
Deep in the garden autumn grass is green,
High on the gates white dew chills.

Pining for you I rise in clear night,
Tighten lute-stops to play *Secret orchid*.
I don't mourn driven tumbleweed's fate,
But suffer the orchid's dereliction.

On campaign he weathers storms,
The traveller who delays with no return.
Outpost trees shed leaves,
Lung peak autumn clouds fly.

In my chill garden evening birds flock,
By the pining window grass insects grieve.
Oh, how I pity his springtime clothes,
What robe will he find against the winter cold?

A stork's cry troubles endless sighs,
I pick beans, sad that time is fading.
I remember when you left on far campaign,
You watched me prepare fine white silk.

Autumn winds blow on green pools,
A bright moon hangs above tall trees.
'Lovely girl, adorn your smooth face,
Come, hold hands, let's do our work!'

I walk down corridors dark unending,
The farewell hall now locked in grief.
To eaves high dusk pounder echoes spread,
In air keen night fulling blocks thud.

Jasper flowers tinkle with each step,
Secret orchid quickens from sleeves;
I pause to fix gold kingfisher pins,
Calmly breathe the coolness of the night.

Glimmering coil smoky patterns,
Gyrating design of tortoise and crane.
Frigid joy of love sleeves,
Ebbing aroma of musk.

I don't resent shuttle and reel labours,
What I mourn is thousand league parting.
Tears spill as I send your parcel,
With bowed head I wait for homeward clouds.

Alone, I never see him
Islet apart, terrace facing winds,
Lake immense, halls that look on water,
Sweet grass grown not yet thick,
Spring flowers falling like sleet.

He used to leave with Lord Chang,
Going back to visit Chao Feiyen.
I served at Eternal Trust Palace,
Who knows of me? Alone, I never see him.

Over passes and mountains
Ch'angan songhouse girls
Come from Yen's deep south.
Though mere goodness makes them lovely,
They are known for natural good looks.

I used to hear of faraway passes and mountains,
But why would you use gold harness?
Each day my heart grows more troubled.
Autumn winds zip through slim boughs.

Parting is wrong
Clouds wispy, warm changing tones,
In grasses green dawn scents revive.
Mountain wastes end their chill gloom,
Orchard ponds glitter with morning beams.
Most spring hearts are aroused,
But I look on nature and feel sad.

Ever since you went away,
Orchid hall stopped humming with the loom.
All he knows is to campaign is right,
Never thinks that parting is wrong.

Despair at Eternal Gate Palace
The jade jar at night softly drips,
Ying Gate is barred and sealed.
Autumn winds toss cassia boughs,
The sailing moon casts pale quivering shadows.
Silken eaves with lucid dew drenched,
Webbed doors plaintive with pining insects.

She sighs to leave the orchid gallery,
Plays in despair her elegant lute.
What would set my dawn belt tinkling?
Will I ever take my night quilt again?
Never remembering my House of Gold,
Will you brighten Eternal Gate's heart?

Let's just say
As I picked white artemesia on an islet
While the sun went down over Chiangnan,
A traveller coming home from lake Tungt'ing
Said he met my old love near Hsiao-Hsiang river.
I had wondered why my old love never came home
Though spring flowers were fading once more.
Don't admit he's happy with his new love –
Let's just say, 'The road he travels is far'!

Getting up in the night to visit
From the city south driver and coach have ceased,
The highway is filmed with pure dust.
Dewy florets gleam on kingfisher webs,
Moonlight streams through an orchid terrace.
My secret room long left unlocked,
Perhaps Ying Gate lies open too?
Creak, creak autumn cassia echoes,
Not you getting up in the night to visit.

Threading needles on Seventh Night
His black horse in autumn did not come home,
His black silk will be threadbare.
Against the cold she prepares the night's sewing,
Lit by the moon she works fine threads.
Lustrous eyes with sorrow glisten,
The line of pining eyebrows puckers.
Clear dew falls on silken clothes,
Autumn winds blow jade lute-stops.
Flickering shade subtly deepens,
Dwindling light seems harder to work by.

The bed
Island in a stream rimmed with light,
Rippling breezes down green waters.
Though not so light as a bed of one cocoon,
I am happy with my blue robe colour.
Specks of dust on my lady's silk sleeves,
Rich tiaras over her ivory bed.
Mistress, when you drink late at night
Bring your lover here to feast awhile.

Chiang Hung

The singer
Jewelled hairpins among pearl blooms,
Discernibly thick beauty-spots.
Near her wispy fringe faint yellow applied,
Light rouge touched on powdered cheeks.
As she speaks fragrance escapes,
Enriched by her own orchid tinge.
Soaring notes release wounded sighs,
Deep chant soft, yet rough.
She turns abruptly, paces swift,
Twin eyebrows swiftly pucker.
She won't show herself full face to me,
But half hides behind sheer silk.

The dancer

Slim of waist, but not a Ch'u lady,
Light of body, but not a Chao girl,
Her sparkling collar strewn with jewel seeds,
From her elbows pearl tassels swing.
With loose sleeves she performs her pose,
Moves her feet in different positions.
Her eyes slant, seem not to notice you,
She goes to turn, then pretends to withdraw.
Why should she blush to soar with cloudy storks?
Is she less lovely than phoenix in alarm?

Red notepaper

Different shades are hardly unusual,
But this red is quite unique.
Flaming, fiery like lotus unfolding,
Flecked with glints like streaking mist.
Embossed tissue rolled with perfumed oil,
Suffused with scent of cut blooms.
Let me record my heart in separation
Enveloped in this my love for you.
If it never reaches my sweet beloved
How will he know of my desirous bed?

A rose

By the door stands a rose,
Branch and leaf curve gracefully.
Unstirred, its scents still scatter,
Windless its flowers flurry at will.
In a spring bedroom disquieted
By her open case she practises *Lady Ming*.
Twisting pools float with spangled glints,
Sloping banks tiered in rich array.
Now she hears sweet bird of passage music,
Then sees mud-carrying birds wend home.
Let's steep ourselves in jugs of clear wine –
For the rest, I couldn't care less!

Kao Shuang

The mirror
When first I went up to phoenix court
This mirror reflected moth eyebrows.
Here it reflects eternal resignation,
But won't reflect eternal love for you.
Empty of love I never pick it up,
Chaste and pure, pointless to hold it.
I won't declare this object obsolete,
But resurrect it next rendezvous!

Pao Tzu-ch'ing

The painted fan
Fine threads light as light can be,
Soft tints barely visible,
Meant to offset red cheeks,
Yet used as a handheld fan.
Instantly raised when Eternal Gates wept,
Offered once at Cypress Rafter's banquet.
Pining cosmetics once revealed it now conceals,
Singing features once hidden, it now shows.
Just paint it with a pair of yellow storks,
Never the waif flying swallow.

Jade steps
Jade steps exquisite
Are more splendid facing Tzu-wei Palace.
North doors open onto kingfisher drapes,
South paths lead to gilded portals.
Pounded into being by sunny rays,

Dappled into hiding with moonbeams.
Light moss stains pearl slippers,
Small puddles lick a silk dress.
I smile in loneliness at K'unlun's crevice,
Watch in vain for the bluebird flying free.

Ho Tzu-lang

Bronze steps
Cassia terrace brushed with clear dew,
Bronze steps moist with fallen flowers.
Her rouge applied, a pretty girl
Holds the hook to roll up fine blinds.
Longing for you she tightens momentary lute-stops
With jade fingers slim, so slim.
Just because of this parting I mustn't
Be foolish and hate you!

A measure of wine
A pretty woman plays in white sunlight,
Glowing, glowing in the spring doorway.
Her clear mirror counters moth eyebrows,
Fresh flowers imaged on jade hands.
Swallows swoop to gather pond mud,
Breezes come to blow slim willow.
Lover, when will you come back
To pour a measure of wine with me?

Moongazing
Clear night. Still not tired
I let the fine blinds hang free a moment.
Chiming jade lake water
Reflects a moth eyebrow moon.
Beaded dewdrops barely in suspense,
Shimmering light gently sinks.
My lovely one, more than a thousand leagues,
Last shadows vain swiftly vanish.

Shen Man-yüan

Her tiara flowers

Pearl blooms ring kingfisher plumes,
Jewel leaves inset with gold jade.
Artificial lotus seemingly uncontrived
Are flowers of apparent natural life.
Lower stems stroke her broidered collar,
Tiny footsteps set the jewels aquiver.
Just let me fix it on her cloudy coiffure,
Then moth eyebrows will be soon painted.

Parody of the other woman

Bright pearl, kingfisher plume bed drapes,
Gold leaf, sheer green silk door tapestries
Lifting now and then with the wind.
I imagine I see your charming face
At dawn when you put on your tiara,
At dark when you slip off your silk dress.
Well, give yourself to Mr Libertine!
Does love have to be selfish?

The coloured bamboo clothes perfumer

Pretty frost-damp texture
Of fine spliced fibre and nicely split strands
Woven to form windblown lettuce,
Wrought into wavy silk lace.
Heavy perfume pours from a pearled quilt,
Brilliant tints tone with a celadon tunic.
Today it sighs vain sighs for lovely gowns,
Why hark back to its cloud-piercing past?

The lamp

On a silk bed the sun is setting,
To chiffon curtains the moon not returned.
Open wax florets cast a stork's glint,

151

Full radiance outshines Ninth Blaze.
Windy eaves fan cinnabar flickers,
Frozen skies attenuate green glimmers.
Don't pity frail moths circling,
Just dread the dawn insects' flight.

Ho Sun

Day and night I stare at the river
P'en city twines P'en river,
P'en river winds like a sash.
Day and night I stare at high city walls,
Far away at blue clouds beyond.

In the city there are many feasts and banquets,
Strings, bamboo blend in constant concert.
The sound of flutes liquid now with rapture,
The sound of strings sharp now with pain.
A singer's kohl contracts as if in anguish,
A dancer's waist threatens to snap.

Mid-autumn's yellow leaves have fallen,
Long winds resentfully murmur.
Early geese emerge from clouds migrating,
Familiar swallows leave their nests to part.
Sad at dawn to live in a strange land.
I dream at night of return to Lo shore.
Lo shore deserted, so deserted.
I get up to look, climb the west storey.
White, white a sail homes for the strand,
Round, round the sun eclipsed by islets.
Who can once metamorphose wings
And lightly rise to drift away in flight?

Reckless
Handsome boys of the east side
Indulge their bodies, reckless of the millions.
Thornwood slings, Lord Sui pearl shot,

White horses, yellow gold harness.
At Ch'angan's nine-radial crossroads
Green pagoda trees stand shading the way.
Wheelhubs at dawn already clatter
Jostling without pause into dusk.
From Racedog Terrace westward for the sights,
From Herdboy Bridge southward bound,
They converge near the sports ground,
Wander around the three markets.

Ivory beds draped with broidered quilts,
Jade dishes laden with fine food,
Singing girls trilling, hidden by fans,
Young wives weaving behind open blinds.
Eyes meet, just a secret smile,
Seeing other people faces turn prim.

Yellow stork mourns its old flock,
Hillside bough sings of first love.
Crows fly, passing travellers disappear,
Sparrows flock, coursing dragons vanish.
With plumed goblets the boys all relax,
This hour's joy has not reached its peak.

Reflecting mirror
When pearl blinds at dawn first roll up,
Silk on the loom lies unwoven by morning.
The jade case open, she studies her image,
Over the jewelled stand she leans to apply make-up.
She faces her image full of lonely laughter,
Looks at a flower, idly twists sideways.
For a moment she creates cocoon-emerging eyebrows,
Cautiously glosses fresh peach tones.
Perhaps plumed hairpins would suit here?
May be the gold hairclasp is too close?
Her wayward lover travels without return,
Tearful cosmetics unbidden soak her breast.

Bedroom regrets
Dawn River dies on a tall ridge-pole.
The slanting moon halfway over an empty garden.
Fallen leaves cross the window sill,

Beyond the blind flitting fireflies are trapped.
Full of love she lowers kingfisher drapes,
Tearful shuts the gold screen.
My long promised love has not come back,
Spring grass though chill is green once more.
My love for you is unswerving,
When will the north star veer?

Seventh Night
Her coach divine halts at seven removes,
Her phoenix carriage leaves the fount of heaven.
The moon shines with a Ninth Blaze glow,
Winds waft perfume of one hundred scents.
The joy to come is a moment's charmed laughter,
Tears of return are on her weeping face.
Lost to sight like Lo river shore,
Sudden disenchantment like Kaot'ang.
They part no more to meet.
River Han steady flows in spate.

The dancer
Pipes blow clear, silk seats move closer,
Strings sound anxious, snowflake sleeves adagio.
Following sung rhythms slim hands interweave,
Answering the melody moth eyebrows move.
Numb passion notes his dropped earring,
Narrowed eyes confide eloquent secrets.
Sunset delays her honoured guest,
She looks at him in this hour of love.

I watch his new wife
Misty twilight lotus arising from a river,
Dawn hazy sun shining on rafters –
Lovelier yet on a night of torchlit splendour
Is a light fan screening her pink face,
And her lover radiant, radiant
Over the couch his brilliant light spreading.
A sad feeling when the tall coach moves
And her waist jewels leave the verandah.

154

The singing-house

Dark, dark tall house benighted,
Blossoming candles by curtains bright.
On the silk drapes a peacock pin silhouette,
From a jewelled lute *Phoenix and chicks* music.
Night flowers show on the branch,
A new moon expands through fog.
Someone is dreaming by the window,
Watching for him, alone, sleek, lovely.

White seagulls, a satire on separated people

How sweet, a pair of white seagulls
Dawn and dusk playing on the river.
By chance they change their nest,
The hen leaves, the cock stays no more.
Bereft flight from shore to strand,
Solitary perch upon Ts'angchou.
East, west, moving on from there,
Shadow, echo for no reason severed.

Green, green riverside grass

Her spring garden somewhat finer each day,
She picks flowers, stares down the long road.
On autumn nights bitter and long
She hugs her pillow, goes to a lonely bed.
In the house of flutes she lowers swift rhythms
To avoid expressing how they parted there.
On the song-mat she hides behind her round fan,
'When will I see you once more?'
Though strings cease, they cling still to the pegs,
Though leaves fall, they but drop against the trunk.
So while I say these things come apart,
Compared to me they aren't quite forsaken.

A satire on the poet Liu Hsiao-cho

Behind bedroom lattice die the flames of night.
Window, door brighten in morning sun.
A charming girl draws the drapes aside,
Steps early from her bed.
Sparrow hairpins slant in dawn curls,

155

Moth eyebrows glint with last night's kohl.
Just audible her jade bangles distant,
Still savoured her kingfisher quilt scent.
How to tell the early dawn courtier?
A straggling line of geese!

Wang Shu

Betrayed
Mornings she gathers hungry silkworm food,
Nights she sews a thousand league robe.
Then up south lane she is heard
Homeward at sunset from picking lotus.
Green moss sheathes the cold well,
Red peonies grow among green fern.
The joys of life are finite,
The hour of love betrayed.
How can I rival new swallows
Flying double, home double together?

To a mulberry picker
I see a girl far off lift her basket,
Young, lithe, so exquisite.
Ready to leave she turns, then turns away,
About to speak, she breaks into a smile.
Just parted from my wife
I have no wish to seek a new friend.
But only for tying your oleaster sash,
Let me thank you with my magnolia spray!

Adorable
Red lotus unfolding in early dew,
Jade face reflecting mists of dawn.
Her Chao Feiyen-in-tears make-up finished,

She turns to insert a tiara flower.
Clustered gold hairpins galore!
Rumpled broidered collar askew!
Sunset return to jasper strung drapes,
To scented lamps ablaze with nine blooms.

Yü Tan

Autumn bedroom vigil
Sparkle, sparkle wide celestial Han,
Fluffy, fluffy clouds from craters,
Moon aslant trees casts shadows,
Winds upon water sketch rippling patterns.
Now she weeps, a wife at her loom,
And mourns the lover of her bed.
Silk tunic ever folded at dawn,
Kingfisher quilt vainly scented at night.
'Futile to draw from the silver curb well.
For whom would I sew gold lamé skirts?'
Her beloved did not come home.
She keeps vigil half the clear night.

One night I dreamed I went home
I sped home in a dream to my love:
With you I draw well water chill,
The bronze bucket's white silk cord,
The lovely well's white silver curb;
Sparrows dart from dense, massed trees,
Insects flit round tortoiseshell rafters.
One apart, you do not see me;
I cannot bear to face the glory of spring.

CHAPTER SIX

Poets of the Southern Dynasties

(early sixth century)

Wu Chün

Spring silkworms
Unhappy, I cannot bear to think
As I pick mulberry south of Weich'eng.
My sash hangs loose broidered with entwined boughs,
My hair is tangled with phoenix pins.
Flowers danced, we snuggled by the long hedge,
Moths flitted, we loved by the green lake.
I have no way to requite your kindness.
With streaming tears I turn to spring silkworms.

I long for Liaotung
Once I was a songhouse girl,
Then I came up to Royal Wei palace.
I've since been honoured in a carved litter,
Achieved the rank of wardrobe mistress.
A jewel of blue peacock, a lotus in its beak,
Gold insects inlaid with precious grains,
I confess they fail to satisfy.
With streaming tears I long for Liaotung.

Spring grass
Spring grass gathered can be bound,
But my heart is quite broken.
From grief green-glinting hair turns white,
Pink cheeks from tears have paled.
Tears not only form beads of pearl,
But I see pearls change to drops of blood.
I long to be a flying magpie mirror
Fluttering to reflect your parted image.

Sweet spring
Where shall I answer your letter?
Left of Lung are five forked roads.
With tears I grind *t'uchih* ink,

160

My brush stains the whiteness of swansdown paper.
On Meng Isle pool float jade-green tints,
Fragrant falls the dew on Tungt'ing lake.
You meant to return but did not return.
Sweet spring vainly spent.

Who can bear?
My home is north of Broadbank,
I blossomed into girlhood at Small Longbank.
Floral hairpins twist with jade arms,
Strings of pearl spangled with gold.
In wispy streaks hang green phoenix plumes,
With arabesque curves flutters my white fan.
Who can bear to look at these for long?
I hate not seeing you!

Her wild husband
The Hsiungnu fate will soon be sealed.
I stand by Jade Gate Pass.
Lotus blooms sheathe my dagger hilt,
An autumn moon clasps my sword pommel.
Your spring loom hums meek and mild,
Summer birds pine with cries of longing.
My wife at home watches for me,
Her wild husband never comes home.

Palindrome brocade
Golden orioles fly in royal parks,
Green plants sprout on islets.
The sun sparkles on K'unming water,
Spring comes alive in Magpie Lodge.
Rocking, swaying white flowers dance,
Rolling, swirling purple plants flow.
My letter woven in palindrome brocade
I have no way of sending to Lungt'ou.
I love you more than the jasper tree.
Not seeing you makes this exile despair.

161

His mop-and-broom

Cracking my whip I approach the great ridge,
Roping horse and men I ford Chang river.
Yen girls and Chao women
Cradle lutes all through the night.
Slim waists trail wide sleeves,
Half foreheads painted with long moths.
A man of course grows travel weary,
His mop-and-broom lives on the tributary shore.
The old one must not be deserted –
A new girl, what could she mean?

Fluttering to you

We live apart, hurt, unhappy.
Toward dusk my heart aches and aches.
Out on the road I question a Chao envoy
And hear you work as a minister.

Scented grass colour has now turned,
Iris blades are not yet even.
Heaped mulberry feeds silkworms into cocoons,
Swooping soaring swallows drip mud.
I long to leave with the spring wind
Fluttering to you in Liaohsi.

Fleeting smoke

White sun hidden by city houses,
Strong winds sweeping chill trees.
We broke apart, east divorced from west,
We last held hands, cold a stranger to heat.
I long for you, breathless, mute,
My hidden room pure and still.
Years have gone swifter than fleeting smoke,
The years to come are like rolling wheels.
The parted stork one thousand leagues will fly,
The waif hen will find no rest at night.

Last gleam

Into a bedroom still and pure
The sinking moon lets a last gleam.
Chill insects hidden by walls are pining,

Autumn moths round a candle flit.
Broken clouds streak then gather,
Scattered birds depart, return once more.
Beloved, where are you now?
Far from my river is your flowing Yih.
Once I play *Parted stork*
Thousand league tears soak my dress.

A few days

Autumn clouds lulled in late skies,
Chill nights form skeins of longing.
I hear you play excited on the flute
Loving you and then *Picking lotus*.
Parting was meant for a few days, no more,
Yet the high moon has waxed three times.
Shying, rearing Yellow river billows,
Plaintive wailing Lungt'ou cicadas.
I'll send you sweet herb leaves,
Pin them on near Bushy Terrace!

Mulberry up the lane

Lithe, lithe mulberry up the path
Shades the path and overhangs the bank,
Long twigs reflecting white sunlight,
Fine leaves hiding oriole yellow.
Silkworm hunger turns my thoughts to love,
I wipe my tears and lift my basket.
How can my past love know of this?
The hate of separation seethes in my heart.

The King of Ch'in wraps a gift robe

Hsienyang spring grass is sweet.
The Ch'in emperor wraps a robe.
Jade studded cord, oleaster case,
Gilt clay, storax scent.
Fresh fragrance impregnates lined drapes,
Last gleams flicker on a jade bed.
He must wait till late levée is over
To take this to his Huayang.

Picking lotus
Brocade sash matching floral hairpins,
Silk dress hanging over a green stream.
I ask, 'Where are you off to now?'
'Out picking lotus south of the river.
To Liaohsi three thousand leagues
I'd send them, but have no way.
Please turn back soon, beloved,
While these lotus are fresh'.

Holding hands
Happy in spring sunlight,
Holding hands along the clear Lo,
At cockcrow the royal park,
At twilight Hsiaop'ing ford.
Long skirts catch the white sun,
Wide sleeves carry sweet dust.
My former mate is just like this :
New love – he stops thinking of me!

Swallow
One swallow comes over the sea,
One swallow rests in a high hall.
One morning both chance to meet,
Surprised to find they are old friends.
She asks, 'Why are you so late?
Were pass and hill so winding or straight?'
I answer, 'The sea route was long,
Winds so fierce made me powerless to fly'.

When we parted long ago I stitched a silk cloak,
Spring winds were first entering the curtains.
By now summer has nearly faded,
Mulberry moths disperse through trees in flight.

Spring
Spring, where does it come from
Stroking a dress and startling plum?
Clouds block Green Chain Gate,
Winds blow Welcome Dew Terrace.
My lovely one a thousand leagues away,
Silk drapes are drawn closed.
No way to speak with her,
I face without hope a loving you winecup.

From a divorcée to her former husband
A deserted wife, I live by the river bridge.
I love you though you are far from me.
Phoenix-mate pins slip down my curls,
Lotus bloom belt sags loose round my waist.
My heart from farewell is broken,
My face with tears wasted.
Remember how we used to be –
Spare me occasional scraps of news!

A boy
Tung Sheng smiles with true charm,
Tzu Tu has such lovely eyes.
A million pays for one word,
A thousand in cash buys surrender.

Don't mention hide-and-seek mallow!
Who cares about virtue meek and mild?
I want you to bring your broidered quilt,
Come lie with your man of Yüeh!

Wang Seng-ju

Spring regrets
The four seasons like torrent water
Hurtle past rushing full circle.
Night birds echo forlorn,
Dawn gleams shine radiant.

I'm bored seeing blossom become fruit,
Have too often watched shoots turn to bamboo.
Ten thousand leagues bereft of news and letters,
Ten years of sleeping apart.

The burden of sorrow sheds my scented hair,
Prolonged weeping ruins my fair eyes.
You left to be in Yükuan,

165

I stayed to live at Hanku.
I only stare at this mossy room
That looks like a spider's nest.

I drink to my echoes in solitary night
And pursue my own shadow.
My ivory bed I've changed for felt and bamboo,
Silk dresses replaced with lined clothes.
Though wind and frost may come and go
I'll live alone, faithful still to you.

His new mistress
Girl of sixteen like a flower,
Moon of the fifteenth like a mirror,
Through parted blinds the very same radiance,
At the doorway both reflect the other.

Expensive women come down from Ch'in and Hann,
Famous ones go up to Yen and Cheng.
Ten cities is the usual asking price,
A thousand gold often makes a bargain.
Your interest, sir, may focus on them,
My heart is not inclined to compete!

Bringing his glamorous lady home
Long had he dreamed of a private boudoir beauty,
Never had he seen one to destroy a city.
For a thousand in gold he frequented gorgeous flowers,
One morning he met perfect glamour.
Her home was beyond Suman,
She came to flirt near Bushy Terrace.
Luckily this Hsiang-ju had no mate,
And this Wen-chün was recently widowed!

My neighbour's wife weaving at night
In a secret room winds blow harsh,
Down a long verandah the moon purer still.
Dim, dim the night garden wide,
Billow, billow the dawn drapes light.

I hear confused insects murmur,
Suddenly I'm pained by one wing of song,

Birdsong unending,
My love everlasting.
Worried you still have no cloak,
Night after night at the window I weave.

Night sadness

Dew on the eaves hardens into pearl,
Ice on the pool sets to smooth jade.
Dawn tears trickle in streams ten thousand,
Night grief deepens from parting a thousand leagues.
Forsaken curtains close, never to open.
Cold tallow gutters, flares once more.
How can I tell my heart and eyes are bewildered?
I see sudden scarlet change to green!

Spring bedroom resentment

Despair visits, no more do I groom my curls,
Spring comes, again I pucker my eyebrows.
Sad to see butterfly dust,
Weep to watch spiders' threads.
Moon shining on cold locust cushions,
Winds blowing kingfisher curtains.
Thoughts hard to trust to skimming carp,
Words no swift wing will bear.

Fulling cloth

Many a time wounded by gold flutes quickening,
Much am I troubled by red gleams hastening.
Dew beads on the purple of the pool,
Winds scurry through green of the garden.

I leave my loom, the slanting moon speeds west,
Pound my block, the glowing sun hurries east.
Sweet sweat like an orchid rinse.
I avoid carved gilt dragon candles.

I play through the *Great mound* variations,
Drum *Angler's south* rhythms.
With *Parted stork* sadness unremitting,
Parted paradise bird breaks, then resumes.
My foot of silk lies in the fish's belly,
My inch of heart relies on the webbed goose.

167

Describing a dream for someone

I've known fancies turn to dreams,
Never believing dreams could be like this!
Fair, fair, immaculate,
Pure, pure perfection,
Intimate by hibiscus cushions,
She turns back the joy of love quilt.
Elegant footsteps most lovely,
Full of whispers enchanting.

What I describe didn't seem to happen fast,
Then, strangely, became a thing of the moment
And I woke to nothingness,
Aware all is empty illusion.

Near, yet far

Girl of Ying in her phoenix-cote,
Lady of Han in Cypress Rafter Hall,
Doesn't she, immortal, conquer death,
Though her voice, her image are still perceptible?

I have a lover single-hearted,
From the same village, not of a strange region.
If a strange region, we'd still not be estranged.
From the same village we stare and stare the more.
If forced to stare like Herdboy and Weaver
We still wouldn't mind their one word of love a year.

Bittersweet

Going outside to admire orchid incense
I lifted the blind and met you.
Composing my features I managed one question,
'Please may I hear of your new mistress?'

'My new one comes full of laughter,
My old love would hide full of tears'.
'My love remains with the cold pine,
Your heart faints with day-lilies!'

Through green wine

Meek and mild, Sung Jung-hua
Sings solo songs of liquid melody.
She turns with a look not without meaning,

Slants her fan to stare back at me.
How is she inferior to Hsü Fei-ch'iung?
She is far better than Liu Green Jade!
How will I send my desire so desirous?
Through green wine in my half-empty winecup.

For a woman to give her lover
Green Jade and Green Pearl,
Chang-nü and Lady Lu –
Her crooning voice has no rival in the past,
Long sleeves have no match in all the world.
She rises as if from a phoenix-cote,
Then appears on Hsiao-Hsiang shores.
Were you to lift your skirt,
I'd whisper one word of passionate love.

Anguish
In a cold tree perches a sheltering hen,
The moon shines, the wind blows too.
Exiled statesmen and deserted wives,
For the fallen my heart can feel.

Seven idle strings on a jewelled lute,
One hundred vain stems of an orchid lamp.
Sulky pertness I won't bother to mimic,
Weeping cheeks are wiped, trickle once more.
My quilt-sharer has become Ch'u-Yüeh,
And yet those foreign lands aren't so alienated!

The one I love
Night breezes puff firefly sparks,
Dawn gleams glint on lichen.
Long faded sweet herb leaves,
Fallen in vain grapevine blooms.

I cannot bear ever to weave white silk,
Who can in loneliness wash sheer silk?
And time, when will it end?
I hope for you soon, but you delay your return.
You are born to wander, I know.
As for me, I'm just an entertainer!

To someone's despairing mistress
Pitiful the lone standing tree
With branches light, roots easily shaken,
Now soaked with dew
And whirled by winds.

Wrapped in my brocade quilt, sleepless
I sit up from night until dawn.
The sad way I am wasting
Is not that you like slim waists!

For a singer who feels hurt
I know in my heart I hate you,
Yet I'm ashamed to look in my mirror.
I used to mope when our love went wrong,
Now I've changed, feel nothing for you.
Take back the earrings you gave me!
Give back the fox-fur I sent you!
A lute string snaps, it can be mended.
Once love departs it is detained no more!

Autumn bedroom regrets
Slanting rays hidden by west walls,
Twilight sparrows up on southern boughs.
Winds come, autumn fans are thrown aside,
The moon appears, night candles are snuffed.

Deep love wells up one hundred times.
Distant tears are not one single trickle.
Useless to worry about unhappiness,
When all is said – you'll never know!

Chang Shuai

We met
We met by Dusk Shadow steps,
As I drove to Peak Cap alone.
The tall gates were all as one,

Stately mansions all of a kind.
I lean on the coach rail. The sun is just setting.
'Where would one visit you, my lord?'

'The place where I reside
Is an easy place to recognise.
My green mansion overlooks the highway,
Gentle terraces look onto winding streams.

'Up in the hall fluent lute studs caressed,
Thundercloud goblets passed round day and night.
Pomelo sweet with blossomed fruit,
Crimson flames blaze on stems of gold.

'Of my brothers two or three
Have tunic belts that glitter with gems.
At dawn they retire from the Forbidden Palace,
Coach and rider cantering abreast,
Golden saddles, agate bridles,
The passersby crowd to watch.

'Entering our gates you see in one glance
Ducks and geese, cocks with their hens,
Many thousand each of cocks and hens
Call to each other fanning their plumes,
Stand in set formation east and west,
Flock on flock in perfect file.

'The eldest's wife embroiders a square collar,
The next wife is nursing her babe.
The youngest wife, still a dear child,
Sits up and flutes a fanfare.
"Gentlemen, come up quick!
Divine phoenix are coming to perch!" '

Wine
From wine I get real pleasure,
And this wine is the finest!
Wine clear as blossom is valuable,
This wine, sweet as milk, is invaluable!

How to attract the best guests?
Make a palm-dancing girl offer them such wine.
Gold goblets clear and full,
Jade tankards slowly edge together.

171

Who would share my late years?
I drink until fragrant dawn.
Before your song has ended,
I'll leave my seat and miss the rafter dust.

Far betrothed
My far betrothed did not return.
Seasonal nature once again is changing.
White dew troubles my unlined gown,
Autumn winds still my round fan.

Who can be parted for long,
In different towns and other regions?
Drifting clouds veil the mountain folds.
I stare after you. When will we meet?
The message I send to a far wanderer:
'Empty bedroom tears like hail'.

Hsü Fei

To my wife
Twilight dreams of your clear eyes.
You slip on shoes, leave your pepper room.
Spinning spiders live in brocade rugs,
Shifting dust shrouds the jade bed.
I cannot perceive your lovely image,
Only a trace of shimmering curtain scent.
This beauty, passionately happy,
Hugs her lute, sitting in the high hall.
How does the bereft mourner forget,
Alone, heartbroken, turned to the corner?
Let me confide through one letter
Despair nine times wreathing my heart.

A poem on sweet promise sent to my mistress
Longing for you I went up the north gallery.
As I paced I glanced at the east house.
Suddenly there was a tree near the eaves
Laden with sparkling sunlit blossom.
Its freshness I'd liken to rouge and powder,
Its whiteness I'd compare to glamorous artifice,
Making my heart's passion stronger still,
Reminding me more keenly of your narrow lane.
Elusive it appears inaccessible,
Wispy, wispy like dawn streaked clouds.
Since stern walls are insurmountable,
I break off my poem for a hempen pledge.

Fei Ch'ang

Fulling cloth in the night
Heavenly gates lower heavy bars,
Cinnabar court exhales a bright moon.
Autumn air freezes in the city,
Autumn blocks thud beyond the wall.
Trailing sounds ring Sparrow Terrace,
Hovering echoes vault Dragon Tower,
Mellifluous, faint, so faint,
They must come from the highway,
Faint, so faint, pathos unending,
Must come from the coach driving district.

In the coach driving district all the world resides,
Their women lovely as dawn mist.
Round jewels sparkle at their ears,
Square collars broidered lie aslant.
Clothes incensed with hundred perfume powder,
Curls quivering with nine stem blooms.

Last evening garden pagoda trees shed.
This morning sheer silks feel thin.
They dust seats, roll out mandarin duck design,
Draw drapes, unfold tortoise and stork motifs.

173

Golden ripples now serene,
Jade footsteps approach block and pounder.
Red sleeves swirl back and forth,
White arms lift in flurried jerks.

I only hear, cannot see.
Alone at night I stand in hopeless despair.
Alone at night, when will it end?
Desire's involuntary wound.

Steps strung with Jade Scales dew,
Garden aflutter with weathervane wings.
Spangled bright shooting stars blaze,
Glistening, radiant Long River glints.

For three winters I have enough to read,
For five days not enough provisions.
Yang Hsiung is now silent and alone
And here you are, 'straight as a bowstring'!

Springtime betrayed
Fragrant trees burst into spring glory,
When Ts'ai Yung stared at her blue dress.
Water carries peach petal away,
Spring with the willow returns.
Willow, when will you return?
You wilt and wilt, droop and droop.
Now the sun shines on Changt'ai lane,
Now sweeps Eternal Gate doors.

All he knows is parting's memory,
Vain regrets of springtime betrayed.
Loyang is far as the sun –
How will I meet Fufei?

In spring suburbs I watch pretty girls
In fragrant suburbs kingfisher plume gatherers
Roll up their sleeves in search of sweet spring.
Golden glints kindle from tiaras,
Red tints dart from tossing ribbons.
Sparkles the sun, sparkles on her canopy.
Flares the dust, flares from horses' hooves.
Dim dusk near the tall house
Tells you my name is Ch'in.

174

Reflection in a mirror
Dawn gleams shine on apricot rafters.
A Chao Feiyen beauty rises for morning make-up.
Careful she spreads wide lines of kohl,
Deft fingers dot her brow with floral yellow.
She fixes jewel pins, studies her image a moment,
Pats with her powderpuff admiring its scent.
But she hates her worn kingfisher plume,
Grumbles at lack-lustre jewels.
'In the city it's half across the forehead for all,
Not the length my eyebrows are painted!'

Sunny spring brings warmth
The sun splendid on Lady Pan's gate,
Winds soft on Tung Hsien's lodge.
Whorlear creeps from the steps.
A shrike squawks on a fence.
Silkworm girl's cassia pole hook,
Playboy's storax shot.
Caressing sleeves mean to delay the traveller,
'Let's meet, don't be mopey!'

On autumn nights chill winds stir
A pretty girl lives at Honei,
Her army husband quells Mayi city.
Fallen dew one morning beads,
By midnight two are shedding tears.
In air crisp bedcurtains are chill,
Under skies cold needle and thread lie inert.
Red cheeks will stay the same a long, long while.
When you come home, how will they greet you?

Picking caltrop
I live near Five Lake estuary,
I pick caltrop on Five Lake shores.
My jade face disdains cosmetics,
Twin eyebrows are natural kingfisher tones.

The sun slants, skies darkening.
Winds roused, waves restless.
There he is midstream!
No good we two falling in love . . .

175

Despair at Eternal Gate Palace
Toward dusk a thousand sorrows stir.
Remorse, can it be quelled?
Sad memories return with me to bed,
My gossamer gown stifles the weeping.
Crimson trees rock gently with the breeze,
Orioles burst into cascading song.
When your House of Gold was to treasure A-chiao,
That didn't mean you weren't to visit!

Mount Wu high
Mount Wu glimmers grow late,
Sun Terrace colours dwindle, dwindle.
The lovely woman's vertiginous eyrie,
How to tell if her heart is true or false?

Dawn clouds strike rocks rising,
Dusk rain soaks clothes sheer.
I long to loosen her thousand gold girdle
And escort her back to the great king.

The one I love
Royal Forest crows about to nest,
Ch'angan sun going down.
My lover I despair of meeting,
Empty dreams of cinnabar court footsteps.

Blinds stirring remind me of your visits,
Sounds of thunder resemble your carriage passing.
In the north there is a lovely girl,
Meek and mild, she makes heads turn.
If my husband is by her bewitched
That won't make mine a jealous heart!

176

Yao Fan

Picking mulberry
Geese homing north of Tallwillow,
Spring returning south of Lo river.
Sunshine on an oleaster collar,
Winds swaying kingfisher hairpins.

Among mulberry I see the gloaming,
In my rooms silkworms will soon be hungry.
If you love me, help me gather!
I can hardly bear to hope for you.

K'ung Weng-kuei

Lady Pan
Eternal Gate and Eternal Trust
At sunset nine-barred, deserted.
Thunderous sounds I hear rumbling, rumbling,
Echoing coaches stop their clatter-clatter.

Favoured light courts skilful dance,
The round fan surrenders to autumn winds.
Glamorous beauty who does not desire?
A man's love will not last for ever.

Liu Ling-hsien

Reply to my husband, two poems

1

Flowery garden lovely with rays slanting,
Through orchid windows soft breezes cross.
The sun sinks. She freshens her cosmetics,
Opens the blinds onto spring trees.
Warbling orioles in foliage echo,
Playful butterflies amid flowers flurry.

She strums her lute in joy's own pursuit,
Her heart for sadness will not be diverted.
Their happy hour together not remote,
Yet her betrothed now she will not meet.
Would you know how much she grieves in secret?
Her spring boudoir is withdrawn and shaded.

2

In the east house a perfect beauty?
Of southern realms the most exquisite face?
In the night moon she appears like a goddess?
In dawn mists she seems to be Fufei?

But I'm looking at my face in the mirror:
Your fond similes I know are false,
Your evocations hopelessly clever,
Your allusions absolutely wrong!
Though you, an intellectual, think me lovely,
I hardly dare to ruin cities!

Ho Ssu-ch'eng

Lady Pan
Hushed, hushed Eternal Trust late.
A sparrow twitters near her secret room,
Spiders spin webs down high galleries,
Lichen carpets long verandahs,
Curtains hang unmoved in empty halls,
Stamens breathe scent on still stone steps.
She watches the sun set for eternity,
Turns again to dust her lonely bed.

Old love
Old love can never be forgotten,
Like the scent of cassia or of orchid.
His new love though he may enjoy her
Is not unlike the dogwood's weak smell.

The song I sing is *Phoenix and chicks*
Not *Mulberry up the lane.*
I gave you my song, you refused.
Cradling my lute I mourn the cold.

In South Park I met a lovely woman
Lo shore seems like driven snow.
Wu Mount like dawn clouds.
Today I first saw a city-destroyer,
Of kingdom-destroyers I had long heard.
Seductive eyes married to shy charm,
Cinnabar lips parted in a smile,
Winds curling her grapevine sash,
Sun shining on her pomegranate skirt.
She has, of course, her dashing husband there,
So a prefect simply need not bother!

179

?Liu Ling-hsien

To my late husband's mistress
Singers attend the Han river girl,
Her painted face enjoys the moon's glory.
Chain-stitch images twin stems,
Lacework forms opening buds.

But widowed rooms dismiss fine silks.
To take your gift would touch a painful wound.
Though I admit not knowing you,
I've heard it said you are well-born.

In the past Huo Kuang halted his coach here,
Liu Hsia-hui used to call in his carriage.
There is no way that we can talk together.
I'm watching sunrise through dawn mist for ever.

CHAPTER SEVEN

Royal Poets of the Liang
(the Hsiao Family)

Hsiao Yen

Fulling cloth
He yoked his carriage north of Yi river,
I escorted him north of the Yellow river.
Dejected thoughts brood on his moving harness,
Tense dreams haunt my lone bed.
When I wake red and green blur,
I begin to sense the wound of plain silk.
From Chungchou trees leaves are falling,
The frontier wall must have early frost.
Shadowy insects grow numb, chilled day by day,
Garden flowers turn a brighter yellow.
Metal winds on clear nights passing by,
A bright moon hanging over the hidden house.

Soft, soft girls of the same palace
Help me prepare his clothes.
Fitful evening pounders irrupt,
Doleful autumn blocks resound.
Light silk billows round jade arms,
Frail plumes curve across rosy faces.
Red cheeks flush ever deeper,
Slanting glances sparkle ever brighter.
We pound with all our 'not a stone'
The pattern forming two mandarin ducks.
The shears we hold would cut metal,
The incense we use is sweet as orchid.

Long has my betrothed not returned.
I will send this cloak to his cold land.
For whom will I make my body lovely?
Longing for you embitters my heart.

A grand house
In Loyang there's a winding lane,
A winding lane no courier can pass.
Suddenly two youths happen to meet.
Reining in, one asks, 'Where is your home?'
'Home is west of Hantan,
Easy to remember, you may know it well.

The eldest's badge ribbons in a tangle,
The middle son's pendants aglitter,
The youngest still in blue silk
And topknot goes out to play at Nanp'i.

'When the three sons enter the gates together
Servants bow down near the gates.
When the three sons go up the hall together
Rich wine would fill a thousand cups.
When the three sons go indoors together
Brilliant light appears inside.

'The eldest's wife is fixing gold kingfisher plumes,
The middle wife is working a bodkin.
The youngest's wife alone has time to spare,
She tunes her pipes, plays by winding streams.
"Gentlemen, stay for a minute,
Phoenix flutes will now give a fanfare!" '

Countless wounding seasons
Round brilliance stares at an empty doorway,
Clear light streams on a bed of love.
A bed of love stares at its lonely shadow,
Bitter remorse and self-pity.
The mirror on its stand soon gathers dust,
The lute in its case has no strings.
Sad desire through countless wounding seasons,
Despair at parting in endless flowery years.

You are like East Mulberry radiance,
I am like West Willow smoke.
Since you left, your path is distant,
Between bright and dark a gulf has grown.
I long to be reins of bronze and iron
Moving you to Eternal Joy Palace.

Green, green riverside grass
Cobwebs' silk strands thick veil tapestried doors,
Far away, far away brooding on promises past.
Promises past, long he is in returning.
His homeland is bereft of news,
Bereft of news, reunion idly delayed.
Half asleep I feel as if he is home,

183

When I wake his image is gone.
Cut off from you all my life,
The moon's rays hidden by clouds,
Leaves' ageing hurried on by frost.
Those on the way are jealous of their own persona,
None will speak for me.

For Su Wu's wife
My lovely one promised to meet me,
I never dreamed time would pass by.
Autumn winds suddenly dismiss the season,
White dew hardens on the front porch.
Wounded, wounded by the one chill pillow,
Hurt, hurt by solitary moon bedcurtains.
Suddenly I hear a northwest goose
As if from the cold desert.
It holds in its beak a ten thousand league letter,
In it are words of lifelong parting.
He only talks of long separation,
No longer says 'I love you'.
Hun sheep he plundered long ago,
Han flags he held in the past.
Before I'd finished reading his words on silk
Tears like silk threads fell down my face.
Useless to cherish our vow unto death,
You reward me from afar with your joint grave poem.

This heart of mine
Flying birds rise in flurries,
Scatter in fear, sudden disarray,
Cawing, cheeping they circle the treetops,
Fluttering, hovering to flock on cold boughs.
Whenever I'm sad from our campaign long
I always feel the pain of the man on the ridge.
I send these words to my love in her boudoir,
'How can you know this heart of mine?
Don't you see the dodder on the pine,
Leaves may fall, but roots will never stray!'

Flower of forgetfulness
To welcome spring there was a flower,
Green its blossoms, many its stems;

184

They say it is the flower of forgetfulness,
It grows beside the north hall.

Flit, flit a pair of butterflies
Bobbing in twos up and down,
Swerving, swooping down then up.
The essence of this scent never alters,
Flitting butterflies, now a pair, now but one.
Here is a heart mankind will never fathom.

Fragrant tree
A green tree starts to toss fragrance,
Fragrance sprung from not one leaf,
Over one leaf pass spring winds,
Fragrance with fragrance joins in close embrace,
Colours mingle in a shifting mosaic,
Massed flowers gay with banks of riches,
Banked riches I cannot bear to dwell on . . .
Who can be calm to dwell on this?

Looking from a high terrace
High terrace half among passing clouds.
I stare, stare from limitless height.
Grass, trees no variation,
Hills, rivers all one colour.
Fuzzy, fuzzy the path to Loyang,
The road is far, hard to make out.
Jade steps, someone I used to desire.
Desire rekindles, does she love me too?

The one I love
Who said lifetime parting is long?
I remember vividly parting from you.
On my clothes your scent still remains,
In my grasp your letter not yet faded,
Round my waist the twin silk belts
I dream wind into kindred hearts.
Often I fear my love will show –
A jasper bloom I cannot bear to pick.

Purple orchid starts to bud
Orchid planted near the jade terrace,
In warm air orchid begins to bud.
Sweet scent spreads with the hours,

Grows lovely and fair to greet the season.
It alone will enrich gilt plumed charm,
Rouse red silk to deeper passion.
Why bother to love the two pleasure-seekers?
Single glance beauty does not ruin cities.
Too shy to be coupled with lotus and iris,
She does not fear the shrike's autumn knell.

The weaving wife

I said goodbye, went out to the south eaves,
Parting thoughts sink heavy in my dull room.
The loaded shuttle lies still on cold nights,
The humming loom stops on autumn days.
My lover is ten thousand leagues far,
With whom to share my woven stuff?
I wish I could once turn light back
To brighten this sorrow and pain.
If your desire is not forgotten,
My heart will endure to the end of time.

Seventh Night

White dew beneath the moon beading,
Autumn winds over trees freshening.
Jasper terrace pregnant with green fog,
Jade curtains begetting purple smoke.
Their meeting rare is not in the sweetest season,
For these sweethearts it's not the best time of year.
The jade pitcher carries night swift,
Orchid tallow till dawn is flaring.
Long ago I was sad how hard it was to cross,
Now I'm wounded how soon it is passed.
Breathless grief, twin rapture severed.
Disenchantment, two lovers sundered.

Bagatelle

Fufei appearing on Lo shore!
Roving nymph rising from Han south bank!
Charms sweeter than at Hsiats'ai,
Wonder more divine than at Kaot'ang.
Mien Chü transformed local custom,
Wang Pao transferred his native culture,

186

How much the more the devas gathered here!
Aren't they all perfect!
Long sleeves make guests linger,
Clear chant ever spins round rafters.
Yen and Chao are ashamed of their looks,
Hsi Shih and Ta Chi shamed by their fragrance.
Though it's only hearsay, that pearl being fondled,
Surely you'll be needing bright earrings?

Hsiao Kang

Love-song
Daybreak's glowing scene is lovely,
A singer is in her phoenix house.
Seen from the front her tapered waist is tinier,
Viewed from the side a flag rolled into nothing.
She apportions cosmetics between faint dimples,
Spreads over cheeks slanting rouge.
She plays her lute with pegs not tightened,
Song and flute never fully finished.

She knows herself that her beloved
Frequents Ch'in palace on duty.
Who says he bows and scrapes to officials?
He moves instead in the highest circles!
His light coach's black awning is festooned,
Reins fly, his greys clatter along,
Gold saddles matching braided tails,
Inlaid jade glinting on plaited manes.
His lance is studded with Ching Mountain jade,
His sword is made of Tanyang bronze.
His left fist grasps storax shot,
Beside him he holds the Great Curve bow.
Drawing the bowstring he relies on Magpie Blood bow,
Wielding the strong bow he uses Oxfly.
For hunting with corded dart he often climbs Lung range,
For drinking deep and song he always goes to Feng.

187

Glimmer, glimmer the sinking sun hides,
Dignified he goes home to boudoir lattice.
Lamps kindle from speculum flame,
Dust scatters in Carp winds.
Coloured plume curtains seasonally lowered,
Ivory bed replaced in its case.

Fog darkens willow before the window,
Cold engulfs catalpa over the well.
Love-vine clings to the fringe of a pine,
Sweet melon creeps east of the well.
Deeply I cherish your favour,
The year fades in hope unending.

The kingdom of Shu

Where Bronzebridge points to Yeh valley,
Dagger Road looks to Central Plains,
Following the stars on high Shu's realm is marked,
Fixed firm in its cities below.
Classical song ensues from good order in the land,
Exotic dance originated in Pa and Yü.
Yang city is the place for fun and pleasure.
With daggers boys ride, racing in swarms.
There five women travelled but couldn't arrive!
One hundred carriages make fine sport.

Sacrifice and prayer on Emperor Wang's feastday,
The ground sprinkled with wine for Lord of Shu's execution.
The river sprites received double betrothal gifts,
The Cho girl longed to lead her chicks.

I stop my strings, strum with plectrum a while,
Cease piping to put on more lipstick.
Spring colours I rinse in Chin waves,
My fan I twirl against the bright bird.
I hear you come home with banners raised,
I'll go down to the corner city wall.

My sad fate

The famous capital is full of lovely talent
Who pride themselves on their looks.
My wastrel travels, never comes home,
A Ch'iu Hu, he won't keep his promise.
On my jade face fade pink cheeks,

Constant frowns furrow kingfisher eyebrows.
In my cosmetic mirror a puzzled morning face,
In the sewing needle brittle old thread.

I'm different from the scolded 'rock-the-boat' girl.
What have I to do with the baby-snatching suspect?
We part for life, but who will pat my back?
If I dropped dead, who would say 'How slow she comes!'
Wang Ch'iang's beauty was extraordinary,
Yet she reluctantly stepped inside felt tents.
Lady Lu married late in the day
When fine spring was no more.
Moving a mountain can still be done,
I'll hope for the unlikely day crows turn white.
My heart suffers for no reason,
The onlookers must be laughing out loud!

Calm Joy Palace newly built
Far away through cloud and mist I see
Carved rafters reflect cinnabar red,
Pearl blinds shot with dawn sunlight,
Gilt flowers brushed by night winds.
You want to know the place for song and pipes?
Come by Calm Joy Palace!

Twin catalpas grow by a lonely well
Late spring moon. Twin catalpas by a well,
New twigs bristling from old stumps.
Late leaves hide nesting phoenix,
Dawn flowers stroke morning rooks.
Once more I glimpse Hsi Shih in splendour,
By the silver curb she draws up the rope.

Sighs of a lady of Ch'u
In her room still the water-clock drips and drips,
Time's infinity, silence of night.
Grass insects flit through the night door,
Spiders entwine autumn walls.
She faintly smiles, but not a happy smile,
She softly sighs, a sigh that turns to sorrow.
Gold pins droop in her hair,
Jade chopsticks trickle on her face.

189

The road to Loyang

Loyang, the place for beauty,
Its highways full of spring glory.
Sportive boys hold their first catapults,
Silkworm girls carry their first baskets.
Golden saddles blaze on dragon horses,
Silken sleeves caress spring mulberry.
Jade carriages race late into town,
P'an Yüeh's fruit fills tall hampers.

Broken willow

Willow tangled into silken strands
Is pulled and broken in early spring.
Foliage thick bird flight hinders,
Winds gentle flower's fall prolong.
Along city walls high, short flutes trilling,
Through forests bare painted horns forlorn.
Tunes that bear no hint of parting
All mean 'I'll love you always'.

Sorrel horse

Getting down from the loom at dawn
I just met my lover coming home,
Green ribbons dangling from jade stirrups,
Scarlet sweat staining perfumed clothes,
Cantering so fast precious cowries jingled,
Prancing so much scattered dust billowed.
'Oatcakes I'm pleased to serve you,
Don't betray past love!'

South lake

On South lake floating-heart leaves
Where sweethearts also seek pleasure.
Silvery fishing lines, kingfisher blue rods,
Jade stern, hibiscus boat,
Lotus scent blending with musk of clothes
To the sound of oars in the water's swift flow.

190

North beach
Along banks shady trail willow fronds,
The smooth river carries whitewashed fences.
Women from near the city I often meet,
See girls many times in their pleasure boats,
Green water spraying long sleeves,
Floating alga staining light oars.

The great embankment
Off to Yi city I stopped midway
Where travellers usually tarry.
Divorced women skilled at plainweave,
Sirens who notch up a fortune,
Cook oatcakes to detain the best clients
Who buy wine to woo these sylphs.

Buying from lotus boats
Where they pick lotus at the riverbend bank
Boatmen often dilly-dally.
Lotus pickers' dresses I can just make out,
Winds soft their scent does not carry.
You want to know where boats slip through?
Just look for lotus leaves that lie open!

I see a dropped hairpin reflected in the river's flow
One by one reflected in green water
They seem to crave a cooling breeze.
The flow trembles, painted image ravaged.
A hairpin drops, coiffure flowers vanish.
Where is her beloved so long?
She suffers in vain for hearts no longer one.

Spring nights
Blossoming trees burst with spring clusters,
Silk bedcurtains ever empty at night.
The wind's voice through bamboo melodious,
The moon's colour with the pool harmonious.
Tinted notepaper vain crumples,
No news will reach Yünchung.

Winter light
Winter dawn sun shines on rafters,
Morosely she gets out of bed,
Lifts from the curtains her bamboo-leaf sash,
Turns to the mirror her caltrop bloom radiance.
Certain there's no one to see her like this,
What's the use of early morning rouge?

Mosaic
Mosaic stamens brighten the south garden,
In the garden a bright scene so sweet.
Prettiest blossom on the bough
Will soon win the spring wind's love.
The spring wind feels passion too:
It kisses drapes, reveals pillars.
Revealing pillars, reveals emerald smoke,
Kissing drapes, kisses hanging lotus,
Making red flowers scatter everywhere
To tumble and flutter, dancing before my eyes.

Before my eyes there is no want of images,
I can stare at patterns kaleidoscopic:
Pearl tassels, kingfisher curtains,
Satin drapes, hibiscus folds,
Scented smoke pours from windows,
The setting sun slants across stairs,
Sun rays depart slower and slower.
Seasonal blooms surround me here:
Peach blossom pink like dots,
Willow leaves tangled like silk thread,
Silken twigs twist toward darkening light,
Shadows fall, dark shades lengthen.

Spring swallows dance double, double,
Spring hearts everywhere wounded.
Wine in plenty, the heart's moment of ease.
The branch of oblivion for sorrow not forgotten.

A singer's frustration
Silk windows look on painted galleries,
Soaring galleries long corridors encircle.
Winds scatter double heart plants,

192

The moon sends out sweet light.
Shadowy inside the blinds appears
A charming beauty quite beyond compare.
Shyly she copies Ch'in Lofu's hairdo,
Bashfully does her Lofu boudoir face.
She slips on her rustling red shawl,
Dabs fresh chic yellow on her brow.

Slanting the lamp she walks through brocade curtains
To her jade bed glimmering with faint incense.
The six-cornered twin tortoiseshell pillows,
Their eight-panelled quilt adorned with two mandarin ducks,
These things can still long since they parted
Comfort love's grief, mementoes of him.
In tears she passes tedious days
So soon transformed from hot to cold.

Jade Gate Pass riders struggle through night snow,
Metal air hurls harsh frost.
Couriers icebound at Fleetfox Pass,
Too distant the Crossriver waterway.
Of my vagrant love there is no news,
Red lips uselessly scented.

Her hidden room

Her hidden room in cold sun grows late,
Declining rays cross the window sill.
Red blinds far do not prevent my view,
Light drapes hang half rolled up.
I know slim hands are tailoring,
Such perfection her finely sewn cloak.
Dragon shears lie across her knees,
Painted rule slips down her skirt front.
Pressing iron, sheen of gilt varnish,
Needle spool cased in ivory.
Cloth cut into a joy of love quilt,
Designed as nestling mandarin ducks.

In sewing she uses double needle thread,
For padding a silkworm's eightfold thread.
Perfume laced with Lich'iu nectar
And musk exhaling Chungt'ai smoke
Now enter lapis lazuli bedcurtains,
Suffuse Mount T'ai rugs.

193

Besides she has a carved stove warm,
Unlike the round fan rejected.
She fears more keenly wartime separation :
An empty bed and futile self-pity.

Bagatelle for a lovely woman
Beautiful Ta Chi and bewitching Mao Ch'iang,
Like them you groom your pretty face,
Like them fix long pins in your hair,
Unlike them you put yellow on your brow.
Your silk skirts are admired for sheer fineness,
Painted slippers prized for high rims.

Too shy to go upstairs,
You go out faintly smiling to the verandah,
Pick flowers to offset haircombs,
Tug boughs and muse on stamen scent,
Sing to yourself one snatch of song,
On dulcet strings tireless play.
You pride yourself on your sweetheart –
At thirty a palace attendant !

Night longing in an autumn bedroom
It's nothing to do with Eternal Trust exile,
Nor that my lover is on campaign,
But sudden from nine-barred rooms he disappeared,
Ten thousand jealousies flourish in my heart.
Twilight gates locked with fish-emblazoned keys,
Nightly bed grieving behind painted screens.
A distant moon peeps through the window,
Moaning insects murmur round the steps.
Early frosts dislodge tiny leaves,
Autumn winds chase scattered fireflies.
Stale make-up still on for several days,
Fresh clothes pleated lie unsewn.
You want to know why I don't sleep?
It's the sound of fulling beyond the city wall.

She ruins cities
A beauty described as sensational
Is lovely as a posy of blooms.
Though she lives north of Li's city,

Her home is east of Sung's house.
She models her singing on the Princess's brother,
Copies the dances of Han Emperor Ch'eng's palace.
She often roams along the Ch'i river,
Loves to stay in phoenix house.

Heels so high seem to go up steps,
Skirts flaring are so nervous of the wind.
Under sheer colours I see her arms,
Pearls amassed, swarming dragonflies!
Fronds dangle around her curtains,
Sunset crosses bedroom lattice.
Cosmetic windows blot out willow colour,
Well water reflects peach pink.
'It's not that I regret the river bank girdle,
But I'm ashamed of my spring bedroom's emptiness'.

Back in town on short furlough
Waters of Han shores early green,
Grass south of the river once more yellow.
In sunshine reedmace hearts grow warm,
From winds blowing plum stamens scented.
Campaign boat moored at the brimming moat,
Homeward gallop to rest by the iron moat.
Dance hall dresses still folded away,
Concert strings yet untouched.
Busily I stride away –
Who cares about women in lonely beds?

For someone's discarded woman
Long ago her jade footsteps charmed.
She swallows her shame by flowery candles.
Don't say his heart has stopped loving!
She bites back tears of self-pity.
She's used to watching joy turn to grief,
It's nothing to do with beauty grown ugly.
A lone goose abandoned midway,
A waif paradise bird dead before the mirror.

195

Bagatelle attached to a letter
Dancing girls and Yen maids,
Singing-houses and women of pleasure
With large plectrums play fortissimo,
With hand mime slowly wind in dance.
Fishing rod from Shu they strum,
Hsinch'eng's *Broken willow* they pipe.
On jade tables Queen of the West peaches,
In pearl-whorl cups pomegranate wine.
Silk curtains different from A to Z,
Front doors magnificent from One to N.
Night after night there is a bright moon,
Season after season I love the change of dress.

Love-song
Cloudy fanlight of cassia its frame,
Flying ridge-pole of apricot its rafters.
Windows aslant let in stamen's breath,
Tiny cracks admit a dusty ray.
She tailors with Empress of Wei measure,
Draws water from Prince of Huainan well-curb.
His green-black horse may come home at dark,
In readiness she perfumes silk skirts.

Regret
Autumn winds and white fans
Are naturally incompatible.
A new woman and past love –
Surely an intolerable idea!
Yellow gold bells behind my elbows,
White jade dishes before the table.
Who would choose to face these alone?
Must I instead bear infidelity?

Night after night
Faint, faint frost in the night,
Not dawn's approaching gleam.
She weeps on her pillow still wearing powder,
Her body won't settle down to sleep in bed.
Orchid tallow gutters, flares again.
Incense burner goes out, rekindles perfume.
Ask but the measure of grief.
It is known by the length of night.

Seventh Night

Autumn promise creeps toward the present.
Through long night moves the River goddess.
Purple smoke soars to phoenix wings,
Shooting light trails her jade coach.
Loyang wonders if she's the sword spirit,
Ch'engtu marvels at the strange star.
The sky shuttle she wove with for long
She stops at last to meet her love tonight.

Spring snow

A late hailstorm hurls silver pebbles,
Floating clouds darken not lifting.
Snow in the pond dissolves without settling,
Dropped and picked up with the wind.
Flowing yellow silk of a woman in love,
Jade mirrorstand of Lady Wen.
The flower she looks at, says she might wear,
Is certainly not spring plum!

Out for a walk in late sunlight

Slender trees engulfed in unspent sunlight,
Spring bedroom suffused with late perfume.
Dainty flowers slip down her curls,
Faint sweat on powder glistens.
Flying ducks tune she soon stops,
Sobbing crow rhythm abruptly changes.
Shamed by the white sun darkening,
Among coach and horse crowds she hopes for him.

Dance

Lowered hands suddenly soar, soar,
Feiyen enchanting on his palm.
Her silk dress lures wayward winds,
Her light sash sways with passionate surrender.
It's not like the land of Ch'angsha
Where dance steps don't make waists whirl.

The harp

Harp pegs slacken, fluting softly starts,
When the music quickens, dancing gets faster.
Bangles jingle in time to strumming strings,
Tunics whirl, half caught in the stops.
You want to know if her heart is excited?
Watch her kohl eyebrows contract!

The dance

How sweet, just sixteen!
Her rhythm like a gliding swan
Is far better than Hoyang entertainers,
Is sultry like Huainan dance.
I see her feet approach in the line,
I watch her chignon vanish with a turn of the head.
On her arm moves Chao Hua jade,
Sleeves follow winds fancy-free.
'Honoured guests, don't get up!
My *Sobbing crow* tune is not ended!'

Spring bedroom passion

Willow leaves slim, slim.
A lovely girl lazily weaves fine silk.
She straightens her dress, turns to her mirror,
To greet spring cautiously lifts the blinds.

She picks plum round and round the trees,
Seeks swallows, peeks up in the eaves.
She simply says, 'In the pursuit of flowers
I'm quite above suspicion!'

Her late boudoir

Pearl blinds were lowered at dusk.
Her charming form I can pursue no more.
Flowered winds in the dark I sense,
Orchid candles through curtains waft.
Within jade windows when again
Night after night will she sew?

Goddess or painting?

Goddess or painting is she, may I ask,
How could such beauty exist?
She ruins cities and she ruins realms.
Like rain is she, and she's divine.
The Han Empress longed for the name Yen,
The king of Chou prized the name Shen.
Cradling her lute once she went to Chao.
Blowing pipes she often entered Ch'in.

By jade steps she always stares at trees,
Down verandahs ever chases spring.
She applies yellow with utmost artistry,
Handles strings with novel technique.
Sometimes to the wind she will stretch her sleeves,
Screening the sun holds out her momentary scarf.
Dainty flowers she inserts to sparkle in her hair,
A fine girdle clasps her body's bright colours.
Who knows when the sun will darken?
She is too shy to speak.

A lovely woman's morning make-up

At the north window she faces her dawn mirror.
Brocade curtains she drapes in a slanting twist.
Sweet, shy, unwilling to come out
She still claims her make-up isn't done.
She spreads kohl wide along her eyebrows,
Yen rouge appears across her cheeks.
No doubt with all this she's sensational,
She deserves to be called 'Adorable'!

Winemaid

On the fifteenth round, quite round,
Streaming light floods Shanglan.
At a stove she serves night wine.
Lodging guests unfasten gold saddles.
Eager to greet them she hugs her lute,
She can't bear to say goodbye with solo song.
'I know love quickly turns to hate,
Still it makes my dress and belt hang loose'.

199

Singers by the wood
Burning rays relent toward twilight.
Near the front pool a casual feast is set.
Fountain and shadow harmonise,
Flower and pretty face enhance each other.
Notes from a flute trilling like birdsong,
Dancing sleeves silhouetted like windy boughs.
In happy joy we get sublimely drunk –
Let it be so for one thousand autumns!

Waning glimmers
Apricot rafters gleam in slanting sun,
Waning glimmers shine on a pretty girl.
She opens a jewel box, takes off precious bangles,
Near the mirror tidies her sheer scarf.
Playful fish stir the pond leaves,
Dancing storks scatter staircase dust.
She wastes sighs on thousand year love,
Longs to reach sunny spring.

Beauty admires a painting
In the hall a painting of a goddess,
A vision of beauty in the palace.
Lovely in every way this painting –
Who could tell art from life?
Each has clearly defined eyebrows and eyes,
The same kind of slim-waisted body.
A special differentiation could be made:
One always has that vital spark!

His favoured boy
His favoured boy's charm is loveliness itself
That surpasses Tung Yen and Mi Tzu-hsia.
Feather drapes fill with dawn incense,
Pearl blinds muffle water-clock sounds at dusk.
Kingfisher quilt charged with mandarin duck tints,
Carved bed inlaid with ivory.

Remarkably youthful like Chou Hsiao-shih,
His pretty face resembles dawn mists.
Sleeves made of twin disc brocade,
Tunic woven from dainty cloth-tree bloom.

When he holds his trousers a light flush mounts,
When he turns his head twin side-curls swing.
Flirting eyes melt with frequent smiles,
Jade hands pick random flowers.

He's jealous not being his lord's latest catch,
His secret love is like the erstwhile carriage.
He's enough to make Yen girls envious,
Or worse, put Cheng women to shame!

Hsiao Lun

A pure wife
A wanderer has gone on tour,
His longing wife keeps to bedroom lattice.
Her dusty mirror dawn by dawn is buried,
The cold bed night on night lies vacant.
If it isn't a new girl he fancies,
Why does he stay so long out east and west?
In case he wonders if somebody loves him,
Tears are spent from weeping in my dreams.

From my carriage I see a fair lady
Captive passion stirs from her eyes and eyebrows,
Tender desire catches her waist and limbs.
Her words, her smile cast a spell,
Her walk is so wigglesome!
I gape up at the sky bedazzled.
Those near the moat don't realise.
Since love from afar is like this,
How would I feel to possess her?

For a remorseful former mistress
Oh let's be ten thousand leagues apart
Rather than this lifelong separation!
How can I bear to see with my own eyes
Past love make way for new?

Spring blossom not yet unfurled tumbles
Suddenly blown down by autumn winds.
Regretful kohl smooth contracts again,
Tearful face wiped weeps once more.
Who can write persuasively for me?*
I'd reward him with yellow gold!

* (Ssu-ma Hsiang-ju, see Notes)

Hsiao I

No more
A tall house, night of the fifteenth,
Shadows streaming into cinnabar court.
Long ago you entertained a certain guest,
Your bridegroom's handsome figure.
Make-up done, cicada-wing curls combed,
Your smiles ceased, moth eyebrows puckered.
From clothes' perfume he knew your steps drew near,
From bangles moving he sensed your walk was slow.
Why did the joy of the dance floor
Change to singing rafter grief I now see?

Still hang the north window curtains,
Unfolded the south eaves drapes.
Hushed, hushed empty streets darken.
No more the season of youth.

Love poem, a bagatelle
As I entered the hall I came across a young wife,
As I left by the gate I met her former husband.
With many words to say she could not speak,
She clutched his sleeve awkwardly.
The fan she twirled was like the moon,
The tears she shed like pearls.
'My love for you now never ceased in the past,
Of your past love for me now remain the lees'.

202

Night visit to Cypress Studio
Candles dim, passersby quiet.
Blinds open, cloud shadows intrusive.
In winds soft the sound of rain slackens,
On nights short the watergauge hastens.

Many times Lady Pan shed tears
And she makes singing-girls weep on.
How much worse for this travelling man
At midnight standing alone.

Spring's beauty
New orioles hidden by leaves trilling,
New swallows toward the window flitting.
Willow fluff leans careless over our wine,
Plum blossom drops sudden into our clothes.
A jade bridle swings with the wind,
A gold saddle glitters in sunshine.
Don't let spring's beauty grow late!
Lonesome I watch for a wanderer's return.

Late nesting crows
Sunset. Wing to fluttering wing
They flock to Shanglin nests.
Winds redouble, the first birds speed forward,
Clouds darken, the last ones get lost.
The way is far, cries go unheard,
Flying off course out of formation.
'You must be back from my home town,
How often did you fly through orchid bedrooms?
May I ask, Is a singing-girl
Worse off than a playboy's wife?'

Cold night
Magpies flying south at night.
My beloved travels, does not return.
Pool water floats a bright moon,
Cold winds carry sounds of fulling.
I long to weave a palindrome brocade
For you and send it to Wuwei.

Autumn night
Autumn night nine-barred room deserted.
Regrets by bedroom lattice for a wastrel.
Lamplight enters sheer bedcurtains,
Blinds' shadows loom on the screen.
Gold studs tuned by jade pegs
Strum *Parted swans* on such a night as this.

Hsiao Chi

Watching a singer
Yen girls play exotic dances,
Cheng women perform clear song.
Responsive shyness shows on glossy cheeks,
Missive flirting hides in puckered eyebrows.
Is this any different from the Falling Rain tryst?
Other than the Crested Wave vision?
I imagine as you mourn the sunset
You must envy Lord Yang of Lu's lance!

Dream in the night
Last night I dreamed you came home:
I had left my humming loom,
Remotely aware your love had lessened,
You did not wear the clothes you left home in.
Why do I say 'Just like my dream'?
Because a letter-goose has flown to me here.

Dawning love
Daybreak birds rehearse in concert warbling,
Dawn flowers tousled are just peeping,
Censer smoke creeps under conical curtains,
Screens conceal the mirrorstand:
Rouge cosmetics spoilt by tears.
Drifter, when will you come home?

From a boudoir lady to a man on campaign
Her frowning beauty's gold star winces,
Grief-shrouded jade chopsticks flow.
I wish you would see a mirage
And think of me up in my tall house.

CHAPTER EIGHT

Twenty Poets of the Liang Dynasty
(sixth century)

Hsiao Tzu-hsien

Sunrise at the southeast corner

A great glow rises far away,
Yang city strikes the soaring vault.
Sunlight shines on a girl at a window
Exquisite like A-chiao.
Her bright mirror with coiling dragons carved,
Hairpin plumes with phoenix attached,
Twisting-fall her Lady Liang coiffure,
Soft and slim her Ch'u palace waist.
Light silk mixed with brocade layers,
Sheer silk mixed with billowing gauze.
Eighteen was she at the end of last year,
Twenty at the start of this year.

In the silkworm yard she gathers sweet cocoons,
Up mulberry lanes picks tender stems.
She comes and goes to the east city quarter,
Walks up and down Lo river's west bridge.
Suddenly she meets a stranger in horse and carriage,
Fluttering canopy sways with tossing blinds.
His seamless robe is of musquash weave,
His precious sword has a cast-iron ramhead.
The stranger's officer is anxious to speak to her,
The coachman reins in the jingling bit.
Through pillars he stares, stares in vain,
Over the parapet he leans, leans a long while.

'My first home was a west side house.
You, sir, court me from a palace.
With Han horse, thirty thousand pairs,
My husband serves in the Ministry of War.
His leather belt-bag broidered with a tiger head.
His left earring fastened with sable tail.
He blows a traverse Dragon-bell flute,
Drums his ivory panpipes.
At fifteen a palace page like Chang Pi-ch'iang,
At eighteen an academician like Chia I.
Everyone laughs at Yen Ssu's wizened looks,
All shout my husband is more handsome than Tung Sheng!'

A beautiful woman
Hantan, stop dancing one moment!
Singers of Pa, rest your strings!
The beauties near Ch'i and Wei rivers
Are more glamorous than Chao and Yen girls.
Their radiance is of plum blossom,
Reflected in water they become lotus.
Mornings they sell wine at Ch'engtu,
Evenings they make a fortune at Hochien.
Though they don't suffer the misery of candle stubs,
Their orchid tallow uselessly flames.

Wang Yün

Spring months, two poems

I

Sun sparkling on mandarin duck halls,
Alga growing on a waterfowl pond,
Drifting dust entering on shafts of light,
Frail willow bending with the wind.
The black hawk hunts fledgling sparrows,
A lone stork mourns its beloved hen.
My quilt-sharer pursues distant pleasure,
From wedded love parted lifelong.
All I see now is swift death,
Why bother with the flower of forgetfulness?

2

The cockleburr's heart has not yet opened,
Sweet herb leaves are ready to unfurl.
Spring silkworms start trailing thread,
First swallows carry mud in busy beaks.
Pheasants of the fields softly call their hens,
Garden birds protect their nesting young.
After you left for Liang
I shut myself in my spring bedroom at noon.
The road to you is blocked by hill and river,
Sweet flowers bloom in idle luxury.

Autumn nights, two poems

1

Nine-barred abiding in the palace lodge by night,
Four walls cruel without light.
Troubled Star turns to sink in the west,
Magpies fly toward the east.
Gliding fireflies slowly garner their flame,
Grasshoppers soon busy at their looms.
At such an hour I think of brocade words
To make a wanderer's cloak,
Hoping my cinnabar heart will reach there
So my fine guest might come back home.

2

Florets of dew start to glisten, glisten,
Cassia twigs go rustling, rustling.
The spirit of death falls from serried eaves,
Light shadows flood four bedroom walls.
Parted favour lengthens distant night,
Far campaign saddens lonely sleep.
Despair wreathes kingfisher wing eyebrows,
Tears flood sidelong rippling eyes.
Eternal Gate visits are sundered,
Passionate I turn back to shuttle and spindle dull.

Roving gaze, two poems

1

The setting sun brightens her rouge
As cradling her zither she faces the window.
She prefers not to sing the *Sweet herbs* song,
All she hears are sighing willows.
In wedded bliss we lived as sweethearts,
Estrangement came from common gossip.
Useless for me to serve dewy mallow broth,
Who will pour the orchidaceous wine?
The day we will meet is far, unpromised.
However will dawn hibiscus last?

Restless in bed for love of you
I soon find myself east of narrow lanes.
Despairing eyebrows imitate Lady Liang's village,
A tall hairdo copies city fashion.
Twin door-leaves catch slanting sunlight,
A solitary stamen enjoys eddying winds.
My lover wrote down the longing in his heart,
Presented his poem to Sweet Springs Palace.
He eats from splendid vessels, I hear.
Does he remember in his spring bedroom?

Liu Hsiao-cho

A dropped earring

Preface. From a distance I noticed my host in a nearby boat throw something into the water. All his singing-girls struggled to retrieve it. One of the guests asked me to write a poem about it.

River flowing peaceful,
Waterfowl crying 'quack-quack!'
Fallen blossom floats away from the banks,
Flying pheasants cross the islet and back.
On such a day as this singing-house girls
Have faces to rival charms of peach and plum.
Their master, sorry to waste a gorgeous earring,
Wishes to exchange it for sweet sedge!
The new fineweave is suspected by the old homespun,
Chao Feiyen in the ascendant causes Lady Pan's downfall;
Flaunted silks compete with hidden plainweave,
Swinging pendants rob the ring-jingler.
The guests' hearts all throb in vain –
The loftiest boughs never can be plucked!

Flirting
Among mulberry leaves first budding, budding,
Surface of the Ch'i not yet flooding, flooding,
A pretty girl seeks a patterned belt,
An honoured guest tempts her with bright earrings.
Day darkens, human sounds quieten.
Soft footsteps leave an orchid room.
For dewy mallows she doesn't need prompting,
Her lilting lute isn't slow to play.
Her kingfisher hairpin fastened now slides down,
Her silk dress stroked releases perfume.
'Why did I marry a playboy?
On spring nights I keep an empty bed.
I will never see my green silk rider,
So why bother with my rouged and powdered face?'

Gleaming gamesboard
Strings and piping of Nanp'i stop,
The final gambling keeps the guests a while.
The sun sinks, the room's lattice darkens,
Lovely girls are sent for flowery candles.
Oblique light illumines the whole board.
Refracted beams half conceal their bodies:
'We don't complain of slender hands weary,
It's just a shame that night turns to dawn'.

Singer in the night
At *Junglefowl* her strings one moment cease playing,
At *Parted stork* she stops a while the lute-studs.
Next there is the melody *A crow weeps,*
Of flying east and west with their back turned.
The singer in despair keeps to herself alone,
Her vagrant lover wanders without return.
If she comes across a lifelong parting tune,
She weeps the long night in clothes of silk.

Left for my love
Hairpins he left carved in tortoiseshell,
Silk he gave woven with mandarin ducks.
These still aren't as good as moist flowering trees,
Branches embracing across my wanderer's bedroom.
Before he went away autumn had fallen,

After he went away spring grew sweet once more.
I can send you nothing, beloved,
Just wistful, heady perfume in my sleeves.

Liu Tsun

Gay

Pretty little Chou
Picks bunches of orchid faintly smiling.
Fresh skin paler than powder white,
Smooth cheeks like peach pink.
He hugs his catapult near Tiaoling,
Casts his rod east of Lotusleaves.
As his arms move he swings his perfume pouch,
Clothes so light are at the kind wind's mercy.

Lucky to be chosen to dust the pillow,
To serve in painted halls.
Gilt screens enclose his kingfisher quilt,
Indigo cloth drapes his incense clothes-frame.
From an early age he knew the pain of scorn,
Kept the words in, ashamed to speak.
Ripped sleeve favours though generous,
Leftover peach love still not ended . . .
Moth eyebrows, what's the use of envy?
New faces stream steadily through the palace.

Back from camp to the city

Han river too deep to ford,
Through vast deeps I see its clear bed.
Brocade rope moors my duck-prow skiff,
Nacreous poles strung with kingfisher pennants.
On shrill whistles the *Fragrant tree* melody,
In liquid song *Picking lotus* music.
Divine the cavalcade sweeps past fleetingly,
Return at sunset to assembled camps.
Why look back in an empty bedroom
Where green moss spreads over the steps?

213

Wang Hsün

If only
In the palace the many divine girls
Till now were beyond compare.
Except there's an exquisite at the window,
She has the prettiest face of all.
Dances she has learned outrival Chao Feiyen,
Powder she applies makes Nanyang's inferior.
A scattering of yellow, two lines of kohl colour,
Incensed clothes, a blend of jujube scents,
Rare hairpins with freshly pressed kingfisher plumes.
She tries to mend her slippers' broken sides.
All morning she counts on her appearance
Or else she'll keep an empty bedroom.
'If only I could count on your love . . .
I wish we could be two mandarin ducks!'

Yü Chien-wu

The one I love
My sweet promise in the end has not come home.
Springtime nature. I sit in scented fragrance.
Dusting a box I find your fan of departure;
Opening a case I see my dress of parting.
Catalpa by the well grows not in full leaf,
The palace pagoda-tree unfurls but sparse.
I will never match mud-bearing swallows,
Together they come, in pursuit they fly.

214

A beauty admires herself in a painting
If you want to know how clever the painting is
Call in real life, let her reflect it!
Side by side they seem bodies of the same mould.
Seen together they look like a mirror reflection.
Arranged hairpins equally spaced,
Collars worn both neat and tidy.
If the Huns had not lifted the siege at P'ingch'eng,
Who'd have survived to rival cinnabar and green paint?

The road to Ch'angan
Double avenues lead to Cassia Palace,
A broad road cuts through to Yellow Mount Lodge.
I hear faraway bells of P'ingling,
Discern distant trees of Hsinfeng.
The assembly hall creates a brilliant glow,
Scattered palaces raise hazy mists.
Sunset song and piping float back to me.
Dust flies from horse and coach passing.

Seeing a woman come back from South Park
A spring flower vies with a jade face,
Both are picked and both are plucked.
Her slim waist accentuates the tight dress,
Long hairpins fix her artistic chignon.
Torches start crossing Lo bridge,
Barriers are about to rise at Black Gate.
The woman inside probably keeps vigil:
'Will my honoured guest come back before dusk?'

I met you in the park
I met you north of the smaller park,
You stopped your coach, asked for the park centre.
Plum blossom new consorted with older willow,
Powder white shone on silk scarf redness.
Your departing shadow moved against the slanting sun,
So scented air there turned windward.
Clouds drifting the steps slowly darkened,
Ice cracking pools half thawed.
'Your departing horse, my boat that won't delay . . .'
Plaintive birdsong unending.
We part wistful from here,
Your coach westward and my horse east.

215

Spring night
Long since my campaigner parted from me
Seasonal fragrance peeps in through my window once more.
Beneath candles I sew clothes at night,
Spring's chill sharply catches my fingers.
I long to reach a homeward flying goose,
Give it my letter to take to Tallwillow.

Winter light
The neighbour's cock sounds its clarion crow,
A dejected woman has not got to sleep.
Moonlight creeps upon her even after dawn,
The frost's glare subsides before daybreak.
With tousled hair she rises to look in the mirror :
'Who can bother to fix flow'ry hairpins ?'

Liu Hsiao-wei

In the wilds on a moonlit night
Magpies' idle flight round trees,
The moon's wheel not yet quite full,
Ch'ang O stares, unable to leave,
Her cassia branch stays hidden.
The sunset glow sends house shadows flickering,
Streaming moon rays set the moat ashimmer.
Stabled horses grieve at Ch'iang flutes,
City wall rooks weep from border cold.

I hear that my wife at loom and shuttle
Frets about my unlined clothes,
That come autumn my silks will be too light,
And, choked with tears, she cannot go on weaving.
She frowns, no doubt unhappy,
While I try to cheer up with sword dances.
'Please let me speak, Hanku officer,
Must we keep on with "a plug of mud" ?'

Winter light
From my home near Loyang city
I often hear dawn bells toll.
The sound of bells was still ringing
When a Han envoy announced your campaign.
The sky grew cold, water in my inkwell froze.
So sad is my heart I cannot end my letter.

For my wife
A charming girl, full of dejected love,
Weaves plain silk as autumn sounds stir.
Passing the yarn-guide her bracelet jade trembles,
Pressing the shears her belt pearls tinkle.
Warp so fine threatens to jam the shuttle,
Woof snaps, she's cross the silk is too thin.
Grapevine begins to look finished,
Mandarin ducks have yet to emerge.

Under cloudy ridge-poles all the weavers stroll,
Silk windows open to each other.
Through window grilles float eyebrow whispers,
From silk so light come smiling eyes.
Blurred, screened by thinnest silk,
Yet clearly glimpsed cosmetic flower :
Sweetheart lotus roots studded with jade,
Loveknot flowers strung with jewels,
Her red gown fastened at the back,
Gold pins slant toward her sidecurls.
From the loom top hangs gay braid,
From the loom's side cascade strings of pearls.
Green silk threads draw in the pivot's crouching hare,
Yellow gold encircles the pulley's Lulu knob.
Rich tints dart from her skirt hem,
Scented gloss glistens on her lips.
One-hundred-city barons ask after her,
Five-horse teams paw the ground before her.

There is only me in my bedroom,
Faithful to past love, not seeking new amours.
In dreams weeping soaks my flowery pillow,
Waking tears drench my silk kerchief.
Sleeping alone is so hard for me,
My double quilt still feels cold.
Even more I desire your skin's marbrous warmth,
More than ever long for horizontal pleasures.

217

I urge on my mount with its gold bridle,
Homeward bound for the city's south end.
The city south, how slow the promised hour!
I imagine you also throb with love.
Your silk bodice must have worn out long ago,
Flower hairpins ready for repair.
On fresh make-up don't add kohl –
I'll come home to paint your eyebrows myself!

Hsü Chün-ch'ien

Sitting out New Year with my wife
Pleasure sweet, excitement without end,
Joy sublime – don't stop the winecups!
From wine we fish daddy-longlegs,
In rice dumplings we search for wild plum.
Blinds open, winds come through the curtains,
Candles die, charcoal burns to ash.
'No wonder pins feel heavy in your curls –
It's from waiting till dawn light comes'.

Out early in spring holding hands with my wife
Coiffure ornaments are the very latest fashion,
The clothes she wears are all new this season.
Through grass short she steps still in slippers,
Plum scent comes slow to touch us.
Trees jutting snag her brocade shawl,
Winds veering slip beneath her red scarf.
Pour to the brim orchidaceous wine,
To look on this makes the soul delirious!

Pao Ch'üan

Watching pleasure-seekers in South Park
In Loyang's Small Park grounds
Coach and horse drive past in swarms.
Along the canal she halts her trotting chaise,
Beside a willow he turns his jingling harness.
Heels so high set pendants all atinkle,
Stockings sheer half hidden by flimsy silk.
'Scudding clouds have no fixed address,
What's the use of making eyes at him!'

At sunset I watch people going home
Sweet charm competing with early spring
Races to the famous festival at Heights Park.
Films of alga change the water's colour,
Mists thicken to screen the sun's disc.
Carved rooftiles deflect sunset rays,
Painted fans brush drifting dust.
Far scent of a dress now drifts toward me,
Distant red of a skirt becomes brighter.
Whose wife are you, girl of the rocking boat?
Where are you going, weaver of fine silk?

Liu Huan

She ruins cities
I don't believe in the Mount Wu sylph,
I don't believe in the Lo river sprite!
But whether other kinds of beings exist –
There's only a woman who ruins cities.
Once she flirted with the Prince of Ch'en,

219

Long ago she came close to Mr Sung.
Before she married her name was Yü,
More recently her maiden name was Ch'in.

Her face seems like powder's sheen,
Red gloss won't do justice to her lips.
Seen from afar a flower appears to open,
Scent I sense and know it differs from spring.
Pins long match coiffure wigs,
Pannier skirt short suits her waistline.
Night after night she exhausts the language of love.
Day after day her behaviour's still quite novel!
Her talent would captivate Hsün Feng-ch'ien,
Her skill would dazzle Shih Chi-lun.
Honoured guests may waste time ogling –
They'll never get to see her horizontal!

Cold bedroom
After we parted the spring pool looked different,
Lotus died, ice seemed to form.
In my sewing-box the shears felt cold,
On the mirrorstand my face-cream froze.
My slender waist become so frail
Can hardly bear the coldness of the clothes.

Autumn night
Over a house stir autumn winds,
Broken despair in an autumn bedroom.
Trickling candles stream into floral clusters,
Incense flares, the censer will soon be spent.
Vain tears cross in two streams
And float the rouge upon her cheeks.

Winter dark
I cannot bear cold nights long
Night after night keeping an empty bed.
Skirt pleats sitting up look sharper,
Hairpin shadows lengthen near the lamp.
No one pities my double brocade quilt,
Why bother to perfume stale air?

Teng K'eng

Just once more

We parted, and though not so long ago
Still, it seems we've long been parted.
Massed cassia many a time stripped of leaves,
Garden trees countless sprays I've picked.
You say my looks have altered,
I fear it's your heart that has strayed.
We need to meet just once more
To get reacquainted with each other!

In the night I hear a singer's voice

Candle florescence like a bright moon,
Chignon shadow higher than a soaring bridge.
A singer's rhythmic dance from Cheng,
Rival beauty copies waists of Ch'u.
For new songs they compose their own melodies,
Familiar zithers need no tuning.
In the chorus no singer smiles:
'Gentlemen, please don't tease!'

Chen Ku

Spring passion

Late last night I raised the blinds to look out
And met my first two swallows returning.
Then this morning I saw peach and plum,
And not just a few flying blossoms.
Now I'm sad spring will soon pass,
No more to send him its fragrance.

Yü Hsin

The dance
In cloistral rooms floral candles bright.
Spoils of Yen, two dancers light
Stamp their heels in time to staccato rhythms,
Lower coiffures on the high notes.
Half a pirouette, step back to position one,
Whirling gowns, melody lingering on.
Paradise birds turn, the mirror will soon be full,
Geese look back, the town will surely fall.
Trained long ago to dance in heaven,
Aren't they like dancers not born of this world?

Seventh Night
Herdboy shines in the distant river,
Weaver is mounting her carriage.
The Bridge of Stars admitted the Han envoy
Who bore away her loom-stone on a magic raft.
Parted by the river they stare so near.
Passing autumn makes parting remote.
They mourn this very night so hated
That makes them wait for next year's flowers.

In mourning
In Purple Gallery dawn levée ends,
At Central Terrace evening memorials lessen.
No more her thousand gold smile!
No use taking a five-day furlough.
The verandah at dawn unswept,
Orchid rooms at dusk with closed doors.
Moss grows where she practised music,
Cobwebs gather on her palindrome loom.
Her old zither's broken strings remain,
Through echoing rafters autumn swallows flit.
Dawn clouds I can bear to watch, and yet

222

It's hard to go near night bedcurtains.
I long to ascend to Sweet Dew Gate
And borrow the dazzling Lamp of Wisdom.
No wonder late in Loyang city
Lone homeward tears soak my robe.

Liu Miao

Mulberry picker

A singing-girl in despair invincible
Descends neatly dressed from her green house
To go with friends west down silkworm paths,
Go hand-in-hand east to the top of the lane.
When leaves are picked she moves to another tree,
If boughs are too high she handles her hook.
Silk ribbons dangle and slip off,
Gilt baskets empty and gather.
Silkworms are hungry now the sun sets,
Why be detained by a prefect?

For a weaver

Slim, slim jade fingers travel,
Throbbing moth eyebrows relax.
Flashing scissors undo crossed yarn,
She stops the shuttle to knot broken thread.
Flowers of the eaves shine with a new moon,
A secluded door still not drawn with curtains.
She works her loom, wipes streaming tears,
Slower than ever weaves plain silk.

Autumn bedroom

Fireflies flit beyond silk windows,
A woman dreams of General Huo.
Before her lamp she measures fauna brocade,

Beneath the eaves floral motif weaves.
Falling dew like light rain,
Long River like wispy clouds.
Autumn brings back a hundred different cares.
No time to perfume his finished robe.

Broken willow
In this tall house ten years ago we parted
When willows were sprouting silky fronds.
Some leaves you picked, amazed they opened so soon,
Broke a twig, hating the long absence.
Year in, year out bereft of all news,
Month by month my looks fading.
Spring comes, who doesn't feel hope?
My love you know by intuition.

Chi Shao-yü

Chienhsing Park
Cinnabar hills embrace the imperial city,
Purple pools enhance Royal Forest Park.
Silver terraces hang down eight hundred feet,
Jade trees tower one thousand yards,
Water flows the shadows of carriage and hat,
Winds unfurl music of song and piping.
Pause to pity a dropped kingfisher plume,
Look back to lament a lost hairpin.
Sunset garden flowers close,
Square coach blinds teem with flickering shade.
Let's say at the last our joy has no end,
Never say you begrudge yellow gold!

224

Fun-loving girls
Garden trees flaunt spring glory,
Fun-loving girls race from looms,
Rummage through boxes, pick out concert fans,
Open cases, choose dance gowns.
'Let mulberry leaves shrivel, we don't care!'
They see sunbeams hurry into dusk :
'We have our private city owners, of course,
No need to dazzle honoured guests!'

Spring sun
A sad woman timidly leans from her window,
Spring beauty is not eternal.
Near the nets fitful steals the sun,
Trembling through blinds creeps the wind.
Fallen flowers whirled back to their trees
Fly light away to vanish in the sky
Leaving a vain trace of jade chopsticks
To hang double in her mirror bright.

Wen-jen Ch'ien

Spring sun
The tall terrace stirs with spring's flush,
Clear pools reflect sunlit splendour,
Green mallow twists toward sunlight,
Kingfisher willow slants with the wind.
In the woods a bird startles my heart,
Orchard's massed blooms captivate my eyes.
Like me they all know this season,
Sigh that you alone keep far from home.
The traveller will not come back today,
Why bother to pick a vain hempen pledge?

225

Hsü Ling

Bagatelle

Today, your being so considerate
Offends, but less than had it been spring.
Candle-trickling tears I shed this night
Are not because you bring her home at dark.
Her dance mat come autumn will fold away,
Her concert fan will gather sheets of dust.
Since time began new love supplants the old,
So why does old love hate to greet the new?
A sliver of moon peeps into her flowery bed,
Slight chill creeps under her shawl and scarf.
Autumn will come when all things wither,
And touch her body with nature's stealth.

The dance

At fifteen she belonged to the Princess of P'ingyang
And so came to enter Chienchang Palace.
The Princess's house taught well the art of dance,
The city perfected the craft of dawn make-up.
With lowered coiffure she nears the silk mat,
With raised sleeves brushes on floral yellow.
Candles cast shadows near the window,
Her dress spreads perfume in her wardrobe.
The reason she attracts guests so well must be
That she makes her dance gown deliberately long.

In her bedroom watching for me

The singer's song and piping over,
She checks her flushed face in the mirror,
Touches up powder, removes fancy flowers,
Takes out pins to make a small chignon.
Lovely lamps left to burn don't go out,
Tall doors stay closed not yet locked.
'Darling, where are you?'
She only sees a moonbeam return.

226

A maid's thanks for a mirror
Your messenger came to bring me a jewelled mirror,
Grand, grand as the round moon.
When a mirror ages it shines the brighter,
When a person ages so passions decline.
I accept your mirror, hang it on the empty stand,
To this day never reopened.
Don't you see that lone paradise bird?
From where will lost love's soul appear?

Wu Tzu

Spring bedroom despair
Jade Gate Pass messengers have ceased.
May I ask, Have you forgotten?
Spring sunshine so indifferent
Peeps through my window to visit.
Long bereft of your news
Suddenly I find the sun veers southeast.
Willow silk strands all tease the swallows,
Mulberry leaves hurry on the silkworms.
Nature's glory in a flash is like this:
Widowhood that cannot be borne.

T'ang Seng-chi

The glint of gold
In olden days a singing-house girl
Picked flowers beside an open well,
And as she picked the flowers she fixed one in her hair,

227

Admiring her image in the well.
She peeps and peeks at her image endlessly,
Smiles and laughs, aware of her charms.
But then her jewelled hairpin falls down . . .
Years not one have passed since her loss.
Though kingfisher plumes dissolved into slime,
The glint of gold still sparkles as before.
This woman today is alive no more.
This object is now her legacy vain.

?Liu Ling-hsien

Lady Pan's regret
Sunset closes Ying Gate.
Despairing love breeds a hundred cares.
All the more since Chaoyang Palace is close,
And winds carry song and piping sounds.
Fickle favour she does not hate,
But her rival's heartless slander so malicious.
She just says she has loftier ideals,
Never envies that light dancer's waist.

?Liu, Wang Shu-ying's Wife

Wang Chao-chün's regret
What is certain, in the end, about life?
The world can never be really secure.
Cinnabar and green missed out her known grace,
A jade coffer turned to autumn grass.
Spilling tears flow at the Pass farewell,
Even now not dried.
'Han envoy, when you go back south of the wilds
I beg you, speak eloquently for me!'

228

CHAPTER NINE

Love-songs in Irregular Metres

(from second century BC to sixth century AD)

Anon. Two Song Lyrics

Eastward flies the shrike

Eastward flies the shrike, westward flies the swallow.
Herdboy and Weaver seldom meet.
Who is the woman living across the gates?
An opening bud shows beauty to dazzle the village.
At south windows, north doors she hangs her bright light,
From sheer curtains, silk drapes scents of lipstick and powder.
This girl, how old is she? Fifteen or sixteen.
Meek and mild, unique, her face is like jade.
Spring's three months ended, flower gone with the wind.
Left all alone, darling, who'll be your mate?

Where the water midstream

Where the water midstream flows east
Is a Loyang girl called Nevergrieve.
Nevergrieve at thirteen could weave fine silk,
At fourteen picked mulberry up south lane,
At fifteen married, became Mr Lu's wife,
At sixteen she gave birth to a boy named A-hou.
The Lu mansion has orchid rooms with cassia rafters,
Everywhere the scent of Yüchin and storax.
On her head twelve golden hairpins,
On her feet silk slippers of five patterns.
From coral hangs her mirror radiating light.
Her slave in a bandeau holds up her shoe box.
A life of wealth and status, what more does she want?
She hates not being married to Wang Chang of the east side!

230

Anon.   Song of the Yüeh Boatman

Song of the Yüeh boatman

Preface. The ruler of Ngo kingdom in the state of Ch'u, Tzu-hsi, was travelling in a blue-plumed boat with a kingfisher awning. The Yüeh oarsman fell in love with Tzu-hsi, and sang a Yüeh song as he plied the oars. The ruler of Ngo was touched. Full of desire he raised his embroidered quilt and covered the boatman. His song went like this:

> Tonight, what sort of night?
> I tug my boat midstream.
> Today, what sort of day?
> I share my boat with my lord.
> Though ashamed, I am loved.
> Don't think of slander or disgrace!
> My heart will never fail,
> For I have known my lord.
> On a hill is a tree, on the tree is a bough.
> My heart delights in my lord, though he will never know.

Ssu-ma Hsiang-ju

Cock-phoenix, Hen-phoenix

Preface. While Ssu-ma Hsiang-ju was travelling through Linch'iung, a rich man there named Cho Wang-sun had a daughter, Wen-chün, who had recently been widowed. She hid behind a screen and peeped through. Hsiang-ju won her heart with these songs:

Cock-phoenix

Cock-phoenix, cock-phoenix goes back to his home town
From roaming the four seas in search of his hen.
Unlucky days – he found no way to meet her.
What a surprise! Tonight up in this hall,
In this very place is a girl sweet and pretty.
My bedroom so near, she so far – it pains my heart.
How can we be mandarin ducks caressing neck to neck?

Hen-phoenix

Hen-phoenix, oh hen-phoenix, come nest with me!
Tail to tail we'll breed, be my bride for ever!
Passionately entwined, bodies one, hearts united,
At midnight come with me! Who will ever know?
Let's rise together wing to wing and fly on high.
Unmoved by my love she makes me pine.

?Hsi-chün

Lost horizon

Preface. In the reign of Emperor Wu of the Han Dynasty during the years 110–104 BC the emperor made Hsi-chün, daughter of the king of Chiangtu, a princess and married her off to Kunmi, the ruler of the Wusun tribe. When she reached their land, she settled in Kunmi's palace. Through all those years she only met him once or twice, but did not speak to him. The princess became melancholy and composed a song which went like this:

My family married me to a lost horizon,
Sent me far away to the Wusun king's strange land.
A canvas hut is my mansion, of felt its walls,
Flesh for food, mare's milk to drink.
Longing ever for my homeland, my heart's inner wound.
I wish I were the brown goose going to its old home.

232

Preface. Emperor Ch'eng's consort, Chao, named Feiyen, had enjoyed his sexual favours in the harem and was with the emperor when he came to and fro from the imperial palace. At that time there was a man, the Marquess of Fup'ing, Chang Fang, who was a clever talker and was graciously permitted to ride with the emperor to Ch'i Gate. Hence in the song it says, 'Lord Chang / Is always having audience'. Feiyen was insanely jealous; she had not borne a son to the emperor. Hence the lines in the song, 'Pecks at princes', and 'flowers, but bears no fruit'. Wang Mang himself said that the man who supplanted the Han Dynasty would have the power of Earth and would prize the colour yellow. Hence the words 'yellow sparrow'. In the end Feiyen was demoted from the rank of empress and died. Hence the line 'she's pitied by all'. [Feiyen's name means Flying Swallow.]

Swallow

Swallow, swallow,
Sleek, sleek is your tail!
Lord Chang
Is always having audience
At timbered gates with green bronze rings.
Swallow flies in,
Pecks at princes.

Cassia

Cassia flowers, but bears no fruit.
A yellow sparrow nests in its crown.
Once the envy of others,
Now she's pitied by all.

Anon.   Two Ditties of the Han Emperor Huan's Era

Tall wheat green
Tall wheat green, so green, short wheat shrivelled.
Who must be reapers? His wife and her mother.
And where is her husband? Out west fighting Huns.
Officers purchased his horse,
The lord confiscated his cart.
What can we do for you? Mutter in rage!

Crows on city walls
Crows on city walls,
Tails down in retreat.
Father became an officer,
Son became a soldier.
One soldier dies,
One hundred chariots retaliate,
Chariots thunderous roll!
At Hochien,
At Hochien a pretty girl makes a fortune,
And with her fortune builds a hall,
Of gold her hall.
Over the door is crushed millet,
Under the millet a hanging drum.
I'd like to beat the drum, but the minister will be angry.

Chang Heng

Four Sorrows, four poems

I

The one I love lives by Mount T'ai.
I long to go after him, but Mount Liangfu is too rugged.
Leaning forward I look east, tears soak my pen.

My handsome one gave me gold dagger coins.
How will I requite him? With fine jade.
The road is far, it won't arrive. I give in to doubt.
How anxious I am, my heart so distressed.

2

The one I love lives in Cassia Forest.
I long to go after him, but Hsiang waters are too deep.
Leaning forward I look south, tears soak my collar.
My handsome one gave me rare gold gems.
How will I requite him? With a pair of jade plates.
The road is far, they won't arrive. I give in to reproaches.
How anxious I am, my heart so tormented.

3

The one I love lives at Hanyang.
I long to go after him, but Lung range is too long.
Leaning forward I look west, tears soak my coat.
My handsome one gave me a sable wrap.
How will I requite him? With bright moon pearls.
The road is far, they won't arrive. I give in to anxiety.
How anxious I am, my heart so disturbed.

4

The one I love lives at Goose Gate Pass.
I long to go after him, but snow falls thick and fast.
Leaning forward I look north, tears soak my scarf.
My handsome one gave me a roll of broidered brocade.
How will I requite him? With a green jade desk.
The road is far, it won't arrive. I give in to deep sighs.
How anxious I am, my heart so tortured.

Ch'in Chia

What's the use?
Hazy, hazy white sun
Trails glimmers west declining.
Sobbing, sobbing cocks and sparrows

Fly in flocks to the pillars.
White, white bright moon,
Twinkle, twinkle serried stars.
Harsh frost biting chill,
Flurrying snow carpets the garden.
Hushed, hushed, living alone,
Bleak, bleak the empty house.
Billow, billow door curtains,
Gleam, gleam flowery candles.
Why should I carefully hang door curtains?
You don't live within them.
What's the use of flowery candles?
You don't make them shine.

Ts'ao P'ei

Your poor wife
Autumn wind's plaintive lute, sky's air chill.
Grass, trees tremble and shed, dew turns to frost.
Flocking swallows take their leave, geese wheel south.
Thinking of your travels, love breaks my heart.
Painful homeward longing, desire for your old village.

Why do you tarry, linger in other parts?
Your poor wife, forlorn, keeps an empty room.
Despair comes pining for you, perhaps you've forgotten?
Tears fall unawares, soaking my clothes.
My cradled lute's singing strings release clear autumn notes.
A snatch of song, soft humming, I cannot go on.
The bright moon, white, white, shines upon my bed.
Starry Han flows west before the midnight hour.
Herdboy and Weaver stare from afar.
What crime is yours, alone denied the River bridge?

So easy!
Day to part so easy! day to meet so hard!
Mountains, rivers far away, the road vast, vast.
My full cup of love for you I dare not confide.
I send words to floating clouds, they stop, never look back.
Tears fall, rain down my face, ruin my kohl.
Who can nurse despair alone with never a sigh?
I open poems, sing clear song, try to relax.
Waves of joy, of grief, dash against my breast.
Restless, I lean on my pillow, sleeplessly.
Throw on my cloak, go out, pace east and west,
Look up at stars and moon, gaze at rifts in clouds.
Flying storks cry at dawn, pitiful sounds.
Numb with remembrance I lose the will to live.

Ts'ao Chih

My sad fate
The sun now departed hides in the west.
They meet once more in an orchid house, secluded room.
Flowery lamps suffuse screens with light,
White as the sun rising from Leaning Mulberry.
Winecups hasten, everyone seated, goblets pass round.
Our host gets up to dance the *Sop'an* dance.
Artistes feel the wrench of parting.
Raised goblets, flying tankards brimful.
Equal measure, same flush, like expression,
Impulse to change cups with a lover.
Scarlet cheeks reveal the orchid's image,
Sleeves move with bodies, faces full of passion.
Wonderful dance divine, divine, bodies so light.
Clothes loosen, shoes slip off, capstrings untie;
Glances up and down, laughter, shouts, abandon.
Fixed stares at lovely women's jade faces.
All alike served from gold tankards, kingfisher plates.
Silhouettes of hands under sheer sleeves barely visible,
Arms too frail to hold pearl bangles.

The seated guests all breathe sighs, soft looks on faces,
With kerchiefs girls put powder on beside them.
Drifting scents of Huona, Tuliang,
Chishe – all blending into one perfume.
A girl moves forward, who is she? Ch'i Chiang?
Generous, deeply in love, unforgettable.
Our host invites his best friends to his private party,
Chants solo, 'Bring the cups! why so slow?'
Guests recite 'Drunk now let's go home!'
Our host responds with 'Dew not yet dry'.

Fu Hsüan

Past autumn's nine

Past autumn's nine, spring's three,
Our kind host greets guests from afar:
'Knowing what you dearly love in your heart,
I ordered fine talented singers,
Who glitter like sun, moon, and stars!'
Laid out are gold jugs, jade goblets.
Guest and host rise together, geese in formation.
Cups fly like lightning flashes,
Pledges made, cups exchanged, clothes in a tangle.
Merry joyful laughter ten thousandfold.
Our host chants a new poem for the rest,
Brilliant as a tiger's marks that change to dragon's streaks,
Mysterious as the time before creation.

Ch'i lyrics, Ch'u dance bright and gay,
Echoes of song swell toward blue clouds.
Eight kinds of music all different styles,
Rare sounds, rapturous, every one novel.
Soft smiles, white teeth, cinnabar lips,
Elusive echoes fly and scatter rafter dust.
Souls are subtly transported to paradise.
The guests all drunk, steeped in joy,
Draw winecasks close, push seats together, look at the eaves,
Bring pledgecups thick and fast, drink each other's health.
With one chorus to you, 'May you live a thousand autumns!'

Let your love be immovable as a mountain!
May your kindness never fail,
Like morning sun, evening moon,
Their light unending for ten thousand leagues.
If you keep for ever our vows of first wine and bound hair,
Why should I fret lest we live as Hu and Yüeh?
Holding my soft hand with its gold bracelets
You'll roam with me through flying turrets in the clouds,
Splendid as mandarin ducks, two birds of paradise.
We'll settle happy in orchid rooms,
Hearts content, joy sublime, fathomless!
Yet I brood on joy that is now sublime,
Our happy hour will vanish sudden like a ruin.
Chill conquers heat, drives light back,
Spring glory chased by blustery winds.
Moved by nature my troubled heart grows sad.

How unlucky is my orphan fate!
A son comes down on earth called 'darling',
A girl, though weak, seems scarcely to survive.
Flesh and blood relations, they are kept apart.
Busy and useful I attach myself to others.
You are like form which shadow follows,
I am like alga floating on a river.
The bright moon cannot always wax full,
No one can keep blooming without roots.
The good times bit by bit give way to bad.
I look back at my broidered collar radiant,
But the white sun turns its slanted rays.
The red flower sudden withers unaware,
Shadow seems to flee form, fly away on high.
Who will say past favours can be retrieved?
Shepherd's purse falls with wheat in summer.
Orchid, cassia pinched by frost grow sweeter.
Destiny depends on inscrutable Heaven.
My heart's bonds of love are true as red and green.
Why do I despair your love will waver midway?

Your carriage is far

Your carriage is far, far horses prancing, prancing.
My thoughts pursue you, cannot forget.
Where do you travel? Westward leads to Ch'in.
I long to be shadow and follow your body,

But you live in shade where shadow can't be seen.
Stay in the light where I want you to be!

Yen women are lovely

Yen women are lovely, Chao girls pretty.
That house so close is bound by towering cliffs.
If clouds were my carriage, the wind my steed,
I'd reach my jade of the hills, my orchid of the wilds.
Clouds don't keep promises, winds have dropped.
Who can cure the trouble of my pining heart?

Four Sorrows, four poems

Preface. Chang Heng previously composed his *Four Sorrows.* They are
small pieces and popular, classified as heptasyllabic. I have composed
impromptu imitations of these, calling them *Imitations of the Four
Sorrows.* They are as follows:

I

The one I love lives in Yingchou.
I wish we were two swans playing together midstream.
Herdboy and Weaver's tryst is in autumn.
Mountains high, rivers deep, no way to pass.
Miserable, unlucky am I, overcome by despair.
My handsome one gave me a bright moon pearl.
How will I pledge him? With eye to eye fish.
The sea is wide, I have no boat. Bitter torment.
I send my message to flying dragons, coursers of the skies.
Winds rise, clouds divide, flying dragons vanish.
Waves in panic dash against skies, coursers not in pairs.
Why do many memories make the heart world-weary?

2

The one I love lives in Chuyai.
I wish we were wing to wing skimming clear pools.
Hard and soft wed powers, conjoin as Heaven and Earth.
Form and shadow once severed will remain apart.

240

Miserable, unlucky am I, my feelings seem numb.
My handsome one gave me orchid plants.
How will I pledge him? With birds of like heart.
Flames are hot, water deep. Overwhelming despair.
My love I show with fine jade, night-gleaming gems.
When Pien Ho died jade was judged no more.
I live like a falling star, sudden lightning expired.
Why do many memories lock loneliness tight?

3

The one I love lives on Mount K'un.
I wish we were the inseparable creatures gazing on Yü Gulf.
Sun and moon return dazzling light, rays brighten the sky.
Antares and Orion wide apart have no way to meet.
Miserable, unlucky am I, burdensome my problems.
My handsome one gave me storax perfume.
How will I pledge him? With kingfisher mandarin ducks.
Hsientu, Jo river, river without a bridge.
My love I show with brocade robes, broidery traced skirts.
The Three Lights course by, rays never lingering.
How mean a thing is human life, so swift it seems to float by.
Why do many memories only bring sorrow?

4

The one I love lives in the north.
I wish we were flying geese both winging south.
I long to appear like the Three Lights shining on mankind.
But Hu and Yüeh are hostile, live in separate parts.
Miserable, unlucky am I, trapped by many cares.
My handsome one gave me feather pennant tassels.
How will I pledge him? With form and shadow.
Thick ice seals despair that rich blooms will fall.
I send my message through sun and moon, vow by bright stars.
But stars darken, sun and moon move on.
My weary horse sadly neighs, ashamed it cannot race forward.
Why do many memories bring disenchantment?

?Su Po-yü's Wife

Palindrome

In a hillock tree a bird sings of sorrow.
In spring water deep carps are sleek.
Swallows in empty barns always feel pangs of hunger.
An officer's wife rarely meets her husband.
She leaves the gate to watch, sees a white robe,
Says, 'That must be him!' But then it isn't,
She goes back indoors sad at heart,
Up the north hall, along the west stairs.
Swift her loom winds silk, the shuttle sounds urgent.
She sighs long sighs, who will she speak to?
'I remember your going away.
There was a day of departure, no promise of return.
You tied my inside belt, saying "I'll always love you."
If you forgot me only Heaven would know,
If I forgot you punishment is sure to follow.
You ought to know I am being virtuous'.

What's yellow is gold, what's white is jade,
What's tall is a mountain, what's low is a vale.
'Your name is Su, courtesy name Po-yü.
As a man you're gifted, quite intelligent.
Your family lives in Ch'angan, your body is in Shu.
How I regret your horse's hooves come home so seldom!
One thousand pounds of mutton, one hundred vats of wine.
You make your horse fat on wheat and millet.
Men today are not wise enough,
Give them a letter – they can't read it!
Start mine from the middle then out to the four corners'.

242

Chang Tsai

Four Sorrows, four poems

I

The one I love lives in southern Ch'ao.
I long to go after him, but Mount Wu is too high.
Climbing a cliff I look far off, tears and snivel criss-cross.
My breast, my heart feel deeply wounded.
My handsome one left me cloth wrapped in a case.
What will I give him? Flowing yellow silk.
I want to cross the far road on a buoyant wind,
In the end it never comes. Desire grows keener.

2

The one I love lives by northern waters.
I long to go after him, but white snow falls thick.
Climbing a cliff I stare for ever, tears and snivel spill.
My breast, my heart feel painfully sad.
My handsome one left me a wing feather from the clouds.
What will I give him? Jade discs of many cities.
I want to cross distant barriers on a homing goose,
In the end it never comes. Despair grows deeper.

3

The one I love lives at Lung's west plain.
I long to go after him, but Mount T'ai cuts me off.
Climbing a cliff I look far off, tears and snivel trickle.
My breast, my heart ache with frustration.
My handsome one left me a pair of horned beasts.
What will I give him? Carved jade rings.
I want to cross ranging peaks on a cloud of passage,
In the end it never comes. Sighs grow longer.

4

The one I love lives east in Yingchow.
I long to go after him, but the long road is perilous.
Climbing a cliff I look far off, tears and snivel flow.
My breast, my heart feel painful despair.

243

My handsome one left me a Greensilk lute.
What will I give him? Twin southern gold bars.
I want to cross the bottomless deep on a surging wave,
In the end it never comes. Moans grow ever louder.

Anon.   A Ditty of the Chin Emperor Hui's Era

That girl
A Yehchung girl, Mo Ch'ien-yao,
Will hug Hun waists three months from now!

Lu Chi

Love-song
The four seasons follow in turn, depart beyond recall.
Cold winds soft, soft falling leaves fly.
Crickets stay in the hall, dew floods the steps.
Remembrance of your far journey is always cruelly sad.
Why do you keep far away, for long not returning?
My poor adoring heart never falters.
The white sun has died. Bright lamps glow.
Cold birds go to the woods nesting in pairs.
Two ospreys – Caw! caw! – nestle on the river's edge.
Despair comes stirred by nature, tears are not a few.
But for remembrance of you, who would I dream of?
So soon the day you part, so late we are to meet!

244

Pao Chao

Magic cinnabar

The king of Huainan
Craving immortality
Drank potions, ate health foods, read arcane tomes.
Of lapis lazuli his drug bowls, of ivory his plates,
Gold cauldron, jade ladle, he mixed magic cinnabar,
Mixed magic cinnabar,
Pleasured in purple rooms,
In purple rooms where exotic girls fondle bright earrings.
Paradise birdsong, phoenix dance broke his heart.

Enter my lord's breast

Vermilion city's nine gates lie ninefold open.
With the bright moon I long to enter my lord's breast,
Enter my lord's breast,
Untie my lord's jewel belt.
I resent you, hate you, need your love!
To build a city look for strength, in a dagger look for sharpness.
We'll both flourish, both fall, not deserting each other.

I'll dance for you

Red lips move,
White arms lift,
Loyang boys, Hantan girls.
The ancients sang *Green river*, moderns sing *White hemp*.
Quicken the strings! Faster play the pipes! I'll dance for you.
Deep autumn's ninth month, lotus leaves yellow.
North winds chase geese away, skies rain frost.
Long night long, wine in plenty, joy's course not run.

Spread jade mats

Spring winds rock and sway, make me love the more,
The sky's coloured pure blue, air soft and sweet.
Peach full of red petals, orchid's purple buds,

The dawn sun glistens, unfolds the garden flowers.
Roll up the blinds, draw the drapes, spread jade mats.
Ch'i song, Ch'in piping, Lu girls' strings.
A thousand in gold for one smile? I'll buy the sweet season!

The road is hard, four poems

1

Five peach trees in the garden
And one is blooming early.
After two or three fine spring months
Windswept flurries of petals fall on the west house.
In the west house a girl in love watches wistfully.
Falling tears dampen her dress, she sighs, soothing her heart.
When first I said goodbye to you outside the door,
Did you tell me you'd delay through changing seasons?
On my bed dust grows, my bright mirror is stained.
My slim waist is gaunt, hair a tangled mat.
Life can never go as we plan!
Disillusion, doubt wound me half the night.

2

Chopped cork stains yellow silk,
Yellow silk tangled cannot be unravelled.
Long ago you and I first met,
I thought then perhaps you loved me.
Tying my belt you whispered to me,
'In death as in life, for better or worse, I won't leave you'.
Today I see my beauty fade,
Your passion sadly different from before.
Take back your jade pin and tortoiseshell jewel!
I can't bear to see them sadden love.

3

I offer you fine wine in a golden cup,
A carved lute in tortoiseshell and jade case,
Feather curtains with seven-tone hibiscus,
A brocade quilt with nine-bloom grapevine.
Pink cheeks wither, the year about to end.
Cold light draws round, the season soon to fail.
I long for you to cut short grief and snuff out pining.
Listen to my drumbeat, my *Road is hard* song.
Don't you see Cypress Rafter, Bronze Sparrow up above?
Suppose we heard clear flutes, music of days gone by . . .

246

4

Jasper room, jade court leading to pepper gallery,
Patterned window, broidered door hung with gauze drapes.
Inside a girl called Gold Orchid,
Dressed in sheer silk suffused with sweet storax.
Spring swallows fitful, winds scatter plum petals.
She opens a curtain, looks at the scene, twirls gold bird pins,
Hums a song, wipes a tear, unable to speak.
In life for how long can we be happy?
Let's be two ducks flying in the meadow,
Never make me a lost stork circling the clouds!

Shih Pao-yüeh

The road is hard

Don't you see the waif goose set out beyond the pass,
Cross plaintive over Yang and Yüeh?
In a lonely town a traveller's heart is broken.
In a hidden room a pining wife nearly expires.
Crisp frost falls by night, brushing her silk dress.
Floating clouds break apart, a clear moon appears.
Night after night faraway futile love,
Year after year hope upon hope, passion undying.
He sent me a green bronze mirror in a case.
My servant for your sake plucks out white hairs.
The road is hard.
The road is hard.
At night to hear Han envoys pass south of town
Makes me stream with tears. I long for Ch'angan.

247

Lu Chüeh

A throne crumbles away

Retinue carriage hanging seats are dusty,
Incense on the panther's tail is fading.
Crimson halls revert to sweet herbs,
Green rush cushions crumble away.
A throne crumbles away.
I stare at sweet herbs,
Look toward cinnabar court,
Weeping on pepper paths.
Widow stork, fettered bird fly then hover.
On carved rafters, kingfisher walls spinning spiders.
Deep in my room on a clear moonlit night
I stare at this, tears like pearls.

Shen Yüeh

Autumn moon

Gaze at the autumn moon!
Autumn moonlight like sheer silk
Shines splendour on Three Sparrow Terrace,
Shimmers on Nineflower Hall.
Nineflower's tortoiseshell rafters,
Flowery beams with jade disc pendants;
The loveliness of these ornaments
Is enhanced by clear moonlight.

Frigid florescence enters axe-print drapes,
Pristine lustre cascades through secret bedrooms.
Long ago it passed by Feiyen's door,
Or lit up Lady Pan's bed.
At Cassia Palace pitter-patter shed cassia boughs,
At Dew Chill Hall numb, numb freezes white dew.

Royal Forest Park's late leaves rustling, rustling echoes,
Goose Gate Pass early geese cross pell-mell.

Curved perfectly round as if by a compass,
It darts pure gleams like white silk,
Lightens thatched shadows of despairing eaves,
Glints on light footsteps up stairs of gold.
Left at home a girl sings laughingly to it,
A separated traveller feels the pain of desire beneath it.

Crossing withered orchards,
Glinting on cold shrubs,
Freezing in clear night,
Trailing autumn winds,
It lends whiteness to garden snow,
Borrows the pink of pond lotus,
Glances on jade court pale, pale,
Breathes on frosty fog a hazy blur.

It blazes down Sky Trails, rocking with the void,
Streaks down Long Han, flickering in the sky,
Steals behind sheer cliffs, yet half reappears,
Screened by curtains it barely filters through.
Spreads pomp and glory over a crimson garden,
Enters green chains with a tinkling clink.

By still steps it saddens a widow swan,
On a sandy bar grieves a stray goose.
Lady of Letters wept in her savage hall,
Ming-chün longed for her Han palace.
And I, what of me
Lingering in these eastern mountains?

Spring wind

Enjoy the spring wind!
When the spring wind stirs spring trees,
Drifting fluff veils like cobwebs,
Falling flowers thicken like fog.
First it skims gulf of heaven pools,
Then slips through slim willow fronds,
Catching butterflies tossed in sprightly dance,
Meeting swallows to ruffle their feathers.

249

It unfurls cassia streamers,
Shakes mushroom canopies,
Opens Yen skirts,
Blows Chao belts.
Chao belts fly jerkily,
Yen skirts fold and part.
It tweaks hairpins and tweaks kohl,
So girls look back dismayed at their faces.
Their faces once so glamorous
The spring wind reduces now to ruins.

A thick flurry of peach and plum blossom,
Green calyx enshrining white corolla,
All that the wind lays open
Is by that wind felled.
Tossing green stems,
Swinging purple stalks,
It makes spring snow dance,
Gliding orioles scatter.

Labyrinthine rooms open, gold knobs rattle,
Gold knobs rattle, a woman's dream shattered.
Catalpa's failing shadow,
Ch'i river's freshening green.
It welcomes falling rain on Kaot'ang,
Escorts migrant geese at Chiehshih,
Passes secret bedrooms,
Rustles white silk,
Troubles hidden boudoirs,
Breathes love on draped veils.

Imagine it roaming through sweet orchards!
Think of it gentle plucking outstretched orchid!
It brushes winter dust from sparkling mirrors,
Smooths autumn creases from silk gowns.
When it swings a girdle jingle-jangle,
Thick heavy scents pour from sachets.
First it enters bedrooms with nervous excitement,
Then slides through cracks with shy hesitation,
Tinkles pearl blinds on broidered doors,
Scatters scented dust on silken mats.

This season depresses pining women.
How can they endure their soldier's campaign?
Yet if lovely women were not here,
Who would the spring wind pity?

On a spring day

[by Shen Yüeh and Hsiao Yen]

Orchid leaves in a tizzy, peach half pink,
Winging scent, waltzing gauze, flirts the spring wind. [Shen Yüeh]
Kingfisher plumes flock in flight unceasing,
I wish we were in the clouds always wing to wing. [Hsiao Yen]

On an autumn day

White dew about to set, grass colour yellow,
Gold pipes, jade lute-stops echo through secret rooms.
Two hearts, one shadow glide round together,
The whispered love I send to you never forget!

Wu Chün

The road is hard, two poems

I

Don't you see the guests in Royal Forest Park?
Frosty gauze, misty silks, ivory seats.
Everyone happy, oblivious to words,
Proud, esteemed, none held in pity.
White wine pleasant, sweet as milk,
Green goblets, white mirrors, lustrous as green jade.
Youth on his dignity is slow to savour –
How could he know the white courser will gallop past the crack?
In a Po Hill censer blended incense,
Yüchin, storax, Tuliang,
Coils sinuous in sweet air round lovely faces,
Slips through green chains, past purple rooms,
Creeps now under bed-drapes of Empress Yin of Chungshan,
Then gets into Lady Pan's imperial bed.
When Lady Pan lost favour her face never relaxed,

251

She served at Eternal Trust Terrace.
Sunset, wide awake she cannot sleep.
Autumn winds cruel visit from four sides.
Jade steps, paths overgrown with fine grass.
Gold censer's scented coals turned to ash.
Love won, love lost in one moment of time,
But that the inch of heart never can foretell.

2

By Tungt'ing lake a lone catalpa
Suffers frost, lashed by waves, buffeted by harsh gales.
Long ago it bared its heart to bask in white sunshine,
This morning it lies down to die in yellow sands.
A famed Loyang craftsman looks on it and sighs.
In a single hack, a single slice he makes a guitar.
On its heart cut from white jade discs he traces a bright moon,
On its face inlaid with tortoiseshell creates windblown blooms.
An emperor sees this treasure unforgettable,
Cradles it and ascends Chienchang Palace.
Terse, piteous, played by a girl musician,
She quickens tense stops, a Ch'u Ming-kuang virtuoso.
Year by year, month by month it looks upon its lord,
Far, far into night on night sleeps at Weiyang Palace.
Glamorous girls of Weiyang play pipes shrill,
Rival glances, timid strokes create a lovely radiance.
Oleaster brocade enwraps it, jade encased,
Why hark back on former days as a withered branch?
Don't copy cassia on Mount Heng's southern range –
One thousand years to this day left unknown.

Chang Shuai

Staring

I'll always love you
However long we're parted.
My beloved's distance is like a drought.
Alone, standing still,

My heart taut inside me,
I stare at clouds gone, gone far away,
Stare at birds flown, flown into nothingness.
Useless staring always ends like this :
Pearl tears that won't be wiped dry.

Pining

I'll always love you
However long we're parted.
Where is my love? Under distant skies pining.
My heavy heart does not know where to look for you.
On jade steps the moon's twilight glimmer.
Through filmy drapes the wind's night-time blowing.
Constantly longing for you I cannot sleep,
I sit and stare at Sky River's motion.

In rhythm

A singer pours out song, her voice near sublime.
A dancer keeps in rhythm, her body light as can be.
Song, dance both well wedded to someone's passion,
Response to strings, to change of key subtly graceful.
Eyebrows raised, she poses, makes eyes at someone.

In unison

Wonderful voices in song after song, light bodies fly.
Trickling sweat stains faces, blending with sweet scents.
They move as one, stop in unison, none out of step,
Enraptured, the honoured guests forget to go home.
Long hours they play through the night as bright stars dwindle.

Fei Ch'ang

The road is hard, two poems

I

Don't you see at Ch'angan's tavern gate
A young singing-house girl called Peachroot?
So poor she spins by night without lamp or candle –

253

Well one day she gets to serve His Majesty!
In His Majesty's palaces, a hundred places or more,
One thousand gates, ten thousand doors never know dawn.
Only the sound of crows heard cawing on city walls.
By a gold well's jade rail she draws the pulley cord.
Near crimson rafters, kingfisher pillars her flowing silk whirls.
Over scented log cassia smoke she cooks wild rice.
That year was topsy-turvy, no set rules.
Poverty in a girl need not be despised!

2

Don't you see how a lifetime flashes past like lightning?
Man's heart a raging tumult – don't you see?
Long ago when I first entered pepper rooms,
Was I less lovely than Lady Pan or Feiyen?
At dawn I trod gold stairs up to my phoenix-cote,
At dusk lowered the jade hook to rest in lovebird hall.
Cypress Terrace day and night perfumed,
Brocade curtains unprompted flared and furled.
On balloon guitars *Mulberry up the lane*,
On flutes, in song *Under the jujube tree.*

Mine was the gift of the emperor's kind love,
I basked in flooding light.
When Empress Yin met with favour, she sought no preferment.
Lady Ch'eng, a favourite, had something taboo.
Once in a thousand years the Yellow river runs clear.
Whether my poor self is lucky again remains an enigma.
Moth eyebrows, halfmoon mouches, these our charms,
Powder and gloss smoothed on – but for whom?
Better to be wild ducks on gulf of heaven waters
Flying away two, homing two, always wing to wing.

Hsiao Kang

Hibiscus my boat
Hibiscus my boat, silk my mooring rope.
Northern Dipper astride the sky, moon about to set.
Where I pick lotus the ferry looks like the Yellow river's.
My love would cross today, but fears the tempest waves.

Floating clouds like curtains

Floating clouds like curtains, the moon becomes their hook,
How can I night after night bear it up south lane?
Yi city's mulled wine is now getting warm.
Unsaddle, tether your horse, nestle overnight!

Black ox, crimson hubs

Black ox, crimson hubs, seven-perfume coach.
How lovely lodging tonight at an entertainment tavern.
In the tall tavern trees are nesting crows.
Silk curtains, kingfisher drapes now bow before you.

A wool-weave screen

A wool-weave screen hinged with silver,
Red lips, a jade face appear before the lamp.
I look at you and sigh, hoping for your love.
Could someone be so shy she won't come closer?

War

Yünchung's watchtower, winged dispatches sound the alarm,
Sweet Springs beacons blaze through the night.
General Li of Erh-shih fame pitches a new camp,
Supreme Commander Huo starts his first campaign.
And there is our Shansi general,
Unsurpassed in valour and renown.
Three battalions drilled in occult tactics,
Five brigades modelled on heavenly armies,
White clouds follow regimental colours,
Blue hills echo to the drumroll.
Sinuous goose-wing array he reviews,
Zigzag goose formation he inspects.
First he will quell Hsiaoyüeh hordes,
Then he will crush Ferghana cities.
Fine horse he'll bring back to Eternal Joy Palace,
Yellow gold pay in to Shuiheng office.
His young Chao wife will drum and play the harp virtuoso,
Maids in first hairpins will render Cheng music.
Garden peach blossom will flurry in heaps,
Pink cheeks all raised to greet him!

Isolated manor grapevines
Isolated manor grapevines pregnant with dangling fruit,
Chiangnan cardamom boughs grown to an embrace.
Insensate, impassive, they are always the same,
Yet he who loves or hates vainly suffers isolation!

Spiders' spun threads
Spiders' spun threads spread through curtains.
Sweet grasses' knotted blades choke the pathways.
Pink cheeks in mute desire weep her life away.
Golden orioles fitful flit, flit past.
Old love though old once was new,
New love though new also must grow old.

Lovely Huai river
Lovely Huai river flows in, flows out.
Spring bank willows cover the river bridge.
Traces of tears still not dry, can they last till noon?
As she walks I hear jade belt jewels coming to meet me.

Peach pink
Peach pink, plum white like dawn cosmetics.
I disgrace my wrecked self next to fresh willow.
I wouldn't mind living a while, then dying before you –
But I'd be in despair without my west Reincarnation scent!

Spring passion
Butterfly yellow, blossom purple, swallows playing tag,
Willows bowing, willows kissing, highway dust in flight.
Now I see a dangling hook hang from green trees.
I know for sure Ch'i river soaks silk clothes.
Two boys parked alongside ask endless questions,
Five horses south of the city not yet turned for home.
Orioles weep that spring soon hastens away.
Nothing for it but to close my futile doors!

Unconscious thoughts
She peeps at rouge in the mirror, winces her eyebrows,
Sorrowful she wipes her tears, unconscious thoughts of him,
Remembering how time passed since he left.
With eloquent eyes, dimpling smiles her love would greet him,

In heartfelt longing, heartfelt passion so plain to see.
Desiring him she cannot bear to speak,
Smothering hate, she stifles her lonely voice.

Or nurse shame

Dawn sun comes slanting up to brighten my door.
Spring birds race in flight out of the woods.
Slivers of light, line of shadow, both lovely,
One echo, one warble inflame my heart.
Royal Forest thick, thick with flowers falling,
Ch'i river veiled, veiled with alga floating.
Years race, seasons flow gentle unto death.
How to bear desire, or nurse shame?

Hsiao I

Moonlit night

K'unming lake's night moon gleams like glossed silk,
Royal Forest's dawn blossom has the sheen of sleet.
Blossom of dawn, moon of night excite spring hearts.
Who can bear loving you, never to meet?

I steal a look

I steal a look at embracing dragon loom brocade,
Glance back at joy of love garden boughs.
Reflected windborne sunlight throws shadows on red cushions,
Tossed flowers, upswept leaves skim gilded pools.
I've never heard parted love must meet many times,
But I regret love's end : to meet becomes to part.

Tangled

Willows before the gate tangled like silk thread
Soon make a beauty lose self-control.
She's just said she'll compose a new *Torn silk* poem,
Little thinking it would degenerate into *Homespun* song!

257

As I dawdle
As I dawdle at sunset west of Wei bridge
I just glimpse the moon sail even with clouds.
Suppose I could make moonlight equidistant
To shine on parted lovers who weep tonight?

Hsiao Tzu-hsien

Holding hands home
Fluttering orioles, passing swallows double wing to wing,
Willow's thousand strands all one colour.
All I see is hands held homeward up the lane.
Who can face this feeling hopeless love for you?

A secret palace
A secret palace where banked grass releases sweet scent,
Golden orioles in sweet trees falling in love,
Speed with the wind, race against the sun, echoes ringing,
Massed flowers, dense leaves won't admit their flight.
You should know this season arouses my love,
Makes my silken sleeve one moment caress your cloak.

Sunny splendoured spring
Chiangtung highway, sunny splendoured spring,
Drooping willow, hanging willow sweep light dust.
Yesterday's farewell at the Ch'i, tears soaked my kerchief.
The rouged face he slept with must be new love.

Why do people part?
Stifled grief, tears wiped, the parted heart knows.
Peach blossom, plum blossom suffer blowing winds.
Though I always knew human hearts aren't like trees,
I wonder – why do people part like torn blossom?

258

No regrets
In my hand a winecup with onyx bells,
On my skirt clustered pendants of amber dragons.
I would send them to you with no regrets
And point to Three Stars, 'What a night is this!'

Tearstained mascara
Tearstained mascara, diluted rouge blotch her petal face,
Distort her looks beyond all recognition.
How can the gold waterclock's night water be so full?
Still, never so full as that far Sky River!

I remember
Windy glimmer's slow dance draws out green mugwort.
Kingfisher birds on orchid stalks carol advent of spring.
Loyang pear blossom falls like snow.
Riverside grass fine, fine and green like a cushion.
Catalpa growing by the well criss-crosses leafy boughs.
Now I see twin swallows suddenly part.

Five-storey flying mansions pierce Han river,
Nine-flower arcaded roads darken crystal pools.
Far away I see a soldier near Whitehorse ford,
He tells of men attacking Huanglung tribes.

The bright moon's golden beams shine vain on me,
Floating clouds' jade leaves you will never know.
I remember you left long ago, willows caressed.
Now in the eighth month you come home to avoid the heat.
Bright pearl silkworm cocoons struggle up the loom.
Yüchin scented petals specially sweeten his robe.

Uptown Loyang cocks are about to crow,
Ministerial office rooks not yet flown.
I dream at night of a soldier as I stitch fox-badger,
And feel for the weaver who tailors scarlet and brocade.
Wu shears, Cheng wadding,
The cold bedroom quilt at night feels thin.
Fragrant season lake ducks in the water.
Sunset. Cold night. Empty city swallows.

Wang Yün

The road is hard
One thousand gates at midnight barricaded,
One hundred cares flock to crush my heart.
I search through boxes, take out shears and rule,
Brush my loom, cut the flowing yellow.
Though I hate my lover for loving someone else,
I dread his having no far frontier clothes.

I have spun silk from one cocoon to make his urgent cloak,
Have pounded mixed scents to perfume his folded robe.
I still remember the size of his waist at parting time,
But don't know his body measurements now.

I've fastened a waistband to his tunic's twin hearts,
Inserted eight pleats both sides of his jacket.
The inside cord fits, I can't bear to sew it!
My needle eye is clear, still the silk won't go through.
Halfmoons two I've joined together on your breast —
They may shine on your breast, but won't light up the sky.
I want you to get their meaning clear :
Don't chase other women! don't forget your former vow!
Mournful, regretful love undying.
Numb, repressed with longing, I'll wait until next year.

A poet meets his former mistress at a party
I delayed my former husband,
Had no qualms.
Deserted by him, I waited up the spring hill
And met him as I picked the sweet herbs.

Liu Hsiao-wei

Poor darling

Nesting double two kingfisher mandarin ducks
Under Mount Wu clouds, Lo river moon, suddenly stare.
Someone's lovely charmer breaks a spray of flowers.
Moth eyebrows, flirting glance arouse my desire.
Green knobs, emerald chains, lapis lazuli doors,
Jasper mats, jade cabinets, gold lamé clothes.
A lovely girl of ten or so
Turns shyly smiling, smooths windblown skirts.
He's off shooting pearl, can't be found.
Left alone, who will comfort her, poor darling?

Hsü Chün-ch'ien

Echoing song

Soaring phoenix mansion
Seen from far floats with clouds.
Echoing song lilts over trees,
Dancing shadows blend with the river's flow.
Leaves fall, I see the village closer.
Skies high, must soon be autumn.

Deliberately

Beauty parlour
Make-up done, she adds a star mouche.
Rouge on cheeks perhaps a bit too faint?
Kohl in eyebrows perhaps not green enough?
Deliberately she leaves her used powderpuff
To dangle on the blind's hook.

Liu, Wang Shu-ying's Wife

In brilliant spring
Cosmetic film, dab of kohl, light brush of rouge.
Bangles jingling, belt swinging she leaves bedroom lattice.
She looks at plum and then looks at willow.
Tears well up in brilliant spring.

Liu, Wang, Bao, Ying, et White

CHAPTER TEN

A Treasury of Short Love Poems

(from third to sixth centuries AD)

Anon.   Four Old Chüeh-chü Poems

Where?

Pounder, where are you now?
Over the hill there lies another hill.
When will you dagger-hilt?
When broken mirror flies up in the sky.

[This poem is a series of puns, which translated read as follows :]

'Lover, where are you now?'
'I have gone away'.
'When will you come back?'
'When the waning moon flies up in the sky'.

What?

Sunset. Autumn clouds darken.
Yangtze river deep, diaphanous.
What will bear my message?
On my tortoiseshell pin – a lotus.

How?

Dodder bent by distant winds,
Root never sundered from host stem.
If insensate things will never part,
How can sentient beings separate?

I'll never forget

One cassia tree on a southern hill,
Two mandarin ducks upon its crown.
One thousand years their necks in long caress :
'Happy love, I'll never forget'.

Chia Ch'ung
Three Linked Verses Composed with My Wife, Lady Li

Why do I sigh?
Who is it in her room
Sighing sighs that echo sad? (Chia Ch'ung's verse)
And why do I sigh these sighs?
I just dread our marriage failing! (Lady Li)

Our marriage
Our marriage is like glue and lacquer.
My 'not a stone' heart won't waver. (Chia Ch'ung)
Who does not fear the end?
Even sun and moon join but to part! (Lady Li)

Your heart
My heart is known to you
As your heart too is known to me. (Chia Ch'ung)
If you don't wish to eat your words –
Let me be the one to share joy with you! (Lady Li)

Sun Cho

A lower-class girl
Green Jade, a lower-class girl,
Doesn't dare cling to kind favour :
'I'm moved by my darling's thousand gold love,
But feel disgraced I'm no city-razing beauty!'

She didn't feel shy
When Green Jade was of broken-melon age
Her lover was mad with passion.
Aroused by him, she didn't feel shy,
But whirled into her lover's arms!

?Wang Hsien-chih

I won't need oars
Peachleaf, oh Peachleaf!
To ferry your river I won't need oars,
Just to ferry, then no more pain,
For I'll be joined to you!

It takes two
Peachleaf, oh Peachleaf!
Peachleaf joined to peach root.
In love it takes two to make love –
Don't make me the only one to try!

?T'ao-yeh (Peachleaf)

Love me!
A seven jewel painted round fan
Glistening with bright moonlight
I send to you to chase away dull heat.
So love me! never forget me!

266

I'll count on its magic!
Green, green bamboo in a grove
Could make a round white fan
To move and stir in my love's jade hand –
Through wafted air I'll count on its magic!

To hide my face
Round fan, oh round fan!
I'll hold this to hide my face,
Care-worn and without make-up –
I'm ashamed my lover might see me!

Hsieh Ling-yün

Someone else's wife
How sweet! someone else's wife
Paddling white feet in green water.
Is the bright moon between the clouds
Far away, unattainable?

Someone else's husband
How sweet! someone else's husband
Sailing his boat on green water.
But since you ask if I'm in love –
That moon sinks into those clouds!

Liu Chün

Halt troops everywhere!
When the viceroy first went on campaign,
How I hated to hear the news!
I longed to create a Shih-Yu gale contrary
And halt troops everywhere!

Pitfalls on campaign
Yellow river's flow is endless.
Loyang's many thousand leagues away!
The snares and pitfalls on campaign . . .
How will I meet my darling?

Round and round
Ever since you went away
Gold, kingfisher grew dull, lack-lustre,
Thoughts of you like sun and moon
Go round and round as day grows into night.

Hsü Yao

The gnarled pillow
A straight tree growing by a river
Fell ill, so became a thing of beauty.
At dawn from cloudy hair it parts,
At night to moth eyebrows draws close.

I've quite forgotten
Once we were like shadow and form,
Now we're like north Hu and south Yüeh.
I don't know if you journey near or far,
I've quite forgotten what year or month you left!

Pao Ling-hui

Sent to a traveller
Cassia breathes out two or three sprays,
Orchid unfurls four or five leaves.
At such a time you're not back home –
The spring breeze smiles on me in vain.

Anon.　Five Modern Western Songs

Stone City
I grew up near Stone City,
Our gates look out on city wall houses.
In the city handsome boys
Drop in as they come and go.

A merchant
There's a merchant who often sends me letters,
No news makes my heart pine for him.
Don't be a bucket fallen down the well –
Once gone, lost without trace!

I heard her name
Sing and dance, all Youth,
Your dazzle won't impress me.
So pretty was that iris flower,
I heard her name, but never knew her.

Fresh flowers
At dawn I left Hsiangyang city,
At dusk lodged in Tat'i.
The girls in Tat'i are all
Fresh flowers to stun a man's eyes!

Old Mother Yang's boy
I went out in front of White Gate a moment,
Where willows could hide a crow.
He uses Sunken-river cologne,
I use a Po Hill censer.

269

Anon.   Nine Modern Wu Songs

Spring song
The morning sun shines on northern woods,
Early flowers of tapestry hues.
Can anyone object to spring love,
Sit all alone and weave at her loom?

Summer song
Muggy, torpid hot midsummer months.
I give a long whistle, set out for the lakeside.
Hibiscus starts to form stamens,
Pureness enshrined, not yet become passion flower.

Autumn song
Through windows enters the autumn wind,
Swaying, billowing lifts silky curtains.
I raise my head, gaze at the bright moon
And send my love on thousand-league beams.

Winter song
Ice on the pool three feet thick,
White snow blanket a thousand leagues wide.
My heart is like the cypress and pine –
And your heart, is it like mine?

Carried by its current
Yellow vines weave a covering cage
As they grow beside Lo river creek.
Flowers fall carried by its current away.
Will I ever see its current carry back to me?

Pomegranate blouson
Her pomegranate twin broidered blouson
Fits tight under her silk jacket.
Soft steps stir light dust,
Silk clothes lift in gusts.

My tiny self
Faraway pillarless sky.
Drifting wide rootless alga.
My tiny self like a firefly spark,
What can I do to repay your love?

Where's your *bed?*
Red silk funnel bedcurtains,
Four corners hung with red pearl,
Jade pillow, Lunghsü grass mattress . . .
'When you sleep, sir, where's *your* bed?'

Sleep alone
Willow tree catches spring winds,
One swing down and one swing up.
Who can love you with hopeless longing
Yet sleep alone through the three months of spring?

Anon.   Three Modern Miscellaneous Songs

He married two
From Chi Pavilion past love has gone,
To Mount Chiuli new love returns.
Divorcing one means he married two –
In not a very long space of time!

Song of spring
Green lotus leaves spread over green water,
Hibiscus sticks up red, fresh.
Forked lotus roots lie side by side beneath,
On top grow lotus blooms with twin hearts.

Silkworm silk
Spring silkworms should not grow old,
Yet day and night they pine always spinning silk.
Why pity their tiny spent form?
Tangled affairs have their natural season.

271

Anon.   A Modern Miscellaneous Poem

I can't decide
Is it jade bangle colour? I can't decide.
Or her gown sheer seeming to show her arm?
She lifts a sleeve as if to defend her shyness,
Keeps turned away, combing tousled hair.

Meng Chu

A pity I didn't
In sunny spring's second and third months
Grass and river are one colour.
On the road I met a kind man roving –
A pity I didn't know him sooner!

Su Hsiao-hsiao

Where?
I drive a glossy panelled carriage,
My lover rides a piebald horse.
Where will sweethearts become one?
At West Mound 'neath pine and cypress.

272

Wang Yüan-chang

Where are you?
Flower-root, where are you now?
This no longer grows by the woods.
When will two topknots hang down?
When the round fan is bright through clouds.

[This poem is a series of puns, which translated read as follows :]

'Lover, where are you now?'
'I live at my old home no more.'
'When will my mirror reflect our two topknots?'
'When the full moon is bright through clouds.'

Ever since you went away
Ever since you went away,
My gold censer has not burned incense.
I love you like the candle bright
Consumed by vain midnight passion.

Autumn nights
Autumn nights long, so long.
Though nights are long, pleasure's not run mid-course.
Dancing sleeves brush bright candles,
Singing echoes spin round phoenix rafters.

Flame
My icy face is disgraced by that far disc,
My aquarian nature surrenders to bright flame.
These shine tonight while I pine for you.
Traveller, I hope you'll be back soon!

273

Hsieh T'iao

Jade steps lament
The twilight palace lowers pearl blinds,
Floating fireflies flit and come to rest.
Through long nights she sews his silken robe,
Longing for you, when will it ever end?

A party at Golden Vale
Nacreous goblets sent round by pretty girls,
Jade cups invite honoured guests.
Once coach and horse go east and west,
And we part, let us remember this night!

A prince went wandering
Green grass plushy like silk,
Dappled trees sprouting pink blooms.
No matter if you haven't come home –
If you had, their scent is now gone!

The one I love
My sweet date made a date but didn't come back.
I hope and hope, leave my humming loom,
Roam restless up east lane.
The moon comes out, travellers sparse.

Yü Yen

The one I love
Mauve wisteria brushes blossoming trees.
Golden orioles pass through green boughs.
Longing for you I whisper a sigh.
Stinging tears by whispers prompted trickle down.

Shen Yüeh

If ever
We let go hands on a peach grove slope,
I wished you goodbye on a steep hilltop.
If ever I want to send you word,
Han river flows toward the east.

Out early, I met my former mistress
Traces of lipstick still show faint,
A touch of powder still shows in smudges.
Where did you sleep last night
That this morning you come home brushing dewdrops?

True and false
A shadow creeps up with the slanting moon,
Perfume drifts in on a distant breeze.
Your promise true now I know is false,
My dawning smile becomes a sob.

Shih Jung-t'ai

Wang Chao-chün
Trailing silk she comes down from pepper gallery,
Lifts her sleeve to flick barbarian dust.
'Oh! Oh!' she touches her heart and sighs.
Moth eyebrows cast a deadly spell on men.

Kao Shuang

Winemaid
Long cushions lie at angles, not close,
The honoured guest can't get near the charmer.
She hands back his winecup without glancing round,
Turns her back with a look so prim and proper.

?The Fairy of Wuhsing

Lone farewell
Jade hairpins hopelessly askew,
Gold flower's sheen getting dull.
I weep a lone farewell to the spring wind,
On fine nights ostracise the bright moon.

Chiang Hung

Just waiting
Winds spring up, green leaves gather,
Waves stir, purple stalks part.
Laden with bloom, pregnant with fruit,
Just waiting for a handsome one to come!

I meet you once again
The white sun calms pure winds,
Light clouds dapple tall trees.
Suddenly, just at that very moment,
I pick caltrop and meet you once again.

Lured (Green river, 1)
Lapping, splashing white and clean,
Light and fresh, such fun!
Perversely, a lovesick bird is lured
To its reflection, and then cruel widowhood.

My grimy face (Green river, 2)
My grimy face I cannot bear to beautify.
I lean over the pool, dream of my wanderer's return.
Who can take green water in her hand,
Wash silk robes in a tedium of despair?

Widow
Living as a widow I hate the four seasons,
Especially in my autumn bedroom.
Frigid leaves flicker with last glints,
An empty garden pokes out cold vegetables.

Winds crush a tree
Against the north window winds crush a tree.
By the south fence cold crickets chirp.
Throughout the garden boundless moonlight.
A pining woman bangs her night pounder.

Her glamour
In her coach she frets about her glamour,
Peers sideways, then right round at herself,
Furious at painted eyebrows' length,
Muttering, 'My face looks even worse!'

Shen Man-yüan

Wang Chao-chün's regret
If only I'd believed the power of paint sooner,
I'd have bribed that Loyang artist heavily!
One thousand gold to buy cicada sidecurls,
A million gold to sketch moth eyebrows.

Wang Chao-chün's dreams
This morning still on Han soil,
Tomorrow dawn she enters the Hun pass.
The high hall's song and piping will recede,
Yet in her dreams this traveller will go home.

Tumbled hair
Fluffy sidecurls fashioned as floating clouds,
Twin moths modelled on new moons.
Where water's smooth she straightens slipped hairpins,
Where duckweed parts tidies tumbled hair.

Ho Sun

South Park
Park gates throw wide their thousand wings.
Park doors open ten thousand leaves.
In mansion and hall are heard pearl slippers,
Bamboo and trees screen filmy clothes.

Bedroom frustration
By her bedroom door passersby cease.
Across her room's lattice moonbeams slant.
Who can go near the north window
And face rear garden flowers all alone?

For someone's pining wife
Swallows play homing toward the eaves.
Blossoms fly landing before my pillow.
My inch of heart you'll never see.
Wiping the tears, I sit and tune my strings.

Spring wind
Audible yet invisible,
May be strong, may be light,
Before the mirror it whirls spilled powder,
Across a lute sounds echoing notes.

278

Autumn bedroom frustration
Bamboo leaves rattle on south windows,
Moonlight shines upon the east wall.
Who knows at night I wake alone
Shedding tears beside my pillow?

Wu Chün

Painful memories
The noon cicada knows painful memories.
Night dew once more soaks a dress.
Leaving me long ago, what was it you said
That made the glow-worm start its flight?

A blur of blooms
On her brocade waist embracing boughs lie,
On her broidered collar joy of love blooms slant.
Though in my dreams I swear I see them,
My vision ends in a blur of blooms.

Spiders dangle
Spiders dangle from the eaves,
Grasshoppers wail by the wall.
When will I get to see my man?
When bright mirror moves from east to my west window.

Wine of our farewell
I weep to hear songs of the night we part,
I grieve to savour wine of our farewell.
From this day on when you have left,
You will still love me, won't you?

Wang Seng-ju

Spring longing
Snow stops, twigs are quite green,
Ice cracks, water quite emerald.
Once more is heard the oriole's voice,
It makes me write a song of loving you.

I ought to go back
It's late in the day, I ought to go back.
The honoured guest is a terrible dawdler.
I slowly feel jade pins weigh heavy,
See my silk tunic gradually go cold.

Liu Ling-hsien

Cloistered
Delightful to send my gaze down verandahs,
Pleasant to enjoy views of spacious halls.
But when will I live in cloistered rooms
Dark and gloomy, far from human noise?

No one suspects
Crying at dusk is not uncommon now,
Weeping in dreams is really rather frequent.
Only my night pillow knows,
Otherwise no one suspects.

A twin-stemmed gardenia
Even if I offer two sprays as a gift,
They won't serve to show our mutual love.
Sweethearts are everywhere at freedom,
But these twin stems capture me completely!

Yao Fan

Powderpuff
About to sob she hangs her head
Afraid and shy her family might know.
She puts her puff in white powder,
Dabs her tears to stop them trickling down.

In a dream I saw my old lover
I woke, and then knew such hatred!
Human hearts are really not alike.
Who can face a pillow of horn
All night long completely on her own?

She didn't come
By dusk the messengers cease,
I choke back remorse, my heart aching, aching,
Swivel the lamp, go to my bed-stool,
Turn my face away to weep in the dark.

Wang Huan

Party talk
Up till now I've avoided party talk –
It reminds me how I wept at separation.
I've no way of following northern geese
That fly straight down toward the Yellow river.

Hsiao Yen

A border guard
The autumn moon risen mid-sky,
Near or far, has no favourites.
It radiates one equal brilliant light
Upon all pining separated lovers.

The candle
In halls fine silken women,
On mats singers and girl dancers
Wait for my waves of splashing light
To shine glancingly for you.

The pen
Once I heard of fragrant orchid months,
Only this is peach and plum time of year.
In case the heart in spring has not been described,
May this feast of love shine just for you !

The flute
At Aspen Pavilion there are marvellous bamboos,
They throb with passion in high and low key,
Sublime sounds pour from jade fingers,
Dragon music echoes with phoenix song.

The dance
Arms delicately lift and drop,
Her body light keeps twirling.
If you mean this to tell of desire,
You must come and join your sweetheart !

He and she
He : She who ruins cities is not of mortal beauty.
    In a thousand years I'll never meet you twice !
She : Though I long for your love in a carriage,
    I'm ashamed of my far from lovely hairdo !

I can't resist
Scent on the stairs invades my breast,
Flowers in the garden shine in my eyes.
Spring love is always like this :
Comes desire – I can't resist !

A sweet thought
Orchid leaves start filling the ground,
Plum blossom has fallen from the bough.
Since they contain a sweet thought,
I'll scoop some up for him who knows my heart.

Sprays to send my darling
Crimson sun glinting on white ice,
Yellow blooms reflected on white snow.
I break plum sprays to send my darling,
We'll meet together in sunny months of spring.

Lotus blooms
Chiangnan lotus blooms are open,
Their red sheen covers jade-green water.
Of like flush and in hearts alike,
Of different roots, their hearts won't differ.

Flowers in her bedroom
Flowers in her bedroom appear embroidered,
Dew on the blinds seems to be pearl.
You want to know if she has a lover ?
She stops her weaving and starts fidgeting.

A jade dish
A jade dish laid with maroon plum,
Gold goblet brimming with white wine.
Though I long to bring them close to her,
I fear her lips still won't find them sweet.

Crimson peach
A day of crimson peach-trees dropping flowers,
A time for oriole's busy flight.
Stop, my lord ! for now your horse is tired,
And I must go – the silkworms will be hungry !

283

Full of laughter

Sash broidered with joy of love knots,
Brocade dress designed with boughs embracing.
Full of passion she goes in with the moon,
Full of laughter comes out with dawn clouds.

Her mouth moves

Iridescent copper gilt pillars,
Florescent white jade rafters.
She sings solo song that won't stop ringing,
Her mouth moves, breathes a scent that lingers.

True love harmonies

Pipes fortissimo can't stop yet !
Strings in finale must start up again !
Both are making true love harmonies,
Each is playing sweetheart melodies.

It's clear

You must believe my vow to clasp the bridge-post,
Don't listen to whirlwind rumour !
In my mirror twin heads of hair –
It's clear our hearts aren't torn in two.

Shy love

Trusting his love she makes as if to draw near,
Then bashful is still reluctant to come close.
Red lips breathe sultry songs,
Jade fingers play flirtatious strings.

Morning sun

Morning sun shines on silk coin windows,
A flickering breeze sways gossamer silk.
Flirting smiles dimple with two melons,
Lovely eyes beam beneath twin moths.

Richer than gold

More flowery fair than apricot or peach,
Her name is richer than gold or jade.
Sublime song she sings – not the low pop,
Full of laughter she plays top-key tunes.

A promise
Sleek, sleek girl in a golden house,
Her heart like jade pool lotus.
With what to repay her lover's favour?
A promise to roam with him in paradise.

Down south
Down south there is a loving you tree
Where shadows join and hearts become one.
A girl of pleasure I cannot court,
So who to rest with in its airy shade?

A round fan
In her hand a white round fan
Pure as the full autumn moon.
Clear breezes woken by her fluttering
Bring seductive perfume with her love.

Jasper
Apricot rafters the sun starts to brighten
Before pleasure nears its peak on orchid mats.
A jasper jewel, she offers golden goblets,
Green wine enhances her flowery face.

A soldier departs
At the end of the lane a soldier departs,
In her room a girl gets down from her loom.
Emotional, she cannot speak.
Farewell has soaked her silk gown.

To let him know
'Plants and trees are not of one fragrance.
Flowers and leaves are of different colours'.
I send these words to my former lover
To let him know my heart remembers him.

Boys
Dragon steeds' copper gilt saddles,
Kingfisher plumes on white jade harness
Sparkle and glitter near twin portals –
I know they are Hsiangyang boys.

Hsiao Kang

Cold bedroom
My quilt is empty, I often wake from sleep,
The cold gets keener, night winds blow.
Gossamer curtains are not a river's swell –
How can I cross to him who once knew me?

Falling rain
I come from the mountain of Wu,
No man has glimpsed my face –
Except the king of Ch'u's courtier
Who said he knew me in a dream!

Rafter dust
Clinging to curtains it mottles deep green,
Soaked in sunlight it stains to pale pink.
It must have risen from the sound of singing,
Not from a round fan that stirs the air.

Florescent moon
A night when hare's shadow looms through clouds,
The hour Ch'ang O's form appears in Han.
Please carry him my thousand league affection,
Don't shine ten years' sorrow down on me!

Night after night
The Dipper star meanders away,
Lamplight half conceals my bed.
Night after night my heart suffers alone.
Slanting moonbeams hit my pillow,

Back from camp I go to the south city wall
Parted for a while we both had doubts,
But I open your blinds, old love rekindles,
As if we'd never loved before,
Like falling in love all over again.

286

Spring river song
Travellers thinking of our homeward path,
Roped together we ford the estuary.
We don't know the girls on the embankment,
But they wipe their tears and wave, pointlessly.

First swallows
New birds return in response to the season,
All flying to the house of flutes,
Entering blinds, startling bangles ajingle,
Coming through windows to collide with dancing dresses.

I play my zither
I play my zither by the northern window,
Echoes of night full of clear tones sad.
The key raised, a string soon snaps
And my heart mourns the melody lost.

Sending her home at night by boat
The brocade-draped barge pushes from its mooring,
Orchid oars stroke the waves in gliding,
Receding torches still dapple water,
Haunting perfume floods our boat still.

A pledge with wine
His hair parted like two topknots,
Long hairpins – signs of puberty.
He takes the winecup, seems to turn round,
Then, wondering if some remains, holds back.

I can sigh
I can sigh but cannot think,
Or can think but cannot see.
A string left broken on my guitar bridge,
A trace of lipstick stains my concert fan.

Soft echoes

Soft, soft echoes of twilight eaves,
Dark, dark colours of drawn curtains.
There's only moss upon the floor tiles,
And I seem to see a spider spinning.

Going through the grove

I'm going through the grove to look at plum buds,
Spring can't be long in coming.
When will I see him – just for once?
That's like viewing plum blossom!

Pleasure-seekers

They dawdle in Longwillow gardens,
Hold hands through Cloud Terrace,
Their pleasure not exhausted
As the white sun sets by western hills.

To a beauty

Your waist and limbs are natural wonders,
Your eyebrows and eyes just amaze me!
I'm convinced there's no one else like you –
And yet, there *is* Lo river goddess!

Admiring from a distance

Loosely her red shawl is draped,
Slantwise are fixed her jade hairpins,
So pretty, no one else like her,
She must be worth a thousand gold!

In her mirror

Long since you left I've looked haggard,
Other people are amazed at the change.
Except there's my mirror in its case.
I take it out again, recognise myself.

Floating clouds
How prettily wispy clouds spread!
One moment banked, then thinning out again.
If I want to relive the king of Ch'u's dream,
These clouds must cross White Emperor city.

Cold bedroom
Green leaves yellow dawn by dawn,
Red cheeks change day by day.
Comparing them figuratively together,
I can't help my thoughts growing sadder.

Chic
Elegantly chic her new chignon,
In a fresh laundered skirt she goes out to have fun.
To her belt front she ties scented herbs,
In her wig pins a pomegranate bloom.

Hsiao Tzu-hsien

Love in a spring boudoir
Gold harness, a gallant knight roving,
Silk loom, a parted girl pining.
Spring passes, he has not returned.
She watches blossom all turned to leaf.

A woman strolling in the park
In the second month of spring her heart excited,
She strolls around admiring early peach buds,
Turns and screens her fan against the sun,
Steps back and straightens her windblown skirt.

Liu Hsiao-cho

From a distance
Caltrop stems sometimes curl round her bangles,
Poked water now and then splashes her make-up.
She doesn't care if red sleeves get soaked,
So long as she can savour green leaf scent.

Children picking caltrop
'Picking caltrop isn't picking beans!'
'It's sundown, let's fill the boat!'
She dawdles, not daring to move closer,
Afraid he might compare her with leftover peach.

Yü Chien-wu

So far away
Singers' voices lilt over painted galleries,
Dancers' sleeves peep from fragrant woods.
Stone City seems so far away,
Ch'iench'i must be very profound.

My lord's young singers
Last year they all had ponytails,
This spring half wear their hair up.
How can I tell their bridegrooms are fine fellows?
They see fit to reject a prefect's advances!

Eternal Trust Palace grass
Fading emerald seems to sense the season,
Heavy scent appears to feel emotion:
Just because slippered footprints are rare,
It seeks to spread all across the steps.

The singer of Golden Vale
At orchid halls honoured guests arrive,
On silken mats clear strings are stroked.
He himself composes *Ming-chün's farewell*,
And asks Green Pearl to dance it once more.

Wang T'ai-ch'ing

Only a single person
Moon idly skimming my tall house,
You're not even a five- or three-year moon!
What's the point of shining on my bed?
It's only a single person sleeping, after all!

Saying goodbye
My frowning face bids you goodbye,
Frowns never to dissolve again.
The only thing to do is wait to see you –
Then will smiles melt my frowns away!

Liu Hsiao-i

Weaver
Gold floral pins now flash and glint,
The white sun has not yet tumbled.
She longs to wait till after the gloaming
To ford the shallow river radiantly.

Rock-lotus
Lotus, your name is worth a million,
Rock, your surname, richer than a thousand gold.
I don't understand how insensate things
Can be so like the heart of man.

Liu Hsiao-wei

Toying with her hair
Bound into braids it's still her familiar hair,
Teased into curls it's silken as before.
From this day on a single comb through is over,
No more can I wind it through my fingers.

Chiang Po-yao

Her exotic gown
Cut and sewn, laid in a bamboo case,
Incensed velvet nap bears a hint of scent.
She opens it and looks, hasn't the heart to wear it,
And from one glance a thousand streaming tears.

Liu Hung

Gay
So pretty he stands out easily from the crowd,
Fair, fair, most exquisite.
Elegant eyebrows arch smooth over twin eyes,
Mellifluous flows his murmuring voice.

Ho Man-ts'ai

Mourning his wife
Slow, slow his robe soaks with tears,
Piteous, piteous regret wreathes his breast.
No more days in her private room,
He hopes still he'll meet her down the hill.

Hsiao Lin

Her petticoat
White, white gold gauze shimmers,
Fine, fine jewelled seams part.
Her slender waist is not a Ch'u model,
Her loose belt is from longing for him.

Chi Shao-yü

Guttering lamp
The guttering lamp still not dead
Now goes out, now rekindles its flame.
Only one or two remaining flickers –
Barely enough to slip her clothes off.

Liu, Wang Shu-ying's Wife

Chill at dusk
Plum blossom emits its own gleam.
The early shrike welcomes the spring.
Colder grows the day, thinner feel my clothes.
He doesn't want to hug my waist.

Tai Hao

Going to bed
She dusts the pillow, perfumes her red hairnet,
Swivels the lamp and slips off her clothes.
Her maids know the night will be long,
But no call means they may go home.

Liu Hsiao-wei (encore)

Remembrance
Dawn sun, fierce wind and frost.
My commitments make us both suffer.
Leaves fall, boughs hang still.
I'm forever getting up to stretch my legs.

Beauty
She's adorable, well worth remembering . . .
Well worth remembering? She cost a thousand cash!
But I must say I do have one regret —
I'm sorry it's not my heart she's after!

Notes

A crow weeps, or *A crow weeps in the night*, the name of a ballad associated with the themes of wandering men, illicit love, or grass widows.

'a plug of mud', in the reign of Emperor Kuang-wu (AD 25–58) of the Han Dynasty, a military officer called Wei Hsiao (d. AD 33) was occupying T'ienshui commandery (in modern Kansu province). His junior officer told him that during that occupation he himself would go and blockade the Hanku Pass for Wei Hsiao with a plug of mud. The term is synonymous with an act of stupidity.

A-chiao, consort of the Han Emperor Wu (r. 141–87 BC), her official title was Empress Ch'en (q.v.), A-chiao being her childhood name. When they were both young, Emperor Wu fell in love with her and exclaimed that he would build her a House of Gold and treasure her there if she became his wife.

alga, a feminine image in love relations, signifying woman's dependence on man, as the alga clings to the surface of water.

always love you (*ch'ang hsiang ssu*), an elaborate pun for the silk floss padding of quilts and clothes, especially of marriage bed quilts. The padding was a pun for never-ending love.

Angler's south, the name of a piece of music based on the name of a Han district in modern Hopei.

Anling, see Lord Anling.

Antares (*Shang*), a star associated in folklore with Orion (*Shen*), believed to be quarrelling brothers who never meet. These two stars are in equinoctial opposition. They symbolise estranged lovers or friends.

autumn moon, on the fifteenth night of the eighth lunar month it is a full moon. Its circular shape gave rise to a pun in Chinese, *huan*, meaning a ring, which was a homophone for to come home. That time of the year was when people traditionally celebrated family reunion at the mid-autumn festival.

Autumn river, a reference to a tune, it is unclear which, perhaps *Green river*, or *Lu river*, an old lute melody.

autumn's nine, the week in antiquity was ten days long, each lunar month having three weeks, and each season three months, making a total of nine lots of ten-day weeks per season, or ninety days.

axe-print, in antiquity was an emblem of high office; later it became a fashion motif for wealthy houses. In some contexts the axe-print denotes a match-maker.

baby-snatching, a reference to the anecdote about a girl from Yüeh state who was the mistress of King Mu of Chou (trad. r. 1001–946 BC). When his con-sort, Queen Chiang, gave birth to a child, the king's mistress stole her baby from the parturition bed and claimed it as her own. The king was very angry with her for this.

295

bamboo leaf, a popular motif denoting frailty because of its slender leaves, constancy because it is evergreen, and long life because it is durable.

banana leaf, a motif denoting frailty because it is easily torn in rough weather.

Beanleaves in my patch, an allusion to poem 186 of *The Book of Songs*, in which a woman expresses her desire to keep her lover near her, likening this to tethering a white colt in her vegetable patch to nibble beans.

Black Gate, the east gate of the ancient city of Ch'angan, the western capital of the Former Han Dynasty. Ancient placenames were often used in poems instead of modern ones or together with them to impart an aura of historical romance.

blue clouds, one meaning of this image is the soaring ambition of a man in politics.

bluebird, the mythological messenger of the legendary figure, Queen Mother of the West, who ruled the paradise of immortals in the western mountains, thought to be the K'unlun range between Tibet and Sinkiang.

bluebottles, blueflies, an allusion to poem 219 of *The Book of Songs*, in which these insects are associated with gossip.

bound hair, at the age of puberty boys and girls bound their hair. The phrase comes to mean marriage. It is sometimes used with another ritual, the first wine of marriage.

Bridge of Stars, see Chang Ch'ien for the anecdote.

bright bird, according to legend, the sun has a bright bird in it.

Bright Cloud Terrace, a reference to the royal pleasure spot of the ancient kingdom of Ch'u mentioned in *Sir Fantasy*, a prose poem by the Han poet, Ssu-ma Hsiang-ju.

bright moons, round pearls of a great size.

Bright Valley, a mythological place where the sun rises, home of the immortals upon whom the sun never sets.

Broadbank, a place near the mouth of the Yangtze river where courtesans and entertainers made assignations.

Broken willow, the name of a flute tune. See willow.

broken-melon age, see melon.

(Bronze) Sparrow Terrace, the name of a Loyang royal building erected in AD 210 by the statesman and poet, and founder of the Wei Dynasty, Ts'ao Ts'ao (AD 155–220). It was famous for the magnificence of the banquets held there. In his last testament Ts'ao Ts'ao instructed that his concubines and entertainers should live in this building as if he were still alive, bringing him food twice each day to his bedroom. On the fifteenth of every month they were to perform dances before invited guests. His sons, Ts'ao Chih and Ts'ao P'ei, and his grandson, Ts'ao Jui, were also ordered to contemplate his tomb from the top of this terrace.

Bronzebridge, the name of a mountain in the old kingdom of Shu, west China, in modern Szechwan.

Bushy Terrace (also translated as Shrub Terrace), a place in Hantan, capital of the ancient state of Chao, famous for the custom of lovers to meet there. It was built by a king of Chao in the Warring States era.

caltrop, or water chestnut, its flower was very pale, a quality admired in a woman's complexion. Women usually picked the caltrops, and this imparts an erotic connotation to them.

candle stubs, see Hsü Wu.

capitals, the most popular capitals mentioned in the poems are Hsienyang of the Ch'in Dynasty, Ch'angan of the Former Han, Loyang of the Later Han, and of the Wei Dynasty, Chienk'ang of the Liang Dynasty.

capstrings, used as a metonym for a man's official rank. To untie them was a ritual gesture, either implying retirement or political opposition. The phrase 'ripped capstring' refers to an anecdote about a guest at the court of King Chuang of Ch'u (r. 613–591 BC), who tweaked the dress of a palace lady when the candles went out at a banquet. In retaliation she ripped off his capstring in order to identify him later. The king, not wishing to disgrace his guest, ordered all his courtiers to remove their capstrings before lights were restored. A man's capstring might be offered to a woman as a love-token.

cardamom, its seeds form clusters, suggesting fertility and abundance. Used as an erotic motif with grapevines.

carp, in the old poems a letter was sometimes carried in a container shaped like a fish, which was said to be 'cooked' when opened. The carp is a prolific fish, and the double carp is probably an emblem of fertility, or wedded bliss.

Carp winds, the name of the wind of autumn in the ninth month of the lunar calendar.

carved litter, a reference to Lady Pan, the favourite concubine of the Han Emperor Ch'eng (r. 33–7 BC), who was invited by him to sit in his royal carriage as a mark of special favour. She refused on the grounds that her status was too lowly for such an honour.

cassia (*kuei*), a pun for come home. Its brilliant red in springtime is a metaphor for happy love, while its autumnal leaf-fall is a metaphor for blighted love. Known as a tree that flowers without bearing fruit, it is a poignant image. The cassia was also thought to grow on the moon, a symbol of immortality.

Cassia Forest, a region in Kwangsi province.

Cassia Lodge, the name of a palace in the Ch'in Dynasty.

Cassia Palace, Yellow Mount Lodge, P'ingling, Hsinfeng, were all sumptuous buildings and places near the capital city of Ch'angan.

Cassia river, in Kwangsi province, it shares a joint source with the Hsiang river which flows south, while the Cassia flows north.

catalpa, a tree invested with grand and noble qualities, especially in the context of music. Expressive lutes were made out of this wood, and often such instruments were *objets d'art*. The best trees were said to grow at Dragon Gate (q.v.), one hundred feet tall and branchless, and favoured by phoenix. The catalpa features in the poems at a wellside, an amorous scenario.

cauldrons, a warrior who lifted, a reference to Hsiang Yü, who became king of Ch'u (233–202 BC). He fought Liu Pang for the empire and lost. He died at Kai-hsia.

Central Plains, the old name of the ancestral heartland of China prior to partition in AD 317 into north and south. It is situated in the basin of the Yellow river in Honan.

Chang Ch'ien, a minister (d. 114 BC) of the Han Emperor Wu sent to explore the regions of west China and beyond. Legend has it that he was ordered to discover the source of the Yellow river, believed to flow from the River of Heaven, or the Milky Way. One version of this legend has it that Chang Ch'ien sailed up the Yellow river and eventually reached the River of Heaven where he met a girl spinning, Weaver, and a boy leading an ox to drink, the star Herdboy. Weaver star gave Chang Ch'ien her loom-stone and told him to tell the astrologer, Yen Chün-p'ing of Ch'engtu, about it when he returned to earth. The astrologer had in fact noted a strange star at the very same time as the voyager's visit.

Chang Fang, when the Han Emperor Ch'eng used to leave the palace incognito to visit Ch'angan's pleasure quarter, he used to leave via Ch'i Gate with

Chang Fang and masquerade as one of Chang's servants. Chang's title was the Marquess of Fup'ing.

Ch'ang O, wife of the legendary figure, Yi the Archer, who had saved the populace from disaster by shooting down the suns when ten suns appeared together in the sky. Later he became the target of popular resentment, and his wife decided to flee their palace, taking with her Yi's elixir of immortality. She took with her her pet hare, and after eating some of the elixir was assumed into the moon as an immortal. But, according to some legends, she was turned into a toad. When the moon is in eclipse the toad is said to swallow it.

Chang of the capital, i.e. Chang Ch'ang (d. 48 BC), a distinguished Han scholar and official, whose weakness for putting kohl on his wife's eyebrows was gently criticised by Emperor Yüan.

Chang Pi-ch'iang, son of Chang Liang (d. 187 BC), who had been ennobled as the Marquess of Liu as a reward for helping Liu Pang win the empire in 202 BC. His son, Pi-ch'iang, had a special status at court.

Chang river, in Hopei.

Chang-nü, it is not clear to whom this name refers, but the context indicates that she was a beautiful person.

Ch'angan, capital of the Former Han Dynasty, situated near the Wei river in northwest China, and known as the western capital. It was near the present site of Sian.

Ch'angsha, one of the southern kingdoms of ancient China, situated in the Yangtze river valley. In the second century BC Prince Ting of Ch'angsha came up to the Han court as the guest of Emperor Ching. At a court banquet the emperor cordially invited the prince to dance and sing. He did so, but only flapped his sleeves by way of dancing. Everyone tittered. The emperor asked him to explain himself. The prince said that his kingdom was so narrow that it was impossible to turn round in it. The emperor took the hint and increased the size of his territory.

Changt'ai, name of a pleasure quarter in Ch'angan.

Ch'angyang Palace, a pleasure spot in a royal park of the same name in Ch'angan.

Chao, a state in ancient China (area of modern Shensi), which was famous for its beautiful women and skilled lutenists. It is usually linked with Yen state of similar fame.

Ch'ao, the name of a state in antiquity, modern Anhwei.

Chao Feiyen, her name means Flying Swallow (d. 6 BC). She was the daughter of a musician. She was attached to the household of the Princess of Yang-a in Ch'angan, the sister of Emperor Ch'eng of the Han. She and her sister were discovered in the Princess's household by the emperor on one of his incognito visits from the palace, and he brought them into his harem. Feiyen ousted his current favourite, Lady Pan, and eventually became consort. After the emperor's death Feiyen was driven to commit suicide by enemies at court, who rumoured that she was to blame for his death. She bore him no children. She was such a good dancer and so light that the saying was coined that she could dance on the palm of a man's hand.

Chao Hua jade, the name of a jewel given by the legendary Emperor Yao to his successor, Shun, when Yao gave him his two daughters in marriage. Yao's daughters were Nü-ying and O-huang.

Chaoyang Palace, the name of the palace where Chao Feiyen lived when she entered Emperor Ch'eng's harem.

Cheng, the name of an ancient state in the region of modern Honan, famous

298

for its new kind of music in the sixth century BC. The 'tunes of Cheng' were abhorred by Confucius (551–479 BC) not because they lacked beauty, but because they 'corrupted classical music'. Other people did not think the music decadent, but erotic and lively, such as the Marquess of Wei, Wen (r. 424–387 BC), who said that he would never tire of the music of Cheng, whereas the classical music of the former kings used almost to make him fall asleep. In these poems they are considered for the most part to be love-songs, or erotic music.

Cheng Chiao-fu, the name of a man of the ancient state of Cheng who lived in the Chou dynasty. One day he was walking along the Han river when he met two lovely girls. He flirted with them and they gave him egg-sized jewels from their belts. He put the jewels in his robe against his bosom and went away. Later he found that the jewels and the girls had vanished. These were the sprites of the Han river.

Ch'engtu, capital of the old kingdom of Shu.

Ch'i, the name of an ancient state in the region of modern Shantung and Hopei.

Ch'i and Wei rivers, in the ancient states of Wei and Cheng (modern Honan), respectively. The rivers were associated with trysting-places for lovers, especially in poems 39, 48, and 58 of The Book of Songs. Ch'i river is particularly associated with remembrance of past love, because poem 58 tells of a divorced wife who forded it on the way to her wedding and the full waters of the river soaked her carriage blinds, a felicitous image.

Ch'i Chiang, the name of a lady of the royal Chiang house of Ch'i state in the Spring and Autumn era, who was famous for her beauty and virtue. Poems 83 and 138 of The Book of Songs refer to a lady of this name who is much sought after in marriage.

Ch'i Liang, the name of a man of Ch'i state who was killed in battle in 550 BC. His wife is believed to have committed suicide by drowning in the Tzu river. She composed a plaintive song before she died, which is said to have made the city wall collapse. Tzu river is in the region of modern Shantung.

Chi Pavilion, in Kiukiang, near Mount Chiuli.

Chishe, an exotic perfume.

Chia I (201–169 BC), a statesman and poet of the Former Han. His early career at court was brilliant. Famous in his native Loyang for his ability to recite The Book of Songs and to compose works in different literary styles at the age of eighteen. He was made a scholar and palace counsellor by Emperor Wen. Later he was disgraced and exiled to the then foreign kingdom of Ch'u, considered by the Chinese as barbarous. There he wrote his famous Prose Poem on the Owl, which foretold his death.

Ch'iang, a tribe to the west of China, considered barbaric by the Chinese.

Chiangnan, a region south of the Yangtze river, associated with love-songs and amorous music.

Chiangtung, the same as Chiangnan.

Chiao-fu, see Cheng Chiao-fu.

Chiehshih, a place on the Gulf of Chihli.

Chienchang Palace, or Palace for Establishing Statutes, built in 104 BC by the Han Emperor Wen. It was a magnificent structure. To be appointed as its supervisor was considered a prestigious post. Empress Wei's (Wei Tzu-fu) brother, General Wei Ch'ing, was so honoured.

Ch'iench'i, a river in the region of Chekiang.

Chienhsing Park, built by the Liang Emperor Wu (Hsiao Yen) in AD 505 in the capital city of Chienk'ang.

Chienk'ang, capital city of the Liang Dynasty. Originally named Moling, it was renamed in the Three Kingdoms era as Chienyeh, then named Chienk'ang in the Chin Dynasty to avoid a taboo name. Near the modern city of Nanking by the Yangtze river.

Ch'ient'ang, modern Hangchow, made famous in poetry by the singer, Su Hsiao-hsiao, who lived there in the Chin and Southern Ch'i dynasties in the fifth century AD.

Chienyeh, capital of the Liang, renamed Chienk'ang.

Child of Night, Tzu-yeh, was believed to have been the name of a professional singer in the Eastern Chin Dynasty in the fourth century AD. A cycle of 42 songs are attributed to her, and they belong to a category of Southern Dynasties folk-songs. Bold and direct in style, they are love poems full of erotic puns and emblems. It is thought that they were originally arranged in a dialogue sequence between two lovers, and that the sequence was disturbed.

Chin, the name of a river flowing past Ch'engtu city, the old capital of Shu kingdom.

Ch'in, the name of a short-lived dynasty (221–207 BC) before the Han. Its capital was Hsienyang. Originally a small state in the northwest of China (Shensi area), it gradually conquered and annexed the various states of feudal Chou by its superior military force and social discipline. When used in the sense of the earlier small state of Ch'in, this refers to the remote border region of China proper.

Ch'in Lofu, the daughter of the Ch'in clan which came from Hantan, capital of Chao state. She married a man called Wang Jen. One day the king of Chao caught sight of her from the pillars and parapet of his palace terrace when she was picking mulberry up the lanes. He was so attracted to her that he asked her to drink with him, hoping he could make love with her. She eluded his advances by composing a song for the lute, *Mulberry up the path*, in which she praised her husband and rejected the casual love of a passing official. The king then desisted from his efforts to seduce her. This song appears in Chapter One of this anthology. The name of Ch'in Lofu occurs in another poem in this anthology, also in Chapter One, where she is said to be the eligible daughter of a family who could become the second wife of Chiao Chung-ch'ing. This poem appears here under the title *A peacock southeast flew*. Ch'in often refers to Ch'in Lofu.

Ching (chou), the Hsiangyang region of modern Hupei. In early times it meant the area of the ancient state of Ch'u in south China.

Ching and Wei rivers, allusion to poem 35, *Valley Wind*, of *The Book of Songs*, in which a divorced woman compares herself to the Ching river and her former husband's new wife to the Wei river. She says that the Ching itself is clear enough, but when it is seen in comparison with the Wei it seems to be muddy.

Ching and Yang, regions of modern Hupei and Kiangsu.

Ching Mountain, in the old kingdom of Ch'u, which is often called the Ching region.

Ch'iu Hu, the name of the husband of a chaste wife,. who came from the state of Lu. Five days after his marriage, he has to go to Ch'en state as an official. Five years later he goes back home, and on the way sees a pretty girl picking mulberry. He falls in love with her and tries to seduce her with some of his gold. She refuses his offer. He goes home, and gives the gold to his mother. Later his wife comes back from her work and goes in to meet her husband. To his dismay he finds that she is the woman he propositioned before. She rebukes him and commits suicide by drowning. She is one of the women praised for their virtue in *A Gallery of Good Women* (*Lieh nü chuan*), attributed to Liu Hsiang (77–6 BC). This was a popular narrative theme and has been treated by Fu Hsüan, Yen Yen-chih, and Hsiao Lun here.

Cho Wen-chün, also called the Cho girl (second century BC), was a recently widowed young woman, the daughter of a wealthy man called Cho Wang-sun who lived in Linch'iung. When the Han poet Ssu-ma Hsiang-ju lost his literary patron, he travelled to Linch'iung and was a guest at the Cho house. He played on his lute and sang, and Wen-chün, who was looking at him from the doorway, fell in love with him. He sent her gifts through her maids, and they eloped that night. Her father disowned her. Later they were reduced to selling wine in the market and Wang-sun was so ashamed that he finally gave his daughter her dowry. The poet's songs appear in Chapter Nine.

Chou, the name of the ancient dynasty (trad. 1111–256 BC), and also the name of the royal state to which the other feudal states owed allegiance. The name is used sometimes to mean China in general. With the Hsia and Shang was considered the Golden Age of antiquity.

Chou Hsiao-shih, or Chou, the catamite of the poet Chang Hua in the third century AD.

Ch'u, the name of a state in south China in antiquity. In the early BC era it was considered barbarous, peopled by an uncouth tribe called the Man. For a long time it was felt that for a cultured Chinese to be posted there was virtual exile. Later Ch'u aroused considerable interest, especially in the literary sphere, since such works as *The Songs of Ch'u* (*Ch'u Tz'u*) originated there. Sometimes Ch'u is used with the southern state of Yüeh to mean a hostile region, and in abstract terms, estrangement between lovers.

Ch'u and Yüeh, the region of modern Hupei and Chekiang. See Ch'u.

Ch'u Ming-kuang, the name of a famous official in the reign of King Chao of Ch'u, and presumably a virtuoso musician.

Ch'ü Yüan (?332–?295 BC), a statesman and nobleman of Ch'u in the reigns of King Huai and Ch'inghsiang. Historical accounts vary, but he was generally believed to have been a favourite minister of King Huai, but later fell from grace and was banished under his son, King Ch'inghsiang. In his place of exile south of Ch'u he is believed to have committed suicide by drowning in the Milo river, a tributary of the Yangtze. It was also generally believed that he wrote a number of poems in *The Songs of Ch'u*, the rest being by his disciples and later imitators. The Ch'ü Yüan literary style is associated with the poem 'Encountering sorrow', an allegedly autobiographical narrative, telling of how he was slandered at court, of the misguided rule of his king, and of his futile search for the ideals of truth and beauty.

Chuang Chou, or Chuang Tzu, was a famous philosopher of Meng state, one of the fathers of Taoist thought, who lived *c.* 399–295 BC. A passage from his writings describes how his friend, Hui Tzu, found Chuang Tzu beating a pot after his wife had died. When Hui Tzu asked him why he was not mourning her, Chuang Tzu replied that he looked on his wife's death as a slumber in the great house of the universe whither her bodily form had been transmuted into its prenatal state. He felt it would be wrong to object to her return to her natural abode by expressions of grief.

Chungchou, the same as the Central Plains.

Chungshan, the name of an important commandery in the Han, in modern Hopei. See Empress Yin.

Chungt'ai, an exotic perfume, probably taken from a placename, of which the place is now unknown.

Chuyai, formerly part of Kwangtung in the far south of China.

cinnabar, a red mineral used in elixirs of immortality. Used as an adjective it sometimes means a lover's faithful heart. 'Cinnabar and green' is a general term for paint.

cinnabar court, the general term for the long courtyard of red sandstone leading to the entrance of a palace.

city tumble, see city-razing beauty.

city-razing beauty, a reference to a woman so lovely that she has the power to destroy a city and a kingdom. The earliest extant mention of this occurs in poem 264 of *The Book of Songs*, which is actually derogatory. A later source for this phrase comes from the biography of Lady Li, concubine of the Han Emperor Wu, and in this context the phrase is one of praise. Before Lady Li entered the imperial harem, her brother, a court musician named Li Yen-nien, sang her praises to the emperor. This song appears in Chapter One here.

clasping the bridge-post, a reference to the romantic hero, Wei Sheng, of the sixth century BC, from Lu state. He promised to meet his sweetheart by Lan bridge in Ch'angan, but she failed to come. He waited for her there, even though the tide rose, and eventually he drowned. He was also known as Wei-sheng Kao.

clear notes of autumn, or clear-tone autumn, the note called *shang*. According to an ancient theory of correspondences in the universe, the autumn season was associated with the second musical note in the pentatonic scale.

clear wine, said to be the drink of autumn, the clear wine like flowers. (Also see wine.)

clock, i.e. waterclock, one of the devices by which time was told in ancient China. It worked by a drip mechanism from a jar of water, and had a day cycle and a night one. When the jar dripped it gradually emptied out into another which tilted when it was full, restarting the drip cycle.

clothes perfumer, a silk-covered bamboo frame placed over a censer. Clothes were laid on top of the frame to be perfumed.

Cloud Gate, the name of the music of the legendary emperor Huangti, or the Yellow Emperor.

Cloud Terrace, a ceremonial edifice in the capital built in the Han Dynasty, so tall it was said to reach the clouds.

cocoon, has several connotations: (1) an early book of marvels tells of a mulberry tree of enormous size. In its top branches silkworms span cocoons three feet long each holding 21 ounces of silk thread. This prolific cocoon is an erotic motif of abundance and fertility. Its silk was said to make a happy marriage quilt; (2) a woman's eyebrows are often likened to cocoons, and more frequently to the moths that emerged from them; (3) clustered cocoons are also an emblem of fertility.

Cold Dew Terrace, built by the Han Emperor Wu at the Palace of Sweet Springs in Shensi on a northwest mountain of the same name. It was the royal summer resort.

cold region, it is a convention of these love poems that an absent lover is often said to be on military duty in the northern border region, where the climate is much harsher than in the heartland of China. The coldness of the region acts as a metaphor for the cooling of love in the man's absence.

Cold Valley, in the ancient state of Yen. The statesman Tsou Yen of Ch'i state was assigned there in the fourth century BC. When he found that millet would not grow there, he blew on his bronze musical pipes to warm the valley, so that millet then grew and flourished.

cold winds, signal the arrival of autumn, with high clouds.

coming down the hill, see *Sweet herbs.*

Consort O, mother of Shao Hao, son of the legendary Yellow Emperor. Sometimes such mythological references constitute polite flattery of a reigning monarch.

cork, has a bitter taste (*k'u*), a pun for bitter in emotional terms.

Crested Wave, one of the emanations of the Goddess of Lo river, as she was described by Ts'ao Chih in his prose poem on the goddess.

cricket, a symbol of poignant suffering and likened to a woman's emotional distress when her lover deserts her. One of the earliest references to the cricket occurs in poem 114 of *The Book of Songs*: 'The cricket is in the hall, / The year draws to a close. / If we don't take pleasure now, / Days and months will pass by'.

Crossriver, a place in Sinkiang, a remote region.

crows, sometimes refer to the anecdote about Chu Po when he became a censor. Several crows perched at dusk on a cypress near the censorial office where he worked, and then at dawn they flew away.

crows turn white, a reference to the heir apparent of Yen state, Prince Tan (d. 226 BC), when he was taken hostage in Ch'in state. He lamented in despair that he would only be freed when crows' heads turned white, when the sky rained grain, and horses had horns. All those marvels happened and Tan did escape. But his father executed him in order to placate the Ch'in desire for vengeance.

Cypress Rafter Terrace (Poliang), where the Han Emperor Wu held a famous banquet; as such it stands for happy banquets of great magnificence in any time or era.

daddy-longlegs and wild plum, it was the custom at (lunar) New Year to put these in wine and dumplings. The name for the insect is *hsi-tzu,* a pun for happiness. Plum is the first tree to bloom in spring, the season of love.

dagger-coin, money was made in different shapes and of different substances in ancient China. One such design was a knife or dagger shape made of metal with a hole for threading into sums of cash.

dagger hilt, literally dagger ring; the word for ring, *huan,* is a pun for return, or come home.

Dagger Road, in Shu kingdom.

dance, one of the skills of a singing-girl, or entertainer, or courtesan, was the performance of a repertoire of dances, besides playing various musical instruments and singing. The gown worn by a female dancer had long wide sleeves that were used expressively to convey different emotions and actions, such as joy or a bird's soaring flight. There were set movements to some dances and a series of theatrical poses. During certain performances, such as at banquets, the female dancer could direct her interest in one of the guests or clients through her dance gestures and through eloquent eye movements.

Dark Dragon, probably the Hsüanyüan stars (Leo), also the placename by which the Yellow Emperor was known (in modern Honan).

303

Dark Gates, one of the names for the Gates of Heaven.

Dark Tower, one of the names for the Gates of Heaven, which like their counterpart on earth were topped with watch towers.

dawn clouds, dusk rain, the natural manifestations by which the Goddess of Mount Wu is known. She is said to have told this to an ancient king of Ch'u when she appeared to him in an erotic dream. The phrase 'clouds and rain' later came to mean sexual intercourse.

Dawn Wind, the name of a bird, the peregrine falcon.

dew, an image that presages in some contexts autumn, since it turns to frost. It also acts as a metaphor for the transience of life. Heavy dew is a metaphor for sexual favours, from a man to a woman.

Dew not yet dry, a refrain from *The Book of Songs*.

Dewdrops, the title of poem 17 of *The Book of Songs*, in which a woman declares that she will not submit to marriage, no matter how influential her suitor's family is.

dewy mallow broth, fare conventionally offered by a woman to a man in the context of a professional courtesan and her client. The image of the mallow is often used elsewhere to suggest through its tendency to lean toward sunlight a woman's emotional need of a man.

Dipper star, see Northern Dipper.

divorced woman skilled at plainweave, an allusion to the first poem in the anthology, *Sweet herbs* (q.v.). This reference varies depending on the context. In some poems the divorced woman featured in *Sweet herbs* is a pathetic person; in others the phrase denotes the sexual attraction of women who conventionally appear to be weaving.

do, re, lit. *kung* and *shang*, the first two notes of the ancient pentatonic musical scale.

dodder, a plant that grows by clinging to a tree or some other natural support. It is used as an image suggesting woman's emotional dependency on man.

dogwood, the same as oleaster in these poems, it has two contradictory meanings. One derives from a passage in *The Songs of Ch'u*, in which Ch'ü Yüan compares the plant unfavourably with cassia and orchid, and in this sense I have translated the plant as dogwood to suggest its derogatory meaning. The other is a vaguely erotic emblem – perhaps the oleaster was used as an ingredient in aphrodisiacs? As such, the emblem appears on several items of woman's clothing, and is translated as oleaster.

double-body creature, or thing, a fabled creature which is an amalgam of two inseparable creatures, the *ch'iung-ch'iung* or the *chü-hsü* and the *ch'üeh*. The first ones are swift, horse-like animals that cannot feed themselves, so they have to have another beast, the *ch'üeh* to help them. The *ch'üeh*, on the other hand, cannot run, so in times of danger the other beasts carry it away on their back to safety. As such this mutual dependence is an emblem of conjugal love.

dragon, a mythological creature with several different connotations: (1) its body is an assemblage of various animal forms, bird-like claws, serpentine body, carnivorous teeth; (2) an auspicious creature, the harbinger of rain and moisture to ripen the crops; (3) a courser of the skies, often described as the steed of the legendary star, Weaver; (4) in spring the dragon rises into the sky, in autumn it disappears into watery depths; (5) interlocked dragons are an emblem of sexual intercourse; (6) a symbol of the emperor; (7) the emblem of the east; (8) with the tiger it is the steed of the legendary Queen Mother of the West, ruler of the land of the immortals.

Dragon Gate, name of a mountain in Shensi, see catalpa.

304

Dragon Tower, Blue (or Green) Dragon Tower Gate in Loyang city.

drapes, often it is not specified whether these are on the door, window, or bed of a woman's apartment. All three or just one is possible. Also, they might mean the flimsy curtains, or heavy brocade drapes, or tapestried hangings.

dried meat, the customary way to preserve meat was to process it so that it was dried out; not a derogatory term, it meant that the recipient was eating well.

drum, there was a custom of hitting a drum to call attention to one's grievances, such as crippling levies expended on extravagant buildings.

'Drunk now . . .', a refrain from *The Book of Songs*.

ducks and geese, or ducks and swans, a reference to an anecdote told in a Former Han sourcebook about a minister called T'ien Jao. He advised the Duke of Lu in the fifth century BC that though a cock had many virtues it should be eaten because it was locally raised and common fare, whereas certain ducks and swans or geese should be allowed to live in the royal ponds because they were rare imports.

Duke Highnose, the nickname of Emperor Kao-tsu, Liu Pang, founder of the Han Dynasty.

Duke Wen of Chin, late seventh century BC, also see Nanwei.

Dusk Shadow, a street in Ch'angan.

dust, flying dust or bright dust on the highway are two images signifying a man's exciting life in the world of politics. Its counterpart is the image of mud in a ditch, or thick river mud, to denote a woman's lowly, immobile position out of the public gaze. Dust sometimes refers to a woman's white cosmetic powder. 'Dust the pillow' is a term meaning to enjoy the sexual favours of one's lord and master. Dust on items of furniture belongs to a complex of neglect images signifying a man's neglect of a woman. Dust flying on the rafters is an image suggesting that a woman's song is so sublime that the rafters resound joyously (see rafter dust).

dust-and-mop, metonymy, in a favourable sense, for a wife or mistress.

earrings, often of large pearls, 'bright moons', they are sometimes said to be behind a woman's ears, rather than on the lobe. A single earring might be thrown by a man to a woman by way of a love-token while she was performing a dance.

East Mulberry, see Leaning Mulberry.

East Wall star, in the last days of the tenth lunar month this star might appear in the south sky, denoting a rare occurrence. Its western equivalent is Gemini.

eight, a propitious number.

embracing boughs, wedded boughs, an erotic emblem of mutual love.

Emperor Ch'eng (r. 33–7 BC), of the Former Han, was named Liu Ao. Of his concubines Lady Pan was his favourite, until she was ousted by Chao Feiyen.

Emperor Wang, said to be a descendant of the legendary Yellow Emperor, was the king of Shu. His name was Tu Yü. When his minister Pieh Ling was away from court, the emperor had an affair with his wife, and when this came to light Tu Yü died of shame. It was believed that when he died he turned into a cuckoo which in late spring weeps and sheds tears of blood, its cry making travellers homesick because it sounds like the words 'better go home!' Another version of this legend goes that his minister went away on flood control and on his return discovered the affair. The emperor made amends by abdicating in his minister's favour. Sometimes the bird he was metamorphosed into is thought to be the nightjar.

Empress Ch'en, also see A-chiao, consort of the Han Emperor Wu. When she

305

lost his favour she retired to Eternal Gate Palace. Her rival was Wei Tzu-fu, and she became Empress Wei. Empress Ch'en had not borne the emperor any children.

Empress Shen, consort of King Yü of Chou (r. ?781–770 BC), was deposed by Paossu, a woman of exceptional beauty. See Paossu.

Empress Yin, this name and title could refer to two historical persons: 1) Lady Yin, a beauty of the Warring States era in the kingdom of Chungshan, became the king's consort. Chungshan was a small kingdom between the northern states of Yen and Chao; 2) Feng Chao-i who bore a son to Emperor Yüan of the Han (r. 49–33 BC), and was promoted to the fiefdom of Chungshan with her son. She is famous for having protected the emperor from a charging bear which had escaped from its cage, putting herself between them.

erstwhile carriage, see Mi Tzu-hsia.

Eternal Gate Palace (Ch'angmen), where Empress Ch'en retired when she lost the affection of Emperor Wu.

Eternal Joy Palace (Ch'anglo), built by the Han Emperor Kao-tsu in 200 BC in Ch'angan. Later it became the residence of the empress dowager.

Eternal Springs, see Yellow Springs.

Eternal Trust Palace (Ch'anghsin), the residence of the empress dowager in the reign of the Han Emperor Ch'eng to which Lady Pan retired when she lost imperial favour.

eye to eye fish, a mythical creature having two fishy bodies and sharing one pair of eyes, their symbiosis denoting marital devotion.

Fairy Radiance, see O-huang.

falcon, an allusion to poem 132 of *The Book of Songs*: 'Swift is the falcon, / Dense the northern wood. / Not seeing my lord, / My sad heart is full of longing'.

Falling Rain, see Goddess of Mount Wu.

fan, usually round, made of sheer white silk, and painted with amorous scenes. Its whiteness and roundness are likened to the full moon. Fans were kept in a person's sleeve or bosom. Used in summer and put away in winter, fans are a frequent metaphor for discarded love, for a woman deserted by a man. These love poems often quote the poem on the fan ascribed to Lady Pan which appears in Chapter One here, entitled *Regret*, and popularly known as the *Round fan poem*.

Feiyen, lit. Flying Swallow, see Chao Feiyen.

Feng, east of Ch'angan, known as Hsinfeng.

Feng Tzu-tu, a slave in the household of General Huo Kuang (d. 68 BC). The general rose to high office under Emperor Wu.

Fenyin, a place in Shansi south of Fen river near the border between China and the nomadic tribes of the northwest in antiquity.

fifteenth, night of, or moon of, usually a full moon, especially in autumn (also see autumn moon).

firewood and feed, a reference to an anecdote about Chi An (d. ?108 BC) who told Emperor Wu that the emperor's method of selecting ministers was like gathering sticks for firewood – he put the last ones on top.

fish's belly, it was customary to send a message in a letter-container shaped like a fish (also see carp).

fish sport, an echo of an old folk-song about fish playing in all directions around lotus leaves (a pun for passion) in the area of Chiangnan.

Fishing rod, the name of an old song for the lute.

Five Elements Theory, in the Han Dynasty, writers such as Tung Chung-shu evolved a system of cosmology relating different categories of natural and celestial phenomena to affairs in the human world. This system drew from many earlier philosophical sources. The five elements were wood (related to east, spring, the number eight, green, note E), fire (related to south, summer, seven, red, note G), metal (related to west, autumn, nine, white, note D), water (related to north, winter, six, black, note A), and earth (related to centre, five, yellow, and note C). Different systems created other sets, but this one is typical.

five horses, a team of five horses indicated the rank of a prefect, or similar status in early China. Sometimes this refers to the rebuffed prefect of the narrative poem in Chapter One, *Mulberry up the lane*.

Five Lake, a general name for the lake district of Wu in modern Kiangsu and Chekiang.

five women, according to legend a king of ancient Ch'in offered five beautiful women to the king of Ch'u, who sent five strong men to greet them. On the way the men stamped and hollered so loudly that the women were petrified and turned to stone.

Flaming Cinnabar, see Huo Tan.

Fleetfox Pass, in the northeast border region, modern Chihli.

flower of forgetfulness, flower of oblivion, a drug that induces amnesia, taken to forget painful events. The earliest reference to it occurs in poem 62 of *The Book of Songs*, in which a woman says she suffers so much from pining for her lord that she wants to plant the herb by her north room, if only she could get it.

flowerboys, some sort of an insect, such as a large species of butterfly or bee, probably the former since this appears as a popular motif in love poetry.

flowing yellow, raw silk or unbleached silk thread.

Flying Chestnut, the name of the famous steed of the legendary Yellow Emperor.

Flying Swallow (Feiyen), see Chao Feiyen.

foot of silk, a foot length of silk was the typical means for writing letters. Paper was invented in the second century AD.

Forbidden Palace, the imperial palace.

Forest Gleam, Linkuang, the name of a Ch'in Dynasty palace.

four points, north, south, east, and west.

Fufei, the name of the Goddess of Lo river.

fulling cloth, the process of pounding the fibres of silk after it had been woven, using a block and a beater of stone. This work was done by women in autumn in preparation for winter clothes. There are many conventional aspects to fulling in these love poems: it is done by elegantly dressed women; it is outside or near the city wall; the sounds are said to be mournful, reminding the women working of their absent lovers; and the words for pounder and silk were puns for a male lover and love or pining, respectively. Fulling is a popular folk-song theme.

General Li, Li Kuang-li, a military commander under the Han Emperor Wu who was sent to Ferghana to obtain a tribute of horses. He captured the city of Erh-shih. He was ennobled for his exploits. Eventually he was killed in captivity after being disastrously defeated by the Hsiungnu in 94 BC. (He was Lady Li's brother.)

girdle, besides a long embroidered sash a woman wore a jewelled girdle. When these were untied, her dress would fall open, and so the gesture comes to imply sexual intercourse. The girdle or its jewels might be offered as a love-token.

girl of Jasper Terrace, Chien Ti, a legendary figure, was the lovely daughter of the Lord of Sung. She was shut away in this building, but a hero, the mythical figure Ti K'u, sent her a swallow. Chien Ti ate its egg and became pregnant. She became the ancestress of the Shang with Ti K'u as its first ancestor.

girl of Ying, see Nung Yü.

god's palm, see Welcome Dew Terrace.

Goddess of Hsiang river, the Hsiang is the second main river of south China, flowing north into the Yangtze, and is one of the rivers of Ch'u. In *The Songs of Ch'u* there is a cycle of shamanistic songs of which the third and fourth are addressed to the Princess of this river and to its Lady. Sometimes these two nymphs are confused with the two daughters of Emperor Yao, O-huang and Nü-ying, because another legend describes how they drowned in the Hsiang when their husband, Emperor Shun, died.

Goddess of Lo river, Fufei. It ran beside the old capital city of Loyang. Fufei appears in *The Songs of Ch'u*, in which the poet tells of his unsuccessful courtship of her. She is also the subject of Ts'ao Chih's famous prose poem quoted in these love poems. Her emanations are a crested wave or driven snow, as Ts'ao Chih describes her.

Goddess of Mount Wu, also known as the divine woman, she haunts the clefts in the rocks of Mount Wu. Traditionally this was believed to be above the Yangtze river in Szechwan. She is said to have met former kings of Ch'u in erotic dreams, leaving them to wake in disappointment. She is also associated with Kaot'ang, a holy hill in Ch'u, and with Sunny Terrace, where King Hsiang of Ch'u saw her emanations as he walked with the poet, Sung Yü. Her emanations were dawn clouds and dusk rain, or falling rain.

gold, currency and a precious metal. Southern gold was considered the finest in quality; it was mined in Chingchou and Yangchow. There was a saying that one thousand gold would buy the fragrant season, or the pleasures of youth.

Golden Vale, a park belonging to the poet and official, Shih Ch'ung, and situated on the outskirts of Loyang in Honan. It was a pleasure park famous for the wealthy poet's extravagant parties. His favourite singer, Green Pearl (Luchu), would perform before his guests there. In about the year AD 296 he held a famous banquet for General Wang Hsü who was on his way back to Ch'angan.

goose, geese, often referred to as carriers of messages between lovers, particularly the wild goose which migrates from the northern region, where men are sent to fight, to the south where the wives and mistresses live. The goose is usually described as a lone bird, a pathetic image.

Goose Gate Pass (Yingmen), a military outpost in Shansi so named because when the geese migrated from the north to the south they seemed to fly through this natural pass.

goose-letter, see Su Wu.

Grand Plains (Kaop'ing), the name of a place in Shantung, suggesting somewhere far from the centre of China.

grapevines, first brought into China by Chang Ch'ien (q.v.) on one of his voyages to the western regions. Vineyards were laid out near the palace. Wine from grapes was not the usual alcoholic beverage in China, but a spirit fermented from rice. The grapevine was used as a decorative motif

308

on women's clothing and furniture, suggesting abundance and fertility through its clustered flowers and fruit.

Great Curve bow (Tach'ü), the name of an archery bow in antiquity.

Great Mound, the name of a suite of music derived from the name of the capital city of Ch'u in the reign of King Huai.

Greater Ch'in, the far-flung provinces of the Roman Empire in the Roman Orient. It is recorded that this region was rich in gold, silver, rare gems, night-shining jade, and bright moon pearls.

Green Chain Gate, the small gate leading to the imperial palace.

Green Jade (Piyü), the name of a concubine of the Prince of Junan in the Chin Dynasty, famous for her flute playing.

Green Pearl (Luchu, third century AD), the famous concubine of the poet and official Shih Ch'ung. She was very beautiful, and was a fine dancer and musician. She is remembered for her performances of dance and music at Golden Vale. Prince Lun of Chao was attracted to her and expected Shih Ch'ung to give her to him. When he refused, and for other, political reasons, the prince had him executed. Green Pearl committed suicide by throwing herself from a tall building.

Green river (Lu shui), the name of a tune to which poems were set. 'Green' could refer to the name of the river or to the colour of the river.

Greensilk lute, the name of the famous lute belonging to the Han poet Ssu-ma Hsiang-ju.

gulf of heaven, or Gulf of Heaven, used figuratively or to denote a constellation.

hairpins, long, elaborately jewelled hair ornaments fixed at chic angles to hold the chignon in place. A popular design was a sparrow, or a peacock, or grains of seed. A dangling hairpin was an allusion to a poem by Sung Yü describing a woman attaching her hairpin to an official's capstring as a love-token.

half-forehead eyebrows, half across the forehead, an allusion to the anonymous song, *A Ditty of the Han Era,* which appears in Chapter One, satirising country girls for their extravagant aping of city fashions.

Han, celestial river, the counterpart of the Milky Way in the West. It is also called Starry River, Long River, Long Han, Sky River, River of Heaven, or Cloudy Han. It was believed that the Yellow river on earth flowed from the Han river in the sky. Usually this reference conjures up ideas of the legend of Weaver and Herdboy stars (q.v.). The Han river is seen as an obstacle between these stellar lovers since it is in full flood every night of the year except the Seventh Night of the Seventh Month (q.v.). On that night the waters ebbed, allowing the lovers to meet. Weaver is sometimes called the girl of Han river.

Han, one of the names for China, derived from the Han Dynasty.

Han (Chung), one of the sorcerers of the first Ch'in emperor, Ch'in Shih Huangti (r. 221–210 BC), sent to find the elixir of immortality. He never returned from his quest, and was believed to have become an immortal. He is associated with the Taoist pantheon.

Han river, terrestrial, rises in Pochiung Mountain and flows into the Yangtze. It was one of the rivers of the old state of Ch'u and was believed to be the dwelling of a water goddess, or two nymphs, known as the Han woman, or the two sprites of Han river. (See Han river sprites.) The course of the Han is in modern Hupei.

Han river sprites, the terrestrial Han river is associated with various

309

legends. One of these concerns two nymphs who rove the banks in human guise, and one day meet Cheng Chiao-fu (q.v.).

Hanku Pass, a natural pass fortified in the Ch'in Dynasty. Sited west of Loyang near the Yellow river, in modern Honan. An important military outpost for the defence of China's northern border against hostile northern tribes.

Hann, name of a feudal kingdom in ancient China, south of the Yellow river and southeast of Ch'in.

Hantan, capital city of the ancient state of Chao in north China, famous for lovely girls and skilled women musicians. Ch'in Lofu, heroine of the influential ballad, *Mulberry up the lane*, came from there.

Hanyang, in modern Kanṣu province, far northwest of China, signifying the remote borderlands.

hard and soft, see *Yin/Yang*.

Heaven's towers, twin towers on the Gates of Heaven.

hemp, hempen pledge, a love-token of hemp was picked by the shaman-poet in *The Nine Songs* section of *The Songs of Ch'u*: 'I pick the glistening bloom of Holy Hemp / To give to one who lives far away'.

Herb poem, or *Sweet herbs* poem, the first poem in this anthology, translated as *Bittersweet*. It tells of a divorced woman who meets her former husband when she has come down from a hill where she picked *miwu* herbs. It has been conjectured by some scholars that this herb might be a fertility drug, implying that the woman was divorced by her husband because she bore him no children.

Herdboy, a legendary star, the equivalent of Altair in Aquila, or Capricorn. Generally called Herdboy, but literally his name is Draught Ox. (See Weaver and Seventh Night.)

Herdboy bridge, built by Cheng, First Emperor of the Ch'in Dynasty over the river Wei, south of the Ch'in capital of Hsienyang.

hibiscus (mutabilis) *(fuyung)*, usually identified as an hibiscus or cotton rose; it is a brilliantly blooming plant of the mallow family, but sometimes also identified as the lotus when it is in bloom. Both plants have red blooms, some double, and are known for their vigorous growth. An erotic emblem because of its colour and prolific nature.

high notes, music has long had allegorical associations in Chinese thought. In the context of love, the analogy is made between the strings of the instrument, such as a lute, and the human heart, and the notes produced are compared with human emotions. Thus when the strings of a lute are tightened and produce a high-pitched sound, this is likened to the tense emotions of a person suffering from the pangs of love. Similarly, as the string of a lute may be broken by excessive tightening and violent playing, so the heart may break from excessive anguish.

Hillside bough, an allusion to the anonymous *Song of the Yüeh Boatman*, which appears in Chapter Nine, in which a boatman in love with a nobleman compares himself to a branch of a tree on a hill.

History, The Book of History, one of the *Confucian Classics*.

Hochien, an ancient province in the state of Chao, modern Hopei. It became a kingdom in the Han and was ruled by members of the royal family. It was the fiefdom of the young Emperor Ling while Emperor Huan was still on the throne. Emperor Ling's mother, or in some versions Tu Nü (q.v.), amassed a huge fortune at Hochien and built an extravagant palace, so the rumour went. Hochien is also associated with the birthplace of Lady Chao, concubine of Emperor Wu of the Han and mother of Emperor Chao. She was discovered by a man who divined strange phenomena at her home in the form of a violet vapour. She was found to have both fists clenched which the emperor unfolded, finding a jade hook.

homespun, or *Homespun* lyric, an allusion to the first poem of this anthology, see *Sweet herbs*.

Honei, the old name of a province in the region of modern Honan where the Shang Dynasty had its capital. It was called one of 'the legs of a tripod in the centre of the empire'.

hook, literally a jewelled brooch worn by a woman, or a hooked pole used for raising window drapes, or for drawing down branches of a mulberry tree. It also serves as a metaphor for a woman's curved eyebrows, or for the crescent moon.

Hop'u pearl, Hop'u was a famous pearl centre and a trading place as early as the Han era, and a pearl of this name means one of the finest quality; situated in the southwest, modern Kwangtung.

horizontal (*hengch'en*), one of the few references to lovers lying in bed.

horned beasts (*chiaotuan*), described in the ancient texts as a creature looking partly like a pig, partly like an ox, with a horn in its nose which could be used as an archer's bow.

House of Gold, a reference to a remark Emperor Wu made when he was still a boy about A-chiao with whom he had fallen in love. (See A-chiao and Empress Ch'en, and Eternal Gate Palace.)

How few!, an allusion to poem 36 of *The Book of Songs*, in which, according to the traditional interpretation, those few who return from an expedition are mourned.

How slow she comes!, see Lady Li.

Hoyang, the name of an old province in the region of modern Honan. It may have associations with the pleasure park of Shih Ch'ung near Loyang where his beautiful entertainer, Green Pearl, used to perform for his guests. (See Golden Vale.)

Hsi Shih (fifth century BC), a beautiful girl from the countryside who was trained in the arts of entertainment and seduction by the state of Yüeh in order to distract their enemy, Wu state. This stratagem was devised by Kou Chien, King of Yüeh who had been defeated by Fu Ch'ai, King of Wu in 494 BC. In 473 BC Yüeh conquered Wu. Both states are in the area of modern Kiangsu and Chekiang. Hsi Shih was noted for the pertness of her sulky face, and later women imitated her frowns in order to appear beautiful like her.

Hsiang river, one of the rivers flowing through Ch'u. Many legends are associated with it, particularly the Goddess of Hsiang river (q.v.).

Hsiang-ju, the first name of the Han poet, Ssu-ma Hsiang-ju. He changed his name to this because he admired the famous statesman of Chao, Lin Hsiang-ju.

Hsiangyang city, in modern Hupei, famous for its knights-errant, and for a certain kind of song sung by women, generally known as Hsiangyang Music.

Hsiangyang Music, according to a record of music, this was a type of music compiled by Tan, Prince of Sui, in about the middle of the fifth century AD, when he was Governor of Hsiangyang. This account says that one night he heard women singing various popular songs and he wrote them down. Music called Tat'i tunes also belongs to this type of song, which appears to be characterised by a local, popular style rather than a formal, metropolitan style.

Hsiao-Hsiang river, the general name for two rivers that flow into lake Tungt'ing from the south in the region of Ch'u, modern Hunan. These rivers conjure up ideas of water-sprites, especially the Goddess of Hsiang river (q.v.), and O-huang and Nü-ying. The Hsiao is a tributary of the Hsiang and rises in north Kwangtung. The two rivers are linked because the main Hsiang carries the waters of the Hsiao into lake Tungt'ing.

Hsiaop'ing ford, this may refer to a ford on the Yellow river north of Loyang city.

Hsiats'ai, a place in Ch'u made famous in literature by being mentioned as a city of alluring beauties by Sung Yü in his prose poem *The Lechery of Mr Tengt'u*. It is in the region of modern Anhwei.

Hsien pool, the legendary pool in which the ten suns (or the sun) were rinsed after their diurnal journal through the sky. In the shamanistic section of *The Songs of Ch'u* the shaman-poet says he will rinse his hair with a deity in Hsien pool.

Hsien-Ch'in, i.e. Hsienyang, capital city of the Ch'in Dynasty.

Hsientu, lit. Suspension Crossing, the name of a kingdom on the western border of the Han empire, east of modern Afghanistan. In Han travel-ogues it was described as inaccessible because of its sheer mountains and dangerous creeks. To journey through this area travellers had to use rope bridges over the mountains and rivers.

Hsienyang, capital of the Ch'in Dynasty, north of Wei river. The heartland of the old state of Ch'in before it conquered the whole of China was surrounded by natural defences of passes, mountains, and rivers, and was called 'within the passes'. The first Ch'in emperor had magnificent palaces built there, the finest being completed in 212 BC. It was said to be one of the wonders of the world, measuring 2,500 feet wide and 500 feet long, and could accommodate thousands of people. Around Hsienyang 270 smaller imperial palaces were built with a network of covered, walled paths.

Hsinch'eng, this placename may refer to a town near Hsienyang which, according to one commentator, used to be called Weich'ing. There is a group of tunes going by the title Weich'ing Tunes. This place is in the Shensi area.

Hsiungnu, usually translated as Huns, this was a nomadic tribe on the northern border of China. Periodically they threatened the peace and stability of China, making incursions into the heartland. The Chinese pacified them by war or appeased them by marriage with members of the Chinese royal family, or by tribute.

Hsü Fei-ch'iung, the name of a fairy.

Hsü Wu, a girl from Ch'i state who was so poor that she had to spin by night using reflected light from a neighbour's house, or other people's candle stubs.

Hsün Feng-ch'ien, a man in antiquity who prided himself on his romantic conquests.

Hu and Yüeh, tribes of the north and south, respectively, they come to represent the north and south. The Hu tribe were nomadic horsemen, the red bird is a symbol of the south, so the Hu horse and the Yüeh bird act as polar opposites when used as dual images.

Huai river, the central river of China between the Yellow and Yangtze rivers of the north and south. It flows eastwards through the region of

Ch'u into the Yellow Sea. There was a popular belief that at one point in the Huai river the incoming tide and outgoing tide met, suggesting the idea of a reunion between lovers.

Huainan, famous in the Han Dynasty as a place where exciting dances originated.

Huaiyin, in the region of modern Kiangsu, famous for its military hero, Han Hsin (d. 196 BC). A man of humble origins, he was ennobled for his bravery. He made a statement about political life, to the effect that when soaring birds have all been killed the hunter's bow is laid aside. Later, when he was executed, he compared himself to such a bird.

Huanglung, one of the various Hsiungnu tribes whose territory was in the region of modern Jehol.

Huayang, the name of a favourite concubine of Lord Ankuo of Ch'in. It has been suggested by some scholars that this might be a confusion with the name of Lord Lungyang, the homosexual lover of a king.

Huhsiang, a place in Honan not far from the old capital city of Loyang. It was the site of several cities in antiquity having different names. This reference might be intended to evoke the idea of the golden age of antiquity, besides the more recent splendour of the city of Loyang.

Hun, a general translation for the Hsiungnu or the Hu tribes, meaning in general the northern tribes.

Hung Yai, the name of the music master of the legendary emperors Yao, Shun, and Wen.

Huo Ch'ü-ping (d. 117 BC), the illegitimate son of Wei Ch'ing's elder sister, and brother of Huo Kuang (q.v.), he rose to the rank of supreme commander of the Ministry of War. In 123 BC he won decisive victories over the Hsiungnu and was ennobled. Miracles and feats of valour are associated with his name.

Huo Kuang (d. 68 BC), brother of Huo Ch'ü-ping (q.v.), he rose to high office under the Han Emperor Wu. When the emperor died, General Huo promoted a royal grandson as his successor, who reigned as Emperor Hsüan.

Huo Tan, Flaming Cinnabar, seems to be the name of an immortal woman. Cinnabar was one of the ingredients for concocting the elixir of immortality.

Huona, the name of an exotic perfume, perhaps patchouli.

I pick beans, or Picking beans, an allusion to poem 226 of The Book of Songs, which tells of a woman unable to do her work of picking beans and indigo because she is pining for her lover.

'In the north there is a lovely lady', the opening line of a song performed by Li Yen-nien before Emperor Wu of the Han, in which he described his sister. She later became the favourite concubine of the emperor, and was given the title Lady Li. His song appears in Chapter One.

Inaction, a reference to one of the meditation practices of the Taoists, in which one attempts to rid the mind of extraneous matters and achieve a measure of mental equilibrium.

incense candle, see sinking incense.

Indigo Field, a mountain in Shensi where fine jade was quarried.

inseparable creatures, see double-body thing.

Iyang, in the region of modern Honan.

jade coffer, or jewel box, or jade in a jewel box, a reference to the halcyon days of Wang Chao-chün (q.v.), before she was sent to be a bride of a Hsiungnu chieftain.

jade disc, a badge of office in antiquity for rulers or high officials having a religious and political significance. Later it became a token of wealth, and even later was used as a design motif in the interiors of grand mansions. A cryptic jade was a jade tablet shaped like a colt, according to one interpretation, and inscribed with a secret message.

Jade Gate Pass (Yümen), in the northwest border region, west of Tunhuang, modern Kansu, where Chinese guards maintained border patrols against hostile tribesmen of the north.

jade jar, a waterclock, see clock.

Jade Scales, the central star of the Northern Dipper constellation, the eighth of the twenty-eight traditional constellations. The Dipper and Scales were considered auspicious stars because they were associated with the tools for scooping and weighing grain in times of a good harvest. Northern Dipper is the equivalent of some stars in Ursa Major.

Jade Tree, grows on K'unlun mountains in the west according to the legend. In *The Songs of Ch'u* there are references to breaking off a branch of this tree.

jasper bloom, an echo of *The Songs of Ch'u*: 'A jasper bloom I cannot bear to pick', it expresses the poet's fear of ageing and losing his beauty. Sometimes, however, this merely refers to the artificial flower in a woman's tiara.

Jo, a placename, in the region of modern Hupei.

Jo river, according to legend this runs through the K'unlun mountains, home of the immortals in the west and realm of Queen Mother of the West.

Jo tree, a fabulous tree, which was red with bright green leaves and red blooms, the branches of which gave off a brilliant red glow.

joy of love (*hohuan*), an erotic emblem appearing on fans, quilts, and curtains. It is identified with the tree *albizzia julibrissin*, a deciduous tree of the pulse family with a tall trunk. Its leaves are like wings, formed as they are from double leaves. At night they close. In summer small flowers emerge with numerous, long, red stamens which later turn to fruit. The ideas of double joining, redness, and fruit are all present in the emblem.

jujube (*tsao*), a tree which is also a pun for the word 'soon', meaning 'better not delay', or hurry up and get married and have children.

Junglefowl, the name of a plaintive and romantic song.

Jutzu, the name of the favourite concubine of Prince Ching of Chungshan. He had another favourite called Ping.

Kaoliu, Tallwillow (q.v.).

Kaot'ang, a mountain associated with the Goddess of Wu Mountain (q.v.), who appeared to former kings of Ch'u in erotic dreams. Wu means shamanka or witch.

keys, the harem doorkeys were emblazoned with emblematic features, such as a crane (symbol of longevity) or a fish (symbol of fertility).

Kiangnan, the name of a region in modern Kiangsu and Anhwei south of the Yangtze given to a type of song, a love-song. (Same as Chiangnan, q.v.)

Kiangtung, the region south of the Yangtze.

kindling, traditionally different kinds of wood were used for making a fire depending on the season. Willow was used in spring, jujube in summer, pagoda-tree in winter, and a species of oak in autumn, besides other kinds of trees for various seasons.

king of Ch'in's daughter, see Nung Yü.

kingfisher, the actual bird does not figure *per se* in these poems, so much as its main attribute, glossy blue-green plumage. The plumes of a kingfisher were prized for ornaments in women's tiaras. Gathering the plumes is a conventional activity of love poetry, associated with the Goddess of Lo river as portrayed by Ts'ao Chih. The word 'kingfisher' came to be used as an epithet for a woman's eyebrows, either their natural green-black sheen, or the blue-black-green colour of kohl.

K'ot'ing, a place in Kweichi, Chekiang.

Kuangchai, the name of a Buddhist temple used by Hsiao Yen, Emperor Wu of the Liang.

Kung Shu, a famous artisan of antiquity who cleverly devised a 'sky-scraping ladder' to attack a city of the old Sung state.

K'unlun, see Mount K'unlun.

K'unming lake, southwest of Ch'angan, made by the Han Emperor Wu for naval exercises.

Lady Fan, concubine of the king of Ch'u, she became a model of virtue when she refused to eat meat by way of protesting against the king's excessive love of the hunt.

Lady Hsü, or Lady Hsü Shu, wife of the poet, Ch'in Chia, she was a poet in her own right. Translations of their romantic correspondence in poems appear in Chapter One.

Lady Ju, favourite concubine of the Prince of Wei state (north of the Yellow river), in the Warring States era. Not to be confused with Jutzu.

Lady Li (second century BC), sister of the court musician, Li Yen-nien, she became the favourite concubine of the Han Emperor Wu. Li Yen-nien composed a song praising her beauty, which is translated in Chapter One. Lady Li died prematurely and the emperor became distraught with grief. One night a magician from Ch'i attempted to bring her spirit back, and the emperor thought he glimpsed Lady Li's shadow. He is said to have composed this poem: 'Is it she, is it not? / I stand and stare. / Swish, swish of her silk skirt – / How slow she comes!'

Lady Liang (second century AD), named Sun Shou, the wife of Liang Chi whose sister became consort to Emperor Shun of the Han. Lady Liang started a fashion in women's coiffure called 'twisting fall' or 'fallen colt', which other women tried to copy.

Lady Lu (second century AD), an imperial concubine, she entered the Han harem at the age of seven, and was transferred to the Wei harem when Ts'ao Ts'ao supplanted the Han. Later she married a man called Yin Keng-sheng.

Lady Lu, either a palace lady in the Wei Dynasty (Lady Lu above), or Lu Mo-ch'ou (Nevergrieve), a girl from Loyang who married into the Lu family at the age of fifteen. See Nevergrieve.

Lady Ming, see Wang Chao-chün.

Lady of Ch'u, or lady of Ch'u, either a possible reference to Lady Fan (?), or a general reference to a Ch'u palace lady.

Lady of Han, ? Lady Li.

Lady of Letters, see Ts'ai Yen.

Lady Pan (first century BC), her first name is not known, but she goes by the name of her rank, *chieh-yü*, meaning Beautiful Companion, the highest among palace ladies. She was the favourite concubine of the Han Emperor Ch'eng. An anecdote illustrating her virtue is told in her official biography: once she had the honour of being invited to ride with the emperor in his carriage, but she refused saying she was not exalted enough for such an honour. Later she was displaced in the emperor's affections by Chao Feiyen (q.v.), and retired to serve the dowager empress at Eternal Trust Palace. Her biography contains a long autobiographical poem attributed to her telling of her sorrows, and a poem attributed to her, called *Regret*, appears in Chapter One. It also goes by the popular title of the *Round fan poem*.

Lady Wen, wife of the statesman Wen Ch'iao (AD 288–329). He gave her a mirrorstand as a wedding gift.

Lady Ying, Nung Yü (q.v.). Ying was the family name of the rulers of ancient Ch'in.

Lant'ien, Indigo Field (q.v.).

latest catch, see Lord Lungyang.

Leaning Mulberry, the fabled tree where the sun rested after being rinsed in Hsien Pool following its journey through the sky. Most early texts place this tree in the east, providing a mythical explanation for the rising of the sun. Some versions of the sun myth relate that there were ten suns, with a black bird in their disc. 'Mulberry-Elm time' means the sunset years of life, or the twilight time of day.

leftover peach, a reference to the anecdote about Mi Tzu-hsia (q.v.), favourite of the king of Wei. One day the two men were strolling in the orchard when Mi Tzu-hsia found a delicious peach. He offered the peach to his lord to savour. The king was pleased with him, saying that he had denied himself the pleasure of finishing the peach so as to give pleasure to his lord. Later, when Mi Tzu-hsia's beauty faded, the king remembered this incident, but in an unfavourable light. Mi Tzu-hsia was executed.

lettuce, windblown leaves of the lettuce or the double heart of the lettuce were erotic emblems.

Li's city, a reference to Li Yen-nien (q.v.).

Liang, in the Warring States era this was the name of a city in Honan, known as Taliang. In the Wei Dynasty it became the capital city, near the present site of K'aifeng, in Honan.

Liaohsi, in the old kingdom of Chao, the northern region of Shensi.

Liaotung, a remote province in the far northeast of China which was administered by the Wei Dynasty. It used to be part of the ancient state of Yen. In modern times it is part of Liaoning.

Lich'iu, a perfume that takes its name from an exotic place, the exact location of which is not clear.

light, a metaphor for the radiant love a man bestows on a woman, be it natural light like sunlight, or artificial light from candles or lamps.

Lin Hsiang-ju (third century BC), prime minister of Chao state under King Hui Wen. He was noted for his bravery. The king of Chao possessed the famous Pien Ho jade and the king of Ch'in coveted it. He tried to win it by a ruse, but Lin Hsiang-ju foiled his plan.

Linch'iung, south of modern Ch'engtu, a town in the old kingdom of Shu, modern Szechwan. It was the birthplace of Cho Wen-chün who was courted by the poet, Ssu-ma Hsiang-ju (q.v.).

Liu Piyü, Liu Green Jade (see Green Jade).

Lo river, associated with the legend of the Goddess of Lo river, and Loyang the eastern capital of the Han which was built on its banks.

Lofu, Ch'in Lofu (q.v.).

Lone stork, the name of a plaintive song.

Long River, one of the names of the celestial Han river (q.v.).

Long Wall, or Great Wall of China, constructed in the Chou Dynasty. Several hundreds of miles of walls were built as defences against northern tribesmen. Their construction, maintenance, and surveillance were carried out by corvée labour. In the Ch'in Dynasty these sectional walls were joined to form one long barrier.

Longwillow (Ch'angliu), the name of a pleasure spot in Ch'angan.

Lord Anling, the favourite of King Kung of Ch'u (r. 492–462 BC). Once when the king was out hunting, he asked Anling who his lover would be when the king died. Anling replied: 'I will die with my lord!' The king gave him a generous fiefdom.

Lord Chang, see Chang Fang.

Lord Lungyang (third century BC), the catamite of the king of Wei, perhaps King Anhsi. One day Lord Lungyang went fishing with the king and when more than ten fish had been caught he started to weep. The king asked him the reason. Lord Lungyang replied, 'When I see you prize the latest catch to such an extent that you throw your first catch back into the water, I realise I am just like the first catch. That's why I'm sad.' From that time on the king penalised anyone daring to mention favourites.

Lord P'ingyüan (d. 250 BC), a nobleman, prime minister of Chao, and also known as the Prince of Chao, he was famous for his generous treatment of retainers, numbering 3,000 men in all. His retainers were so well dressed that even their shoes were embroidered with pearls. He was also famous for his humble recognition of the ability of men inferior in rank to himself.

Lord Sui, owned a fabulous pearl given to him by a wounded snake he had cured. Lord Sui pearl (or jade) is said hyperbolically to be used as a catapult pellet.

Lord Yang of Lu's lance, when the sun started to set while Lord Yang was still battling with Wei state, he hurled his lance at the sun to hold it back.

lotus, an erotic emblem. Its brilliant red colour is the colour of passion, its name, *lien*, is a pun for sexual love, and its other name, *ho*, means sexual union. Lotus leaves are also an erotic emblem, denoting passion. The roots, *ou*, are a pun for mates.

Lotusleaves, or lotus leaves, either a placename in Chiangnan, or a general term. The phrase often suggests an echo of the old folk-song about fish sporting around lotus, an erotic image of lovers' pleasure.

loving you (*hsiangssu*), the name of a tree associated with the legend of a wife who pined to death for her husband while he was away from home in Wei state fighting against the Ch'in in the Warring States era. It is identified as the *abrus precatorius*. According to legend this tree grew on the wife's grave, its branches stretching forward toward the place where her husband had gone to war. These outstretched branches figure as an erotic motif on women's clothes, boudoir objects, and utensils such as a winecup.

Loving you, the name of an old love-song.

Loyang, the ancient capital of the Later Han and a major city or capital of the Wei and Western Chin dynasties. It was built on the banks of the Lo river, which had legendary associations.

Lu, the name of a state in antiquity, modern Hupei.

Lu Pan, a clever artisan of antiquity who designed a wooden kite and made it fly.

Lu river, see *Green river*.

Luchiang, the home of the Chiao family whose story is told in the anonymous narrative poem translated in Chapter One, *A peacock southeast flew*. Its site is in the region of modern Anhwei.

Lulu, the name of a dagger. Its hilt was shaped like the pulley of a well. The

317

word for the ring of the pulley was a pun for return, or reunion (*huan*). One of the romantic scenarios of the love ballad was a well, usually under moonlight, and embellished by a silver well-curb, silver bucket, and silk rope.

Lung, the name of a mountain range west of the region of modern Kansu. The Lung hills were guarded by Chinese border patrols, and had beacons for military alarms.

Lungyang, see Lord Lungyang.

magpie, allusion to the legend about two lovers who kept half a mirror each as a love-token when they had to part. Later the woman fell in love with another man. Her half of the mirror turned into a magpie and flew off to her former lover and told him what had happened.

Magpie Lodge, a tower for viewing the panorama around Sweet Springs Palace (q.v.), the summer resort of Han emperors in the northwest.

mallow, usually an allusion to poem 1 of *The Book of Songs*, in which culling water mallow is a metaphor for finding a good wife: 'In patches we grow water mallows, / To left and right we must seek them'.

Man of Pa, the name of a piece of music, classified as coming from the state of Cheng. The poet Sung Yü told King Wei of Ch'u that in the capital city a thousand people were singing lyrics to such music, whereas only a few tens of people were singing lyrics for classical tunes such as *Sunny spring*.

man of Yüeh, a reference to the *Song of the Yüeh Boatman*, see Chapter Nine.

mandarin ducks (*yüanyang*), *aix galerculata*, frequently mentioned in love poetry and serving as a symbol of conjugal fidelity because the birds stay together until they die, or pine to death if separated. Their brilliant plumage is often used to describe something glossy. These birds feature on such items as a marriage bed quilt or drapes.

Mao Ch'iang (fifth century BC), a woman of legendary beauty, she was the favourite concubine of the Prince of Yüeh. The philosopher Chuang Tzu wrote that all creatures fled from her beauty – satirising conventional concepts of beauty and ugliness.

mat, the usual name for a bed. The word also signifies a seat, or a floor for performance of dance and song.

Mayi, a place in the far north, modern Shansi, which was subject to invasion from northern tribes.

meet a minister, a phrase which occurs in a collection of stories about virtuous women, *A Gallery of Good Women* (*Lieh nü chuan*), implying that honest work in the mulberry fields is not so good as the lure of marrying a minister.

melon, in poem 57 of *The Book of Songs* a lovely girl is said to have teeth like melon seeds. 'Two melons' is a flattering term for the two rows of teeth. 'Broken-melon age' means sixteen, melon being an anagram in Chinese for that number. The numerous seeds of the melon denote fertility.

men of learning, a reference to the gathering of scholars and poets around their patron, Ts'ao P'ei, who ruled as Emperor Wen of Wei in the third century AD.

Meng Chu, probably the name of a female singer of around the fifth century AD, who is said to have come from Tanyang, part of Yangchou in the region of modern Anhwei.

Meng ford, north-east of Loyang city.

Meng Isle, probably near Yünmeng, a place in the Tungt'ing lake area.

metal, metallic, according to the Five Elements Theory (q.v.), autumn is associated with the element of metal because it is a season of harsh weather.

Mi Tzu-hsia, a favourite of the king of Wei in the Warring States era. The king promulgated a law that no one should use his royal carriage under any pretext. Mi Tzu-hsia, however, relying on the king's favour, appropriated the carriage when his mother fell ill. The king admired his courage. Later when Mi Tzu-hsia lost the king's favour, this incident was recalled in an unfavourable light and Mi Tzu-hsia was executed. (See leftover peach.)

Mien Chü and Wang Pao, cultured men of antiquity famous for bringing their skills to different parts of China. Mien Chü settled in Kaot'ang and gave the people of Ch'i the art of song. Wang Pao settled by the Ch'i river and gave the people there his technique in song.

Millet thick, an allusion to poem 65 of *The Book of Songs*, in which the heavy ears of ripe millet contrast with the feelings of someone suffering from love.

Ming-chün, see Wang Chao-chün.

mirror, the early Chinese mirror was a bronze circular object, flat and shiny on one side, and elaborately decorated on the other. Fixed on a stand, usually made of jade and elaborately decorated with motifs such as twin dragons and phoenixes, it was an *objet d'art*. Its shiny surface had to be kept polished to prevent it from becoming tarnished or dirty. It is a frequent metaphor for the full moon, while a broken mirror stands for a waning moon. The mirror could also be hung at a window for the application of morning make-up. A dusty mirror is a typical metaphor for a woman neglected by her lover. Also see magpie, paradise bird.

moon, a protean image in Chinese literature, it can denote (1) a mirror, (2) a round fan, (3) the legend of Ch'ang O, (4) a woman's eyebrow, (5) a boudoir curtain hook or hook brooch, or (6) reunion, based on a pun for circle (return). The single source of light at night, the moon acts as a focal point of communication between parted lovers. (See autumn moon.)

moth eyebrows, thick, dark eyebrows were a mark of feminine beauty. To accentuate this feature, kohl was applied in a broad line over and beyond the natural line of the eyebrow. In some cases the eyebrows were described as 'cocoon-emerging', meaning the moth that emerges from the cocoon, or, more precisely, the wings of the moth.

Mount Chungnan (South Mountain), occurs early on in *The Book of Songs*, poem 172, where the blessings of long life and happiness are invoked. It became a symbol of longevity. It stood south of Ch'angan.

Mount Heng, a mountain south of Ch'angsha in Ch'u, modern Hunan. One of the five holy mountains of China.

Mount Hua has two connotations, (1) the name of the holy mountain in Shensi, (2) a mountain in Luchiang, Anhwei.

Mount K'un (K'unlun?), in the far west of China, see Mount K'unlun.

Mount K'unlun, believed to be the land of the immortals in the far west of China, upon whom the sun was said never to set. Also see Queen Mother of the West.

Mount Sung, the highest of the five holy mountains, in Honan.

Mount T'ai, one of the five holy mountains, in Shantung. Mount Liangfu is a small mountain nearby.

Mount T'ang, said to contain vast stores of cinnabar, the precious mineral used for concocting the elixir of immortality. Believed to be where the immortals lived.

Mount Wu, the home of the Goddess of Shamanka Mountain, traditionally believed to be above the Yangtze in Szechwan. See Goddess of.

319

moving mountains, allusion to the story in the *Lieh Tzu*, a collection of Taoist writings dating around AD 300 based on earlier materials. Master Simple decided when he was almost ninety to remove two mountains which were blocking the road. He and his family started moving the mountains one by one, stone by stone, clod by clod. He reckoned it would be done in time after several generations. The gods intervened in this huge endeavour and had the mountains shifted for him.

Mr Sung, see Sung Yü.

mulberry, one of the traditional symbols of a woman's life was the mulberry grove where she picked leaves to feed silkworms, and women were often called 'mulberry girls'. In *The Book of Songs* the lanes where mulberry grew were a rendezvous for lovers.

Mulberry up the lane, an anonymous ballad which had an important influence on the development of love poetry. It was imitated by poets frequently, and there are many versions in this anthology. The original appears in Chapter One. It is a narrative poem about a girl called Ch'in Lofu who is courted by a prefect while she is picking mulberry. She rejects his advances, saying she already has a fine husband.

Mulberry-Elm time, is a phrase meaning twilight, when the sun sinks, or the last years of life.

Nanp'i, in the area of modern Tientsin, Hopei, it is a place where Ts'ao P'ei used to go on excursion with his literary coterie.

Nanwei, or Nanchihwei, the name of a beautiful woman, the favourite concubine of Duke Wen of Chin during the Warring States era. The duke was very much in love with her, but kept her at a distance for fear that her beauty would cause him to neglect affairs of state.

Nanyang, a region south of the Yellow river in modern Honan which produced a fine cosmetic powder.

narrow lane, a euphemism for the brothel district of a city.

needle, often associated with the celebration of Seventh Night (q.v.), when the legendary Weaver star met her lover, Herdboy. Girls would compete on this night with embroidery patterns, using double needles and seven-colour thread. Double needles and threading needles, besides silk thread, were all erotic emblems.

needle and drugs, acupuncture and elixirs.

Nevergrieve (Mo-ch'ou), seems to refer to two separate people. One is mentioned in the poem, *Where the water midstream*, translated in Chapter Nine, either anonymous or attributed to Hsiao Yen. She comes from Loyang and is unhappily married to a rich man called Lu. She is sometimes called Lady Lu. She had wanted to marry the boy next door called Wang Chang. The other is the name of a female singer from Stone City, whose name appears in the title of a song in Chapter Ten.

Ngo, in Ch'u state, the region of Wuch'ang in modern Hupei. See *Song of the Yüeh Boatman*, Chapter Nine.

night of the fifteenth, usually this refers to the eighth lunar month when the autumn moon is full. See autumn moon.

Nine autumns, the name of a tune.

nine blooms, the legendary Queen Mother of the West is said to have lit a nine-branched lamp when she met the Han Emperor Wu. The many lights of a candelabra or the nine-flowers of a woman's jewelled tiara probably derive from this mythical source.

Nine chord, the name of the music of the legendary Yellow Emperor.

nine death sorrow, an allusion to poem 4 of *The Nine Declarations* of *The*

Songs of Ch'u, which describes the exile of the Ch'u courtier, Ch'ü Yüan: 'His soul sped forth nine times each night', as he longed to return to his capital city Ying. He was believed to have committed suicide by drowning in the Milo river.

nine heavens, the number nine is associated with paradise in some contexts. Sometimes it merely denotes a vast distance.

nine-barred, a palace gate or door closed with heavy bars.

nine-flower, used as an epithet to suggest something decoratively splendid, similar to nine blooms.

Nineflower Hall, the name of the palace built in Loyang during the Wei Dynasty, and associated with the founder of the Wei, Ts'ao Ts'ao, who used to hold magnificent banquets.

Ninth Blaze, the name of the fabled torch lit by the legendary Queen Mother of the West when she met the Han Emperor Wu.

north, traditionally related to the female principle known as *Yin*, the cosmic force operating with *Yang*, the male principle. The women's apartments were situated in the north part of the family complex of buildings. The north also has connotations of hostility in terms of the invading nomads such as the Hsiungnu.

Northern Dipper, eighth of the twenty-eight traditional Chinese constellations. See Jade Scales.

'not a mat', a phrase from poem 26 of *The Book of Songs*, in which a girl declares: 'My heart is not stone, / You cannot roll it away. / My heart is not a mat, / You cannot roll it up.' The term comes to mean constancy, or to stand for the heart.

'not a stone', see 'not a mat'.

Nü-ying, Maiden Bloom, one of the two daughters of the legendary Emperor Yao of high antiquity whom he gave in marriage to Emperor Shun, his successor. When Shun died, his two wives drowned themselves in the Hsiang river. Sometimes they are identified as the nymphs of the Hsiang. The tears they shed when Shun died fell on a bamboo and speckled the leaves, and this species of bamboo was named after them.

Nung Yü (seventh century BC), daughter of Duke Mu of Ch'in. She was taught by Hsiao Shih, the master flautist, to copy the phoenix cry. She married him and the duke built a phoenix terrace for them. One day when Nung Yü and Hsiao Shih were playing the flute, the phoenixes that used to perch in their home flew away with them, and they disappeared.

O-huang, Fairy Radiance, one of the two daughters of the legendary Emperor Yao, see Nü-ying.

oatcakes, food conventionally served by a girl to her client in a brothel.

office swagger, a phrase echoing the last quatrain of the anonymous narrative poem, *Mulberry up the lane*, used to describe in flattering terms the husband of the folk heroine Ch'in Lofu.

Old Man of Heaven, his name features in one of the earliest recorded handbooks on sex listed in the Han Dynasty, *The Erotica of the Old Man of Heaven and Other Experts*.

oleaster, see dogwood.

orchid, a sweetly scented, gorgeous flower, noted in love poems for its vulnerability in autumn frost. It is a metaphor for a lovely girl. The name of the tragic heroine of the anonymous narrative poem, *A peacock southeast flew*, is Lanchih, *lan* being the word for orchid. The word is also used as a general epithet like jade to mean lovely or fragrant.

Orion (*Shen*), a star associated in mythology with Antares (q.v.).

Pa, the name of an ancient state in the region of modern Szechwan.

palindrome brocade, Su Hui (*c.* AD 350) was the wife of Tou T'ao, an official. She was jealous of her husband's favourite concubine and refused to go with him on a new assignment to a remote region. Later she sent him a palindrome brocade she wove herself which formed an apologetic poem. Her husband forgave her.

palm-dancing girl, see Chao Feiyen.

P'an Yüeh, see biography of this poet under Background to Poets and Poems.

Paossu (eighth century BC), the favourite concubine of the king of Yu in the Chou Dynasty. She displaced the queen. The king was so entranced by her that he would do anything she asked. Being of a sulky nature, she refused to smile unless something extraordinary happened. The king was anxious to amuse her, so he permitted the beacons to be lit. This did effect a smile. Later when they were lit in earnest during an invasion, people just thought it was Paossu's tricks, so they ignored it. The king's realm was eventually ruined.

paradise (Fant'ien), one of the names of a Buddhist paradise, based on the name of Brahmadeva, a Buddhist deity.

paradise bird, one legend tells of a king of ancient Kashmir who found such a bird. It refused to sing, so his wife told him to do something to stop it pining for its mate. They set a mirror up in front of the bird, hoping it would sing to its reflection. The bird did sing, but its song was so sad that it died of a broken heart. It was believed that a pair of these divine birds (*luan*) danced and sang in happy times. Sometimes this bird also represents the female of the male and female phoenix, or lovebird.

Parted paradise bird, the name of a tune for the lute.

Parted stork, the name of a tune for the lute.

pat my back, see wardrobe mistress.

Peachleaf (T'ao-yeh), the name of a concubine of Wang Hsien-chih, a painter and poet of the fourth century AD. Their poems appear in Chapter Ten.

Peak Cap, the name of a district in Ch'angan city.

pearl, see Chiao Cheng-fu, bright moons, and Lord Sui.

pearl shot, see Lord Sui.

pebbles, possibly an image denoting constancy and integrity.

P'en city, in the region of Kiukiang in north Kiangsi.

pepper, the bedroom walls of a palace lady were impregnated with a species of pepper plant, making them fragrant and conveying the idea of fertility.

pheasant, in pairs denote conjugal harmony.

phoenix, a mythological bird denoting love, especially when a pair is mentioned, the *feng-huang*. It responds to the sound of a flute when played exquisitely, and often features in the legend of Nung Yü (q.v.), or the poems entitled *A grand house.* The phoenix was particularly attracted to the catalpa tree. The word is sometimes used to refer to the bedchamber of an imperial concubine or empress, and has as its male counterpart the dragon.

Phoenix and chicks, the name of a tune, symbolising a happy family.

phoenix court, the imperial court.

phoenix fluting, see Nung Yü, or the poems in the series *A grand house,* or phoenix.

phoenixboys, either an insect, such as the huge brilliantly coloured butterfly, or a young bat.

Picking beans, or *I pick beans,* an allusion to poem 226 of *The Book of Songs,* which tells of a woman unable to do her work of picking beans and indigo because she is pining for her lover.

Picking caltrop, a popular song title, see caltrop.

Picking lotus, the title of a love-song, see lotus.

pictures, erotic illustrations of sex manuals.

Pien Ho jade, Pien Ho (eighth century BC) was from Ch'u. He found a piece of jade of very fine quality and wished to present it to the king, according to custom. His jade was judged to be inferior, so he suffered the penalty of having his left foot cut off. When another king came to the throne, Pien Ho submitted his jade again, but was once more punished by having his right foot amputated. Later, when another king came to the throne and Pien Ho offered the jade again, he wept tears of blood because his jade had been misjudged. This time his jade was found to indeed be of the finest quality and was accepted by the throne.

pillow, a hard object made of horn, tortoiseshell, or some other expensive material, with a concave niche for the neck. For a double bed two pillows were put together, making a felicitous six-angled arrangement. 'Pillow and mat' was a phrase meaning a bed in general. 'To dust pillow and mat' was a phrase used of a woman or catamite to mean service to their lord.

P'ingch'eng, in the reign of the Han Emperor Kaotsu (202–195 BC), the Hsiungnu tribe north of China besieged P'ingch'eng near the border. The emperor was advised to offer the portrait of a beautiful Chinese girl from the palace to the wife of the Hsiungnu chieftain. This he did. When she saw the painting, she reasoned to herself that if the siege were not lifted, lovely girls such as the one in the painting would become the booty of her husband, and she would be sure to lose his favour. So she urged her husband to lift the siege. This traditional account is probably apocryphal.

Po Hill censer, hill-shaped censers date from as early as the Chou Dynasty. The typical Po Hill censer was of bronze, conical in shape to represent a holy mountain, studded with jewels, and decorated with fabulous fauna. Po Hill was a mountain in the region of Shantung.

pole-star, it was customary for people to make an oath on the pole-star because it was fixed in the firmament, symbolising fidelity to one's vow.

pomegranate, red and full of seeds, this was a symbol of love and fertility. The word is also used to describe the colour of red clothes. Pomegranate wine is occasionally mentioned.

pounder, an instrument used for beating silk fibres and softening them. One word for pounder was an elaborate pun for a lover, or mate, and silk fibre was a pun for love.

pounding block, an object used with a pounder for fulling cloth.

prefect, see *Mulberry up the lane.*

Prince of Ch'in's daughter, Nung Yü (q.v.).

Prince of Ch'en, Ts'ao Chih, see Goddess of Lo river.

Prince of Huainan, Liu An (d. 123 BC), was a prince of the Han royal family. He dabbled in elixirs to attain eternal youth.

Princess's brother, see Wei Tzu-fu who first served in the household of the Princess of P'ingyang, sister of the Han Emperor Wu, and later became his consort.

purple, the imperial colour, and used as an adjective to mean imperial.

Queen (Mother) of the West, a mythological figure said to rule the land of immortals in the western region of the K'unlun mountains. She grew peaches which conferred immortality, but the trees bore fruit only once every 3,000 years. Originally, she was depicted as a wild creature with dishevelled hair, tiger's teeth, and the tail of a leopard. Later she was made more civilised, and the only remaining suggestion of wildness was her long, unbound hair and serpentine lower body. She figures in a legendary account of a banquet she gave in honour of King Mu of Chou (trad. r. 1001–946 BC), at which she sang for him. She also gave a banquet in honour of the Han Emperor Wu, at which she gave him five peaches of immortality. Her guardians were the tiger and dragon.

quilt, a padded bed cover, sometimes made into a double, fitted garment. The padding was of silk floss, a pun for everlasting love. The cover was usually decorated with erotic motifs, such as mandarin ducks or lotus.

quince, in poem 64 of *The Book of Songs* the poet says a woman he desired threw him a token of a quince, then of 'a peach, and then a plum, and he requited her with different kinds of precious stones.

Racedog Terrace, part of a Han Dynasty palace.

rafter dust, an image of good fortune deriving from a legend about a woman called Han O who sang so marvellously that the echo circled the ridge-pole for three days, making the dust on the rafters leap. Sometimes the poems refer to a male listener in this context; he says he must leave his seat before the rafter dust leaps, meaning that he cannot bear to experience such sublime music.

rafters, usually described as being of some rich wood like apricot and carved with erotic motifs, such as a lotus, and gilded. Also see rafter dust.

rain, often suggests the legend of the Goddess of Wu Mountain.

rear, the location of the women's quarters in a family house.

red, the colour of passion. A bride wore red at her wedding. See lotus, pomegranate, and hibiscus.

Reincarnation scent, a Buddhist term used in a secular way as a name for a perfume that was fashionable in the Southern Dynasties.

ripped sleeve, see Tung Hsien.

River, sometimes this refers to the celestial Han river, or the Yellow river.

River of Heaven, see Han, celestial river.

river sprites, see Han river sprites.

rock-lotus, two puns are involved here: rock was often used to suggest constancy, and lotus was an emblem for passion.

rock-the-boat, a reference to the anecdote about the Lady of Ts'ai who went boating with Duke Huan of Ch'i (d. 643 BC). She started to rock the boat and refused to stop, even when the duke clearly was not amused. He finally grew so enraged, he sent her back to Ts'ai state, in modern Honan.

roots of the lotus, *ou*, their interlocking growth suggests the intimate bonds of love and entwined lovers.

rose of sharon, a flower that blooms at dawn and is dead by dusk.

Round fan poem, ascribed to Lady Pan (q.v.), translated as *Regret* in Chapter One, also referred to as the *Torn silk poem*. (See fan.)

Royal Forest, see Shanglin Park.

same heart, a recurring phrase meaning lovers of one mind and heart, that is they are so close that they do not see things differently. Difference, it is suggested, leads to quarrels, and then to estrangement. This idea is conveyed by such motifs as same heart lettuce, flowers, and so forth. Often translated as sweetheart.

Scales star, see Jade Scales.

Secret orchid, the name of a tune. A lovely girl is often called an orchid, and she is generally described as living in seclusion, or in a secret room.

seven removes, a phrase occurring in poem 203 of *The Book of Songs* which describes Weaver star. It is taken by some commentators to mean that Weaver's movement through the firmament is like a shuttle passing the weft through the warp of other stars, and that she makes such a move once a month, or seven times a year. The number is clearly linked to Seventh Night, when Weaver is permitted to see Herdboy. Sometimes this phrase is taken to mean that Weaver rolls up her sleeves to weave seven times.

Seven spirals, the name of a dance.

Seventh Night, or the Seventh, the night of the seventh month when Weaver star was allowed to meet her lover, Herdboy. Also see Weaver. Women celebrated this night by embroidery competitions in honour of Weaver, using double needles threaded with seven-colour silk thread.

shadow and echo, a double metaphor for intimate love and friendship, or estrangement. Shadow may be bound to form, or separated; echo may be bound to sound, or separated. Usually woman is represented as shadow and echo, man as form and sound.

Shanglan, a Han Dynasty palace in the Royal Forest.

Shanglin park, the Royal Forest in Ch'angan where Han emperors used to hunt. The park had an imperial zoo. Several handsome lodges were built in the park.

Shansi general, there is a proverb that goes: Shansi produces generals, Shantung produces ministers.

Shanyin, a place in the region of modern Chekiang.

Shanyü, the title of the chieftain of the Hsiungnu tribes.

Shih Chi-lun, see Shih Ch'ung.

Shih Ch'ung (d. AD 300), courtesy name Chi-lun, a statesman and poet of enormous wealth. He had a pleasure park called Golden Vale near Loyang where he held lavish parties. His favourite singer used to perform there, delighting his guests with her dance and music. See Shih Ch'ung's biography in Background to Poets and Poems, also Green Pearl and Golden Vale. His famous poem on Wang Chao-chün appears in Chapter Two.

Shih-Yu gale, reference to the anecdote about a certain Mr Yu who married a Miss Shih. When he had to leave home on business she pined so much that she died. As she was dying she vowed she would become a contrary gale and stop boats from sailing away from wives at home.

shrike, there was a saying that the shrike calls in spring and then flowers will grow; it calls in autumn and then flowers will die.

Shrub Terrace, see Bushy Terrace.

Shu, an ancient kingdom in southwest China, part of modern Szechwan. It has many associations. Ssu-ma Hsiang-ju, the Han poet and wooer of Cho Wen-chün, came from its capital, Ch'engtu. The astrologer who divined the sky voyage of Chang Ch'ien also came from this city. Tu Yü, Emperor Wang, ruled the kingdom and turned into a cuckoo (or nightjar) when he died.

Shuiheng, the name of an office that was in charge of the Royal Forest Park during the Han Dynasty.

silk, sericulture was originally the task of women. It has acquired many erotic associations. Women used to pick mulberry leaves for hungry silkworms, a sexual metaphor. The silk thread of the cocoon was a pun for pining love. After spinning, women would weave cloth, often said in these poems to be clothes for their lover who was away fighting, and so forth. If a man loved a woman, he would show this in a visible way by wearing the clothes she prepared for him. Many of the poems contain several stages in the process of sericulture and tailoring: silkworm care, weaving, fulling, cutting material, sewing, embroidering, wrapping and perfuming the garment.

silkworm, in spring, the season of love, the silkworms grow quickly and feed hungrily on mulberry leaves. Girls tending them are called 'silkworm girls'. Also see cocoon, mulberry, silk.

single glance beauty, a reference to Lady Li, a phrase taken from the song her brother sang to Emperor Wu describing her beauty. See Lady Li, and 'In the north there is a lovely lady'.

sinking incense, a reference to a type of incense candle, often decorated with jewels such as pearl bands, used for perfume and for marking the time. When the candle burned down, the jewels would slip, appearing to sink.

Sip Dew Terrace, probably another name for Cold Dew Terrace.

Sky River, see Han, celestial river.

Sky Trails, in popular mythology this was a constellation which led to outer space.

Small Longbank, probably a region near Chienk'ang (modern Nanking), capital of the Liang Dynasty.

smoke, often associated with mountain mists and the Goddess of Mount Wu, it has erotic overtones.

Sobbing crow, a tune, perhaps the same as *A crow weeps.*

solar-ray, see speculum.

songhouse, the usual euphemism for a courtesan's residence. She was called a singing-girl, a singer, or artiste. Originally a green-painted house indicated the residence of a nobleman, but later this fashion was adopted by courtesans.

Songs, The Book of Songs (see below).

Sop'an dance, either a transliteration of a Central Asian word, or a descriptive term meaning a gyrating type of dance.

south, when contrasted with the north, it may denote a male image, compared with the feminine image of the north, or else the north in a hostile relationship with the south. Sometimes the south suggests an exotic region. When birds migrate south, the image conveyed is one of homecoming, or the pursuit of warmth.

South Mountain, see Mount Chungnan.

South Park, an amusement park for city people in Chienyeh, or Chienk'ang, the Liang capital.

Sparrow Terrace, see (Bronze) Sparrow Terrace.

speculum, a highly polished bronze mirror used as a reflector to catch solar rays in order to generate fire.

Spreading Scent Hall (P'ihsiang), a harem residence in the Han.

spring's three, the three months of spring.

Ssu-ma Hsiang-ju, the Han poet famous in the literature of love for his courtship of Cho Wen-chün and elopement with her. He courted her with two songs, featured in Chapter Nine. For his biography, see Background to Poets and Poems. He is also known for writing a moving entreaty on behalf of Empress Ch'en with the result that her estranged husband, Emperor Wu, felt affection for her again.

stars, in the ancient Chinese astronomical system, the sky was divided into four 'palaces', namely Green Dragon in the east, Vermilion Bird in the south, White Tiger in the west, and Black Tortoise in the north. The sky was further subdivided into twenty-eight 'mansions', or constellations, conceived of as resting-places for the sun, moon, and planets. The planets moved in a sequence of 360 degrees. Of the constellations, the most popular in love literature were Herdboy, Weaver, Three Stars, Antares, Orion, Warp, Tzu-wei, Troubled Star, Northern Dipper, and Jade Scales. It was also believed that the earth was patterned on the heavens, and that each locality had its counterpart in the sky. Thus Shu kingdom was the earthly equivalent of Wall star. Pole-star, being fixed, was often used as an emblem of constancy for swearing oaths.

steps, usually described as being of jade, connected with a palace or palatial ambience, and leading to a woman's bedroom. They are often featured with a film of heavy dew or coated with frost, showing clearly the absence or presence of footprints. They are an erotic image, connected with the erotic appeal of the foot. A poem by Hsieh T'iao (Chapter Ten) made this image famous, and set the style for many later imitations. Usually a woman is pictured waiting near the steps for her lover on an autumn night.

Stone City (Shihch'eng), a place in Hupei, which gives its name to a type of popular music. A girl called Nevergrieve is said to have come from here.

storax (*suho*), a perfume, originally imported from Rome and Parthia, it was scented resin, a dark purple in colour.

stork, a symbol of longevity, often also called a crane, and linked in this context with the tortoise. The cry of a stork was thought to be particularly plaintive, and usually considered to be of a bird parted from its flock or mate. This meaning derives from poem 156 of *The Book of Songs*: 'A stork cries on the ant-hill, / A wife sighs in her bedroom.'

straight as a bowstring, a simile from a ditty circulating in the reign of the Han Emperor Hsün (r. AD 126–144): 'Straight as a bowstring, / You'll die by the wayside. / Crooked as a hook, / You'll be dubbed a duke!'

stuff, material, lit. a bolt of cloth, *p'i*, a pun for a mate.

Su Hsiao-hsiao, a singer of the fifth century AD who made a pact to be true to the grave. She died young and her spirit was said to hover around her grave waiting for her lover to join her. See this entry in Background to Poets and Poems.

Su Wu (first and second centuries BC), a Chinese envoy captured by the Hsiungnu in the reign of the Han Emperor Wu. After many trials and tribulations during nineteen years of captivity, he was released and returned to China. It was believed that while in captivity he wrote his wife at home a letter of sorrowful pining, and a poem on the same theme; the latter is featured in Chapter One. He is also believed to have sent his love poem by a goose's foot.

sulky pertness, see Hsi Shih.

Sumen, in the ancient state of Yen, northeast China.

Sun Terrace (Yangt'ai), where the Goddess of Mount Wu is believed to have appeared to a king of ancient Ch'u in a dream, telling him that this was her abode at dawn and dusk. It was thought to be located in the region of Szechwan or Hupei.

Sung, see Sung Yü.

Sung Jung-hua, the name of a woman singer at the time of Ts'ao Ts'ao in the late Han and early Wei eras.

Sung Yü (? third century BC), a courtier poet of Ch'u, perhaps during the reign of King Ch'ing-hsiang. He is thought to have been a literary disciple of the semi-legendary poet and statesman, Ch'ü Yüan. Tradition has it that Sung Yü was a romantic and a flirt. A number of prose poems are attributed to him, *The Lechery of Mr Tengt'u, Mount Kaot'ang, The Goddess*, and others. The first piece is supposed to have been occasioned by a counsellor called Tengt'u denouncing Sung Yü at court as a lecher. The poet responded by saying that while he himself had lived chastely next door to a really lovely girl, Tengt'u had sired five children by his unbelievably ugly wife. The last two pieces are on the theme of the Goddess of Mount Wu. Sung Yü's name is also connected with two tunes, *Man of Pa* and *Sunny spring*.

Sunny spring, a classical tune on the theme of love.

supreme commander, Huo, see Huo Ch'ü-ping.

Sweet Dew Gate, Lamp of Wisdom, Buddhist terms denoting the stage of enlightenment, when earthly cares have been left behind and sorrow no longer pains the human heart.

Sweet herbs, or sweet herbs, both the name by which the first poem of the anthology is generally known and a herb called *miwu*, the purpose of which is not understood. Some commentators suggest it might be a fertility drug, arguing that the person featured in that first poem was divorced because she bore no children. This important poem contains several features which later poets developed: (1) an encounter between a divorced woman and her former husband, (2) the suggestion that as the first wife she was more honest and down-to-earth than his second wife, (3) she wove more homespun cloth than the second wife, who wove a fancier cloth, a theme much quoted in love poetry in general, (4) the idea that the first wife was still in love with her former husband.

Sweet Springs Palace (Kanch'üan), a summer resort of the Han emperors situated on a mountain of the same name in Shensi. Built in the Ch'in Dynasty, it was reconstructed by Emperor Wu in 121 BC.

sweetheart string, string tied in a knot suggesting the bond between two lovers.

sword spirit, see swords.

swords, a pair of magic swords, a reference to the story about the third-century AD astrologer, Lei Huan, who was asked by Chang Hua, the poet, statesman, and scholar, the meaning of a purple vapour in the sky. Lei Huan explained that it was the spirit of a magic sword in the Ch'u city of Fengch'eng. Sent there as a governor, he found two swords, one marked 'Dragon Fount', and the other marked 'T'ai-a', made by Kan Chiang for the Ch'u King. Lei Huan put one sword in his belt and gave Chang Hua the other. Hua commented that because the swords were magic the time would come when they would reunite. When Hua died, his son wore his magic sword, but one day it vanished into a river without a trace, leaving two dragons in its place. The colour purple was imperial, and one meaning of dragon was also imperial.

Ta Chi (twelfth century BC), a famous beauty, concubine of Chou Hsin, last ruler of the Shang Dynasty who was condemned as a tyrant. She was said to have been so beautiful that she caused the downfall of the dynasty. At the end when the Shang was in ruins, no one dared to execute her, except for one aged counsellor on the victor's side who was immune from her charms.

T'ai Yung, master of music to the legendary Yellow Emperor.

T'aiyüan, the region of modern Shansi.

Tallwillow (Kaoliu), a place in the region of modern Shansi. Represents the border region where the Chinese had to mount patrols to guard against invasion from northern tribesmen.

Tanyang, part of the region of Yangchou, modern Anhwei.

Tat'i city, associated with Hsiangyang music, situated in modern Hupei. The city gave its name to a collection of popular local tunes.

The Book of Songs (Shih ching), one of the *Confucian Classics*. Traditionally thought to have been compiled by Confucius from an earlier collection of over 3,000 folk-songs gathered from the different feudal states of Chou China. The present collection contains 305 songs, hymns, dynastic legends in verse, and ceremonial odes. The material is believed to date from about the early Chou era, perhaps between the ninth and seventh centuries BC. One section of this collection is devoted to songs from different regions, 160 from fifteen northern states, and contains many love poems, quoted often in the love poems of later periods. As a *Confucian Classic* it formed part of the basis for education, and young people were expected to be able to recite from it by heart.

thread, see silk.

Three Gods, the three spheres of Heaven, Earth, and Human Life.

Three Hills, an allusion to poem 110 of *The Book of Songs*, which describes a man on military campaign pining for his family as he looks homeward from three types of hill: a tree-covered hill, a bare hill, and a ridge.

Three Lights, the sun, moon, and stars.

Three Rivers, the Yellow, the Lo, and the Yi, which flow near Loyang, and come to represent that city.

Three Sparrow Terrace, see (Bronze) Sparrow Terrace.

three springtimes, the usual meaning of this phrase is the three months of spring, but it may also mean three spring seasons, or three years in some contexts.

Three Stars, or Triad, usually involves an allusion to two poems in *The Book of Songs*, either poem 21, in which a nobleman's concubines complain that just as the small stars fade at dawn, so they have to leave their lord early, whereas his senior wife like the Triad star may stay with him until late morning. Or the allusion may be to poem 118 in which a nobleman rejoices to see the charming concubines, like the Three Stars, whom he receives on his wedding night together with his senior wife.

thundercloud, an ancient art motif featured on ritual bronzes of the Shang and Chou dynasties, it later became a fashion detail on such objects as a winecup. A symbol of good fortune signifying fructifying rain.

Tiaoling, an allusion to the philosopher Chuang Tzu who is said to have shot 'a peculiar magpie' there.

tiara, a woman's jewelled headdress; called a 'quiverer' because its delicate assemblage of kingfisher plumes, pearl pins, and gilt artificial flowers would quiver as she walked.

tigers roar, a propitious image deriving from the fact that in mythology the tiger was the guardian and steed of Queen Mother of the West, ruler of the land of the immortals.

toad and hare, two of the mythical creatures on the moon. When Ch'ang O (q.v.) fled to the moon with her husband's elixir of immortality, she took with her a pet hare, and, having taken a dose of the elixir, she changed into a toad. The hare is sometimes depicted holding a magic herb. The toad is one of the emblems of immortality. It was believed that an eclipse of the moon was caused by the toad swallowing the moon. Also, when the moon wanes, the toad and hare disappear.

top-key, the music from local areas was considered popular, or even lowbrow, compared with the classical, metropolitan music. For example, *Man of Pa* was popular, *Sunny spring* classical.

Torch Dragon (Chulung), according to a sourcebook of myths, *The Classic of Mountains and Seas (Shan hai ching)*, this was a deity with a human

329

face and a snake's body which dwelt on the Changwei hills beyond the northwest seas. It controlled wind and rain and lit up the Nine Darknesses. Its eyes were so bright that when they were open it seemed as light as day, and when they were shut it seemed as dark as night. Its name was used to describe intense or brilliant light.

Torn silk poem, see *Round fan poem.*

tortoise and stork, emblems of longevity.

Trinity Prayer, in legendary antiquity a guard is said to have met Emperor Yao on the border of Hua and prayed that he would have long life, wealth, and many children.

Troubled Star, the first star in the handle of the Northern Dipper. It was believed to herald autumn when it pointed southwest.

Ts'ai Yen (*fl. c.* AD 190), the daughter of the famous literary figure, Ts'ai Yung (AD 133–192), she was captured by the Hsiungnu and married to one of their chieftains. When he died, she married her first husband's son by another wife, a custom of that tribe. Eventually, she returned to China. A long narrative poem ascribed to her tells of her ordeal in captivity. She is generally known by the title *Wen-chi,* or Lady of Letters.

Ts'ai Yung (AD 133–192), a famous man of letters. He wrote a poem called *A blue dress.* His biography appears in Background to Poets and Poems.

Ts'angchou, one of the places known as the land of the immortals.

Ts'ao Chih (AD 192–232), one of the poets translated in this anthology, he is quoted in many love poems in connection with his *Prose Poem on the Goddess of Lo River,* a fanciful evocation of the deity as she appeared to him in a vision.

Tu Nü, the name of a girl mentioned in a ditty circulating in the reign of the Han Emperor Huan (r. AD 147–168): 'Tu Nü of Hochien cleverly amassed a fortune.'

t'uchih ink, it is not clear what this name means; perhaps it is a transliteration of a Central Asian word. The context in which it is mentioned indicates that an exotic ink is meant.

Tuliang, the name of an exotic perfume, probably deriving from the name of a place, the site of which is not known.

Tung Hsien, the catamite of the Han Emperor Ai (r. 7–1 BC). One night as they lay sleeping together, the emperor's sleeve got caught under the boy's body. When the time came for the emperor to go to the dawn court ceremony, rather than waken the boy, he ripped his sleeve off and slipped away quietly.

Tung Sheng, this may refer either to Tung Yen or Tung Hsien, but in any event both lovers were famous for their handsome features.

Tung Yen, the name of the catamite of the Han Emperor Wu.

Tung-men Wu, a man named Wu from the Tung-men area in the Wei era was so stoical that even when his son died he showed his fortitude by refusing to grieve.

Tunghsia, the old name for a region in modern Shantung, famous for the manufacture of silk thread.

Tungt'ing lake, in the kingdom of Ch'u, modern Hunan. It formed a confluence for several important Ch'u rivers which were associated with various legends, namely the Han, Hsiang, and Hsiao, besides the Yangtze. It is mentioned in two of the shamanistic songs of *The Songs of Ch'u* addressed to or about the deity of the Hsiang river. Elsewhere in that anthology it is associated with sad journeys undertaken by men in the vain pursuit of happiness.

Tungyang, the old name of a region in modern Chekiang.

turrets, in popular mythology the sky was divided into different palaces, each having gates with turrets above them. The mythical Gates of Heaven is a general name given to a region of the sky, and these are also said to have turrets, or flying turrets.

T'u-shan, when Yü saw the daughter of the T'u-shan clan, he left for a tour of the south before marrying her. She longed for him and sent a messenger with her song of love. Yü was the legendary founder of the Hsia Dynasty.

twentieth, the moon of that night.

twin hearts, an emblem of good fortune, of devoted love; a typical example is a double-flower plant.

twisting fall hairdo, see Lady Liang.

two boys, an allusion to the anonymous ballad, *A grand house*, translated in Chapter One. It tells of two youths whose carriages get stuck in a narrow lane, and who start chatting to each other about where one of them lives.

Two Discs, sun and moon, symbols of constancy for their supposed regular motion in the skies. A sun and moon motif, or Two Disc motif, was fashionable in the Southern Dynasties for items of clothing and furnishing.

two pleasure-seekers, the Han river sprites (q.v.).

Tzu river and Sheng river, an allusion to an anecdote about Yi Ya (seventh century BC) who was head cook to Duke Huan of Ch'i. His sense of taste was so subtle that he is said to have been able to distinguish between the waters of these two rivers. When the duke said he had tasted everything except a boiled baby, Yi Ya served him his own baby on a dish.

Tzu Tu, a good-looking man in antiquity.

Tzu-wei star, the name of a constellation, and a general name for an imperial palace, partly deriving from the word for purple in its name (*tzu*).

Upper Palace (Shang kung), a trysting-place for lovers, and an allusion to poem 48 of *The Book of Songs*, which tells of a man's assignations with lovely women among the mulberry near Upper Palace and along the Ch'i river.

Vast Wave (Hungpo), the name of a Ch'in Dynasty terrace, a pleasure spot of Chao Chien-tzu.

Wan-shan, a place in Hsiangyang.

Wang Chao-chün (first century BC), courtesy name Chao-chün, given name Ch'iang, her name was changed from Chao to Ming because it violated the taboo name of Ssu-ma Chao, posthumously entitled Emperor Wen of the Chin (AD 211–265). She was a palace lady in the harem of Emperor Yüan of the Han. Because she refused to bribe the court painter, Mao Yen-shou, he depicted her with a blemish. Later when the Hsiungnu demanded a Chinese bride, Emperor Yüan picked out Wang Chao-chün's portrait and sent her off in marriage to the tribal chieftain. When the emperor saw her leaving the palace he realised that hers was no flawed beauty and deeply regretted her departure. She had to leave China, however, and in due course married the chieftain, bearing him a son. When he died, she married his son by another wife. Her story is told in Shih Ch'ung's long narrative in Chapter Two.

Wang Ch'iang, see Wang Chao-chün.

Wang Mang, usurped the Han throne and set up his Hsin Dynasty for a short-lived interregnum AD 9–23. He took as his emblematic colour yellow, symbolising the earth (see Five Elements Theory).

Wang Pao, see Mien Chü and Wang Pao.

Wang (Tzu-ch'iao), called by his other name of Wang Tzu-chin (sixth century

BC), son of King Ling of the Chou Dynasty. He studied the occult arts for thirty years and then, according to legend, flew away on a white stork, the symbol of longevity, and became an immortal. Other versions of the legend say that Wang was a sorcerer or a Taoist immortal, who changed into a rainbow serpent, then into a shoe, and then into a great bird. He figures frequently in *The Songs of Ch'u*, riding the clouds as a divinity.

wardrobe mistress, a reference to the career of Wei Tzu-fu (second century BC), who was originally employed in the household of the Princess of P'ingyang, the sister of the Han Emperor Wu. One day when the emperor was returning from an outing, he visited his sister and she showed him her ladies-in-waiting. He was only interested in Wei Tzu-fu. Later she helped him change his robes, and the emperor made love to her in the corridor. He gave his sister 1,000 weights of gold, so she offered him Wei Tzu-fu. As the latter was about to enter the carriage taking her to the imperial palace, the Princess patted her back encouragingly and told her not to forget her bene-factress. Eventually Wei Tzu-fu displaced Empress Ch'en who was childless. As Empress Wei she bore the emperor a son and he became the heir apparent.

Warp stars, the seven luminaries of the sun, moon, and five planets, move on the woof of the other stars' trajectories.

waterplant, see alga.

Weaver, stars in Vega and Lyra, associated in folklore with the wife of Herdboy. The legend goes that when they married they were so happy they would not work. The king and queen of Heaven were so angry with them that they separated them. The queen drew her silver hairpin across the sky and created the Han river, or River of Heaven, to divide the lovers. But the king was moved by their plight and allowed them to meet once a year on the Seventh Night of the seventh month of the lunar calendar. Then the water of the river would abate, and Weaver could cross in her divine carriage to Herdboy. The sky would form their boudoir with clouds forming thick bedcurtains. During the rest of the year Weaver is shown fidgeting at her task of weaving, never completing her pattern because she is pining. She is the patroness of embroidery, and on Seventh Night girls compete in embroidery patterns using double needles (probably to represent the two stellar lovers) and seven-colour thread. Sometimes Weaver is called the girl of the river Han in the sky. Most poems on this theme stress the brevity of the joy of Seventh Night.

Wei, the name of the dynasty founded by Ts'ao Ts'ao in AD 220 and ruled until 265 by the Ts'ao family with their capital at Loyang.

Wei and Cheng, names of ancient states and of sections of the 160 regional songs of *The Book of Songs*. The songs and music associated with these states were traditionally considered to be licentious, or enjoyable, according to the listener's point of view. (Also see Cheng.)

Wei Hsiao (d. AD 33), a military man who once occupied T'ienshui, see 'a plug of mud'.

Wei river, a traditional rendezvous for lovers, often coupled in this context with the Ch'i river. It flowed north of Ch'angan.

Wei Sheng (sixth century BC), see clasping the bridge-post.

Wei Tzu-fu, see wardrobe mistress.

Weich'eng, the name of a city near Hsienyang, capital of the Ch'in Dynasty, north of Ch'angan.

Weiyang Palace, a Han palace, residence of royal ladies.

Welcome Breeze Lodge, a Han summer residence in Sweet Springs, Shensi.

Welcome Dew, a reference to the bronze pillar built by the Han Emperor Wu, on the top of which he had erected an image of an immortal holding its palm up to the sky to receive dew. Dew was believed to be the nectar of immortals.

Welcome Dew Terrace, a terrace where the bronze pillar was built bearing the same name.

Wellpath, the name of a district and of a mountain north of Hantan, capital of Chao state.

Wen-chün, personal name of Cho Wen-chün (q.v.).

West Mound, a place west of Ch'ient'ang river, modern Hangchow area.

West Park, in Yeh city during the Wei Dynasty.

Western, usually means Central Asia in the context of traditional China.

West Willow, a mythological tree in the west where the sun sets. Called Hsi-liu, a pun for Slim Willow.

whistle, whistling, has a romantic connotation in these poems, sometimes expressing wistfulness or deep feeling. In the context of reclusion, whistling summons a wizard or an immortal.

White crest song, the name of an anonymous folk-song, also entitled *White as snow on the hills*, translated in Chapter One as *Today a keg of wine*.

White Elm star, its location in the sky is not certain.

White Emperor city (Paiti), in Kweichow, where Mount Wu was thought to be.

White Gate, the southwest gate of Chienk'ang, formerly Hsüan-yang Gate.

White Girl (Sunü), the name of a goddess entrusted with the arcane mysteries of sexual techniques. She is linked in this context with the Dark Girl.

White hemp dance, considered a modern tune in the fifth century AD. Possibly performed by youths wearing white hempen robes. White was the colour associated with autumn. Hemp was usually worn in summer.

white horse(s), a traditional image of time's swift passage, usually described galloping past a crack in the wall.

White snow, the name of a melody.

white sun vow, an oath sworn by pointing up at the sun (and/or the moon), symbolising constancy and fidelity to one's vow. Poem 73 of *The Book of Songs* contains the couplet: 'You thought I had broken faith; / I was true as the bright sun above'.

White-brass-shoes, it is not clear if this is a placename in Shansi in the Han era, or refers to an object. Attached to a song, the name seems to indicate a traditional air.

Whitehorse ford (Paima), near the Yellow river.

willow (*liu*), a pun for to detain, to keep someone from going away on a journey. Since the Han Dynasty it was the custom for a person escorting a traveller part of his journey to give him a twig of willow. 'Broken willow' or 'Breaking willow' denotes a parting theme. The willow was also an image of feminine grace and slenderness. The willow, like the plum, heralds the spring with its green fronds and fluff. Its silky strands are often compared with silk thread, a pun for love.

window, the panes of early Chinese windows were of silk. The frame was wooden. Sometimes there was a wooden fretwork or lattice, a pun for cage, *lung*. In a woman's sheltered life the only time she might be seen by outsiders was at her window, where she applied her make-up, sewed, and stared into the distance.

wine, although the grapevine was introduced to China during the Han Dynasty, wine from grapes was not the usual alcoholic drink. Fermented rice wine was more usual. This is sometimes described as white or green.

Sometimes wine is generally said to be 'orchidaceous', meaning fragrant. Mulled wine was served in wineshops by women. 'First wine' meant the first ritual sharing of wine by bride and bridegroom at their marriage, and came to mean marriage itself, like the phrase 'bound hair'. There was an old song which said that clear wine like flowers was the drink of autumn, wine sweet like milk was the drink of spring. Lovers pledged with wine, the male or master offering a cup of wine from which he had drunk the first half. The cup was supposed to be drained.

Wu, see Mount Wu, and the Goddess of Mount Wu. Wu is often linked with Lo, meaning Lo river and its goddess.

Wu, the name of an ancient state in the region of modern Kiangsu and Chekiang. In some poems the region is mentioned in connection with the production of tailoring shears, for which it was famous. Also, the region is associated with Hsi Shih (q.v.).

Wunü, the name of a star.

Wuwei, the name of a place in modern Kansu.

Yang city, in the old kingdom of Ch'u, modern Honan. Sometimes used as a general placename for lovely women, deriving from Sung Yü's mention of it in *The Lechery of Mr Tengt'u*, in the same way as Hsiats'ai (q.v.) is mentioned.

Yangchow, in the Southern Dynasties era this placename was synonymous with Hsiangyang, modern Hupei.

Yang Hsiung (53 BC–AD 18), poet and philosopher of the Han Dynasty, his courtesy name was Tzu-yün. Though poor, he was a man of honour and integrity, preferring to live quietly and modestly, rather than pursue fame and fortune.

Yeh valley, a very long valley in Shensi.

Yehchung, capital city of the Wei Dynasty in the third century AD, it was taken over by Shih Hu of the Chieh tribe of the Hsiungnu.

yellow, it was a cosmetic fashion in the Southern Dynasties for a woman to attach a beauty-spot of different shapes and colours to her brow. The usual colour was yellow, and the shape varied between a mountain, flower, moon, or star.

Yellow Emperor, Huang-ti, legendary sage-king of ancient China, believed to have bestowed upon mankind various benefits, including sericulture (invented by his wife). The philosophical school of Taoism is often referred to as the Teaching of the Yellow Emperor and Lao Tzu, or Huang-Lao. The titles of many arcane texts bear his name.

Yellow river, the northern river of China, the basin of which formed the central heartland of ancient China, known as the Central Plains. The capital cities of Hsienyang, Ch'angan, and Loyang were all situated in this region. The river is often mentioned in love poetry as an insuperable obstacle for one seeking to follow a beloved traveller. The Yellow river was believed to be a continuation of the Han river in the sky. Another popular belief was that the normally muddy Yellow river flows clear once in a thousand years, a symbol of rare good fortune. The river is also used to symbolise the flow of time.

Yellow Springs, the afterlife, considered as a lower world beneath the world of men. Also called Eternal Springs.

Yellow stork, the name of a song composed by a girl called T'ao Ying from Lu state when her husband died and her relatives tried unsuccessfully to make her remarry.

Yen, see Chao Feiyen. (Yen means a swallow.)

Yen, the name of an ancient state in northeast China annihilated in the third century BC by Ch'in state. It was famous in its heyday for its lovely women, and is linked in this context with Chao state. A Yen song is about parted lovers.

Yen Ssu, a man who served the Han Emperors Wen, Ching, and Wu, who successively ruled 180–87 BC. He lived so long that he became a symbol of decrepitude.

Yi city, south of Hsiangyang in Hupei.

Yi river, in the region of Hupei.

Yih river, perhaps southeast of Shantung (different from Yi river).

Yin/Yang, one of the earliest cosmological ideas in ancient China was that the universe operated according to the interaction of two primeval opposing forces in a complementary way, *yin* and *yang*. *Yin* stood for the feminine cosmic force, being dark, cold, north, submissive, weak, soft, negative, woman, and the moon. *Yang* stood for the male cosmic force, light, hot, south, dominant, strong, hard, positive, man, and sun. Their interaction was believed to cause the phenomena of the universe. (Also see Five Elements Theory.)

Ying, capital of the kingdom of Ch'u, usually associated with the rhapsodies and shamanistic chants of *The Songs of Ch'u*. Sung Yü was sometimes called 'the man from Ying'.

Ying Gate, the main south gate of a palace.

Yingchou, one of the names for fairyland in the east, thought to be one of the three sacred mountains in the Gulf of Chihli, the other two being P'englai and Fangchang.

Yingchow, a place in the region of Ch'i, the eastern state of ancient China, modern Shantung.

Yingmen Pass, see Goose Gate Pass.

Your collar, the title of poem 91 of *The Book of Songs*, in which a girl imagines the blue collar and belt jewels of her lover who has gone away.

Yü, a place in the region of modern Szechwan.

Yü, a princess, daughter of King Fu Ch'ai of Wu in the fifth century BC.

Yu and Chi, names meaning the north in general.

Yü Ch'ing (third century BC), a minister in the court of King Hsiao-ch'eng of Chao.

Yü Gulf, a mythological place where the sun sets.

Yüeh, the name of an ancient state in the region of modern Chekiang.

Yükuan, in modern Suiyüan, north of the bend of the Yellow river.

Yünchung, in the Pingchou region of Shensi, the border area where military defence was regularly maintained.

Yungchow, ancient name of the region west of the Yellow river.

APPENDIX

Hsü Ling's Preface to
New Songs from a Jade Terrace

Now,
Cloud-conqueror and Sun-high
Are palaces such as Yu Yü never glimpsed.
Their ten thousand gates, one thousand doors
Were once rhapsodised by Chang Heng.
On King Mu of Chou's jade-disc terrace,
In Emperor Wu of Han's House of Gold
There are jade trees with coral boughs,
Pearl blinds on tortoiseshell frames,
And within live beautiful women.

These beauties
Are aristocrats of Wu-ling,
Chosen for the imperial harem
From the best families of the Four Clans,
Celebrities of the seraglio.

There are also beauties from Ying-ch'uan and Hsinshih,
Lovelies from Hochien and Kuanchin
Who have long been called 'gracefully fair',
And named 'charming smiles'.

They are like ladies of King Ling of Ch'u's palace
Whose slender waists none failed to admire;
Or like beautiful girls of Wei kingdom
Whose delicate hands all marvelled at.
Our beauties are well-read in *The Book of Songs,* polished in *Rites,*
Quite different from the east neighbour who did her own matchmaking!
And they are nice, refined,
No different from Hsi Shih after she had been trained.
One beauty had a brother who harmonised the pipes,
So she studied singing from an early age;
Another grew up in Yang-o,
So from the first she was skilled in dance.
One beauty's new song for the lute
Did not wait for the poet Shih Ch'ung.
Another lady's lute medley
Did not look to Ts'ao Chih.
One lady inherited her drumming on the guitar from the Yang clan,
Another learned to blow the flute from the daughter of Ch'in.

So it seems that
When a favourite became well-known to Eternal Joy Palace
Empress Ch'en knew and grew disturbed.

339

And when a painting revealed a goddess,
The *Yen-chih* stared at it in distant envy.
The east girl with her charming smiles
Came to serve the royal bed at the Robe-changing.
Hsi-tzu, puckering her eyebrows,
Was bedded within luxurious curtains.
Another lady accompanied the emperor to Saso Palace
Where she moved her slim waist sinuously to *Whirlwind Music*.
Forever happy at Mandarin Duck Palace,
A lady plays new music to rhythmic tunes.

A beauty dresses her hair into wispy chirping cicada side-curls,
Sees reflected her tumbling fallen colt locks,
Inserts gold hairpins at the back,
Fixes a jewelled comb slantwise.
Black kohl from a southern city
Accentuates twin eyebrows,
Yen rouge from a northern place
Brings fine colour to two cheeks.

Also there are
A divine youth on a mountain peak
Who shared his drug pills with the Wei Emperor;
And one with a precious phoenix at his waist
Who presents his calendar to Hsüanyüan.

Gold stars rival the brilliance of the Wunü star,
Musk moons compete with Ch'ang O's sweet light.
From the flirtatious sleeves of a startled phoenix
There once hovered incense from Secretary Han.
The long skirts of a flying swallow
Were meant to be clasped by the Prince of Ch'en's girdle.
Though never painted in a portrait,
Our beauties are no different from that of the lady which hangs in
    Sweet Springs Palace.

So, although they are far from being goddesses,
They are indistinguishable from her who played at Sun Terrace.
They may truly be called
Beauties who ruin realms and cities,
Matchless and unique.

Besides,
Divine is their brilliance,

340

Exquisite their mind.
They superbly appreciate literature,
Are skilled in the craft of poetry.
Their coloured glass inkstone-case
Is beside them all day long,
Their kingfisher jade pen-case
Never for one moment leaves their hands.
The fine literary pieces cramming their cabinets
Are not just about peony blooms!
Their new compositions, verse after verse,
Are a marked advance on *The grapevine ode!*
When they climb a height on the Double Ninth
They often produce a poem of feeling.
On the Princess of Ten Thousand Years
They would not be shy of eulogistic phrases.
Our ladies' beauty is as I have described before,
Our ladies' gifted natures, too, are as I have just described.

And so,
Through labyrinthine spirals of pepper palaces,
Up mysterious elevations of thorn-tree halls,
Scarlet Crane keys impose privacy at dawn,
Bronze Clam knockers fall silent at noon.
Before the Three Stars twilight hour
The ladies are not summoned to bring their quilt.
Even five days seems too long –
For whom will they comb untidy hair?
Languidly idle with few distractions,
In quiet tranquillity with hours of leisure
They loathe Eternal Joy Palace's tardy bell,
Are weary of Central Hall's slow arrow of time.
So weak are their slender waists
They are daunted at washing clothes in Nanyang.
Brought up in secluded palaces
They delight in the Fufeng woven brocade.

Also, suppose
A palace lady is Jade Girl playing tosspot –
Her interest will flag by the hundredth throw!
Or she is a girl of Ch'i competing at draughts –
Her interest will die on the sixth move!
The palace lady takes no delight in idle hours,
But devotes her mind to the latest verse.
For poetry can

Be a substitute for the flower of oblivion,
And can banish the disease of ennui.

Yet
The famous works of former eras
And the artistic compositions of today,
Being as they are variously deposited in Unicorn Gallery
Or scattered in Hung city,
Unless I anthologise these literary pieces,
Our beauties will have no means to peruse them.

Therefore
Have I written, burning the midnight oil,
Wielding my pen over tomes at dawn.
I have selected love-songs,
Ten books in all.
They could never compare with the *Odes* and *Hymns,*
But they do reach the strict standard set by poets of the *Airs.*
Like the hiatus between Ching and Wei rivers
Is my method of selecting good from bad among love-songs.

Afterwards
These books were put under golden casing
And bound on luxury rollers.
Like the magnificent calligraphy of the Three Chancelleries,
Their script is in Dragon-coiling and Wriggling-caterpillar styles,
Written on coloured floral sheets
Of paper from Hopei and Chiaotung.
In lofty rooms red rouge
Revised copyist errors in the script.
Musk and the freshest incense
Will ward off Yüling bookworms.
Together with *Divine Flight* and *Titular Six*
My book will be kept in a jade box;
Together with *Brilliance Vast: The Art of Immortality*
It will always be tucked away in vermilion pillows.

So it seems that
Inside our ladies' black-ox curtains,
When their lingering lyrics have ended,
Beside the Vermilion Bird Window
When their cosmetics have been applied,
This is the very time when they will first undo bright book wrappers,
Scatter braided ribbons
And for long hours be diverted behind their reading drapes,
My book always open in slim hands.

Certainly my book will be quite different
From Empress Teng's study of *The Spring and Autumn Classic,*
For a scholar's attainments are too hard to acquire!
And my book will differ from Empress Tou's specialisation in
   Huang-Lao –
The art of gold-and-cinnabar can never be mastered!
Then, of course, my book will be superior to the case of
The well-born man of Western Shu
Who devoted his feeling to exhaustive recitation of *Lu Palace!*
And to the case of the Crown Prince at his imperial lodge
Whose repertoire of chant was limited to *The Cloistral Flute!*

Lovely the ladies of Ch'i!
They will always help to chase away the hours.
Pretty her red pen holder!
Beautiful her scented vanity-case!

Notes to the Preface

(in the order of their appearance in the text)

Yu Yü. In the Spring and Autumn era (722–481 BC) he went to the Jung territory of the west and was asked by their king to visit the Ch'in state to see the court of Duke Mu. There Yu Yü criticised the luxurious buildings of Duke Mu, noting that they could cause civic unrest.

Chang Heng. See Background to Poets and Poems, p. 350. Wrote *Prose Poem on the Western Capital* which has a line similar to this about gates and doors.

King Mu of Chou (trad. r. 1001–946 BC). Built a terrace of layered ceremonial jade-discs for his favourite concubine.

Emperor Wu of Han (r. 141–87 BC). See Notes, A-chiao, p. 296.

Wu-ling (Five Mounds). The burial place of Han emperors, situated in the suburbs of Ch'angan. Nearby was the residential area of the aristocracy. The five burial mounds were for Emperors Kao-tsu, Hui, Ching, Wu, and Chao who reigned between 202 and 74 BC.

Four Clans. The four most prominent non-imperial clans of the Later Han were the Fan, Kuo, Yin, and Ma.

Ying-ch'uan. A river in Honan. Said to be so pure that the legendary sage Hsü Yu rinsed his ears in it when he was sullied by Emperor Yao's offer to make him his minister. It is also an area famous for beautiful women. Hsinshih is in Hopei.

Hochien. In Hopei. One of Emperor Wu's consorts, Lady Chao, was discovered here through an omen. Kuanchin in Hopei was the birthplace of Empress Tou, consort of Emperor Wen of the Han, and mother of Emperor Ching.

slender waists. The fashion for slim waists was such in Ch'u state that courtiers starved themselves to look beautiful.

The Book of Songs, Rites. Two of the *Confucian Classics.*

east neighbour. In earlier literature there are many references to the east neighbour, implying a woman of doubtful morals. It was one of the rules of social decorum that marriages were conducted through the matchmaker.

Hsi Shih. See Notes, p. 312.

brother. See Notes, Lady Li, p. 316.

Yang-o. In Shansi. Probably a reference to Chao Feiyen, who came from here, was a skilled dancer, and became Emperor Ch'eng's concubine. See Notes, Chao Feiyen, p. 299.

Shih Ch'ung. See Notes, p. 326. His poem, *Wang Chao-chün's Farewell*, appears in Chapter Two. In his preface to that poem Shih Ch'ung pretends that he is merely citing the words of Wang Chao-chün herself.

lute medley. Probably a reference to a widow's lament for her husband who drowned, *Master, don't cross the river*. It was set to a tune called *Lute medley* by Li-yü, wife of a Korean who had heard the lament. Ts'ao Chih wrote a poem of the same title, but it is a feasting song. Its last couplet has a sepulchral tone.

Yang clan. Yang Yün of the Han Dynasty was from Chao state and was a skilled performer on the *se*, a stringed instrument.

daughter of Ch'in. See Notes, Nung Yü, p. 322.

Eternal Joy Palace. A reference to the success of Emperor Wu's new favourite, Wei Tzu-fu, who ousted Empress Ch'en from her position at court. Empress Ch'en retired to Eternal Gate Palace. Wei Tzu-fu had a son and, because Empress Ch'en was childless, became Empress Wei.

The *Yen-chih*. Title of the consort of a Hsiungnu chieftain. For the anecdote, see Notes, P'ingch'eng, p. 324.

Robe-changing. The girl associated with this phrase is Wei Tzu-fu, who was favoured by Emperor Wu when she helped him change his robes. In this context the 'east girl' is meant to be flattering (cf. pejorative usage, on p. 344).

Hsi-tzu. See Notes, Hsi Shih, p. 312.

Saso Palace. Pleasure resort of Han emperors.

Mandarin Duck Palace. See Notes, mandarin ducks, for meaning of the name, p. 319.

fallen colt locks, wispy chirping cicada side-curls. Two popular hair-styles in the Southern Dynasties period. See Notes, Lady Liang.

Yen. See Notes, p. 335.

divine youth, precious phoenix. This passage seems to be an interpolation, the meaning of its reference being unclear. The previous passage had been describing women's cosmetics, and the Preface continues in this vein after the interpolation. It may be that these lines are meant to suggest that the love poems include the theme of homosexual love.

Hsüanyüan. Another name for the Yellow Emperor. See Notes, p. 335.

calendar. A man called Ling Lun made twelve bamboo pipes and fixed their pitch according to the notes of male and female phoenixes. He paired these pipes with the calendrical months.

Gold stars, Musk moons. See Notes, yellow, p. 335.

Wunü star. See Notes.

Ch'ang O. See Notes.

startled phoenix. Descriptive phrase suggesting the nimble grace of a female dancer.

Secretary Han. He stole incense which was a tribute gift to the emperor – a crime. He gave it to the woman he loved, the daughter of Chia Ch'ung in the Chin Dynasty. Their affair was discovered.

flying swallow. A descriptive phrase suggesting a woman's graceful appearance.

Prince of Ch'en. One of the titles of Ts'ao Chih, see Notes. In his prose poem on the goddess of Lo river he described how he offered his jewelled girdle to the goddess as a love-token.

Sweet Springs Palace. See Notes. When Lady Li died (see Notes), Emperor Wu enshrined her portrait there.

Sun Terrace. See Notes.

ruin realms and cities. An allusion to poem 264 of *The Book of Songs*: 'The wise man builds a city, / The clever woman ruins it. / Lovely is that clever woman, / But an owl is she, a hooting owl!' See Notes, city-razing beauty.

peony blooms. Hsin Hsiao, the wife of Fu T'ung of the Chin Dynasty wrote a poem called *Paean to the peony*. The flower was given as a love-token.

The grapevine ode. An unidentified piece. See Notes, grapevines.

Double Ninth. A festival held on the ninth day of the ninth lunar month, when it was customary for people to go on an excursion. They would climb a height, drink wine with chrysanthemum petals, and compose poetry.

Princess of Ten Thousand Years. The title of the Chin emperor's daughter. When she died, the emperor requested his concubine, Tso Fen, who was a literary woman, to compose a lamentation for her.

pepper palaces. See Notes, pepper.

thorn-tree halls. The official name of the Shanglin Palace. The leaves of the thorn-tree were used for feeding silkworms.

Scarlet Crane, Bronze Clam. See Notes, keys.

Three Stars. See Notes.

five days. According to an ancient book of rites, a husband must make love with his wife at least once every five days until she reaches the age of fifty.

untidy hair. An allusion to poem 226 of *The Book of Songs*: 'My hair is untidy, / I go home and wash it. . . . / Five days he promised! / Six days and I still don't see him!'

Eternal Joy Palace. See Notes.

Central Hall. Name of an imperial harem.

washing clothes in Nanyang. South of the Han river there was a hill called Mount Maid, and its crest was called Maid Peak. At its bottom was a shrine called the Maid Shrine with a stone, Fulling Stone. There was a legend that Chang Lü's daughter used to wash her clothes there by beating them on the stone. Later she gave birth to two dragons. When she died her funeral carriage suddenly ascended the mountain, and she was buried there. Also see Notes, Nanyang.

Fufeng. A commandery in Shensi. An allusion to Su Hui's romantic palindrome woven in brocade. See Notes, palindrome.

Jade Girl. A reference to the legendary game between the Lord of the Eastern Kings and Jade Girl, in which there were 1,200 throws.

Unicorn Gallery. In the Han Dynasty there was a hall called the Unicorn where the archives were stored.

Hung city. The name of a palace gate building in the Han where books were stored.

Odes and *Hymns*. Comprise three of the four sections of *The Book of Songs*. Of the 305 poems in that collection there are 145 odes and hymns.

Airs. One of the sections of *The Book of Songs*, comprising 160 poems out of the total of 305. The airs were generally lighter verse than the odes and hymns, and many of them were folk love-songs traditionally believed to have been gathered from various parts of ancient China.

Ching and Wei rivers. In Shensi. There was a proverb that the Wei river is muddy and the Ching clear, but although the two rivers flow together for a hundred miles of their course they never become intermingled or confused. This simile implies that this modern selection of love-songs will not tarnish the traditional image of poesie.

Three Chancelleries. Imperial offices of the Han.

Hopei and Chiaotung. In Hopei and Shantung.

red rouge. Metonym for female copy editors.

Yüling bookworms. An allusion to the story of Emperor Mu whose books were riddled with bookworms when he was on his travels.

Divine Flight and *Titular Six*. Taoist classics. The Titular Six were divinities of the Taoist pantheon whose names were formed from compounds of the Ten Celestial Stems and the Twelve Branches. A court lady is said to have locked her copies of these books in a jade box.

Brilliance Vast. An esoteric book written by Liu An, Prince of Huainan (d. 123 BC), but no longer extant.

vermilion pillows. Pillows were hollow, vermilion was imperial.

black-ox. The Taoist philosopher Lao Tzu is said to have ridden a black ox, so it has become part of reclusive hagiography.

Vermilion Bird Window. This was probably a south facing window, since the attributes of the south included the colour red and the vermilion bird. An anecdote about the Han courtier Tung-fang Shuo tells how he peeped through such a window on the occasion of the legendary visit of the Queen Mother of the West (see Notes) to Emperor Wu.

Empress Teng. Said to have received instruction from Pan Chao (d. 116 BC, sister of the famous historian, Pan Ku), in the *Confucian Classics,* of which this was one.

Huang-lao. See Notes, Yellow Emperor, p. 335.

art of gold-and-cinnabar. The alchemical arts.

man of Western Shu. Liu Yen taught countless slave girls to recite the poem, *Prose Poem on Lu Ling-kuang Palace,* composed by Wang Yen-shou of the Later Han.

Crown Prince. Emperor Yüan of the Han (r. 49–33 BC) was so enamoured of this poem when he was Crown Prince that he made all his harem ladies recite it. The poem was a prose poem by Wang Pao.

ladies of Ch'i. Allusion to poem 39 of *The Book of Songs*: 'Lovely, all the Ch'i ladies! / I want to make plans with them!'

Background to Poets and Poems

Anonymous, *A Ditty of the Chin Emperor Hui's Era* (r. AD 290–307).

Anonymous, *A Ditty of the Han Era*, late first century AD. This originally appeared in 'The Biography of Ma Liao' in *The History of the Former Han* by Pan Ku (AD 32–92). Its other, more popular title was *The City Rhyme*, translated here as *Half across her forehead!*

Anonymous, *A Modern Miscellaneous Poem*, fifth century AD.

Anonymous, *A peacock southeast flew*, third or fourth century AD. A long narrative poem, rare in Chinese literature, it has 355 lines. The poem goes by another title, *An Old Poem Written for Chiao Chung-ch'ing's Wife*. The formulaic opening of the narrative contains an image popularly used in the folk-song tradition, that of a bird which becomes separated from its mate or its flock. The theme of separation is echoed in the closing section of the story when Chiao Chung-ch'ing commits suicide on a 'southeast' bough of a garden tree.

Anonymous, *Eight Old Poems*, middle of the Later Han, around AD 100. The first poem in this set is one of the most influential of the early love poems. Refrains from it appear in many poems in this anthology, imitating the bittersweet theme of a reluctant divorce. The fifth poem was also popular among later imitators, having the theme of a gift sent from a lover to his lady. Poems 2, 3, 4, and 5 are the equivalent of poems 16, 8, 17, and 18, respectively of *The Nineteen Old Poems*. The old poem, or *ku-shih*, is a five- or seven-syllable verse form. The last word of each couplet usually rhymes. The rhyme category may be the same throughout, or it may change in the course of the poem.

Anonymous, *Five Modern Western Songs*, ? fifth century AD, 'Western' in this context means the region of Hsiangyang, modern Hupei. Stone City gave its name to a certain kind of folk music and song to accompany dance, but later lost the association with dance. The third poem in this set was believed to have been composed by Liu I-ch'ing, Prince of Linch'üan (AD 403–44), the famous author of *New Tales of Society* (*Shih-shuo hsin-yü*). The fifth in the set is said to be a children's rhyme, and refers to the story that in AD 494 of the Ch'i Dynasty Yang Min, the son of a shamaness, was the Empress's lover.

Anonymous, *Four Old Chüeh-chü Poems*, ? third century AD. From their position in Chapter Ten, prior to poets of the third and fourth centuries, these four poems appear to belong to the third century, or slightly earlier. As such they would be the earliest prototypes of that verse form. The *Chüeh-chü* began as a short song in the popular tradition, linked to the folk-song, having four lines, with five or seven syllables per line. The name itself means 'cut-off lines'.

Anonymous, *Nine Miscellaneous Poems*, ? first or second century AD. Traditionally attributed to Mei Sheng (d. 149 BC), they are now, except for poem number 6, classified as anonymous poems in *The Nineteen Old Poems*. Poems 1–5, and 7–9 appear as poems 5, 12, 1, 6, 2, 9, 10, and 19, respectively of *The Nineteen Old Poems*. These are all seminal poems in the development of medieval love poetry, and attracted many later imitations.

Anonymous, *Nine Modern Wu Songs*, fifth century AD, from the region of Nanking. Wu was the name of the old kingdom on the southwest coast, south of the Yangtze river, in the region of Chekiang and Kiangsu. Such songs are sometimes also called 'Chiangnan Songs'.

Anonymous, *Six Old Folk-songs*, ? *c.* AD 100. The first is the famous narrative poem about Ch'in Lofu, of which refrains occur in many later love poems. It goes by several other titles: *The sun rises from the southeast corner suite, The Lofu Love-song suite,* and *Mulberry up the lane.* 'Suite' means a series of related stanzas linked to make one long poem. The second poem in this set is another favourite. Its theme is of marital harmony in a wealthy household. The fifth poem was traditionally thought to have been composed by Cho Wen-chün, wife of the Han poet Ssu-ma Hsiang-ju, when he tried to take another girl as his new bride. 'Folk-song' is used as a general term for the poetic form called *yüeh-fu*. Originally this term meant the Bureau of Music established by the Han Emperor Wu *c.* 120 BC. It then came to mean those anonymous folk-songs collected by officials attached to this Bureau. Later still the term meant folk-songs in general, whether they were genuine folk pieces or polished imitations by named poets. They are characterised by narrative, formulaic, and musical elements, by simple diction, bold imagery, and punning devices. The earlier type of *yüeh-fu* was metrically irregular, while the later version was metrically inseparable from the old poem or *ku-shih*.

Anonymous, *Song of the Yüeh Boatman*, first recorded in the first century BC by Liu Hsiang, it derives from an earlier oral tradition of Yüeh, and was then transcribed into the Ch'u dialect. It has in its present form elements of the *sao*-song style, similar to some poems in *The Songs of Ch'u*. This poem is often quoted in later love poems having a homosexual theme.

Anonymous, *Three Modern Miscellaneous Songs*, fifth century AD. They are songs for accompaniment to percussion, bells, and wind instruments, but not for strings.

Anonymous, *Two Ditties of the Han Emperor Ch'eng's Era* (r. 33–7 BC). The first of the rhymes appears at the end of Chao Feiyen's biography in *The History of the Former Han*, where it is implied that she was instrumental in causing the death of Emperor Ch'eng. That version ends with the couplet: 'The princes died, / Swallow pecks their turds'. Similarly, another version of *Cassia* starts with the couplet: 'Crooked paths ruin fine fields, / Gossiping tongues confuse honest men'. Such rhymes were believed to be prophetic and were often included by historians into their biographies of the famous or infamous. Despite the historian's censure in her biography, Chao Feiyen enjoys the status of a romantic heroine in the pages of these love poems.

Anonymous, *Two Ditties of the Han Emperor Huan's Era* (r. AD 147–68). During the years AD 151–3 the Ch'iang tribe of Kansu rebelled and invaded Szechwan and Shensi, inflicting great damage. Chinese punitive expeditions against them failed. Because of all this military activity, the seasonal labour of harvesting was neglected and the work had to be carried out by the

349

womenfolk. Local officials requisitioned all forms of transportation, making farming even more difficult.

Anonymous, *Two Song Lyrics,* ? Han Dynasty, or ? Liang Dynasty. Their position at the beginning of Chapter Nine prior to a poem datable from the first century BC suggests that they are of that era or slightly earlier. Their form, however, the regular seven-word metre, clearly indicates that they are much later. One popular theory is that they belong to the sixth century AD and were put in the wrong chronological section. Another theory is that they were written by Hsiao Yen.

Chang Heng, courtesy name P'ing-tzu, AD 78–139, from Honan. A poet, astronomer, and mathematician of the Later Han era, he wrote famous prose poems on the twin capitals of Ch'angan and Loyang. His poem in Chapter One is entitled *Like sounds,* a phrase originating in *The Book of Changes (I ching),* one of the *Confucian Classics.* The original passage is: 'Like sounds accord with each other, / Like minds seek each other out'. His four poems in Chapter Nine called *Four Sorrows* were based on the *tristia* of *The Songs of Ch'u,* and were themselves imitated by later poets.

Chang Hsieh, courtesy name Ching-yang, *fl. c.* AD 295, from Shantung. Younger brother of Chang Tsai. Known with him and Chang Hua as the 'Three Changs' of literature. Ranked as a major poet in the Southern Dynasties, only twelve poems survive.

Chang Hua, courtesy name Mao-hsien, AD 232–300, from Hopei. Rose from poverty to wealth and status through literary talent. (See Chang Heng.) Served as minister of state in the Chin Dynasty. Became a famous scholar and was appointed as junior tutor to the heir apparent. He wrote the *Treatise on Investigating Phenomena (Po wu chih),* which survives in a reconstructed fragment. Executed for espousing the cause of Empress Chia against the Prince of Chao. The first line of the first of his series of five love poems echoes that of Li Yen-nien in Chapter One.

Chang Shuai, courtesy name Shih-chien, AD 475–527, from Kiangsu. Served the Liang as deputy of the imperial chancellory and later became a prefect of Hsinan. Transferred for irresponsibility, he became an official for Hsiao Kang in AD 509 for a decade. His poetry won the admiration of Hsiao Yen, Emperor Wu. He was a prolific writer and his lifetime compositions amounted to thirty tomes. His first poem in Chapter Six is an imitation of the old ballad which appears in Chapter One as *A grand house.*

Chang Tsai, courtesy name Meng-yang, *c.* AD 289, from Hopei. Older brother of Chang Hsieh, also a poet. He attracted the attention of the Chin Emperor Wu by his moral inscription on a mountain pass in Szechwan. He served the heir apparent as secretary, but retired early from politics. His four imitative poems may be compared with those by Chang Heng and Fu Hsüan in Chapter Nine, entitled *Four Sorrows.*

Chen Ku, ? *fl.* early sixth century AD. Biographical data scant. One of his poems is modelled on one by Hsiao Kang, suggesting a possible connection with the Liang court.

Ch'en Lin, courtesy name K'ung-chang, d. AD 217, from Kiangsu. One of the 'Seven Masters of the Chien-an Era (196–220)'. He held office with Yüan Shao and Ts'ao Ts'ao as secretary. The poem by him in Chapter One is not in the regular five-syllable metre featured in this part of the anthology, but in a mixed metre. Because it belongs to an early period *vis-à-vis* the Liang, and because it comes immediately after one having the same title by

Ts'ai Yung (?), it remains here rather than in Chapter Nine which features irregular metres.

Chi Shao-yü, courtesy name Yu-ch'ang, c. AD 535, from the area of Chienk'ang, the Liang capital, modern Nanking. While Hsiao Kang was Crown Prince, he became an erudit in the Eastern Palace, the heir apparent's official residence, in AD 541. He also served other Liang princes, such as Hsiao Chi and Hsiao Lun, also poets. The theme of Chienhsing Park in the capital city was popular, and Chi's treatment of it may be compared with that by Yü Chien-wu in Chapter Eight.

Chia Ch'ung, courtesy name Kung-lü, AD 217–82, from Shansi. He inherited the title of Marquess. He served the Ssu-ma family and helped them defeat the last Wei emperor, thus inaugurating the Chin Dynasty. Enfeoffed as the Duke of Lu and made prime minister. Said to have died from shame when the Chin attack against the kingdom of Wu, which policy he had vetoed, met with great success. Branded as a traitor in some later histories. His wife, Lady Li, was the daughter of Li Feng who had been executed for a crime.

Chiang Hung, c. AD 502, from Honan. Served the Liang Dynasty, but died because of his involvement with a political scandal. His name was linked with the poet Wu Chün, and the few details known of his life mostly appear in the latter's official biography.

Chiang Po-yao, ? mid-sixth century AD. Biographical data scant. Invited by Hsiao Kang to become one of the 'Ten Scholars of the Lofty Studio' to work on the imperial library.

Chiang Yen, courtesy name Wen-t'ung, AD 444–505, from Honan. Probably a poor orphan, he rose to high office because of his wide scholarship. Served the last Ch'i emperors and Hsiao Yen, the first Liang emperor. He was one of the 'Eight Comrades', a literary group whose patron was Hsiao Yen. Ennobled as the Marquess of Liling. His poetry, prose poems, essays, and so forth, amounted to over a hundred volumes, two volumes of which survive. He admired the poet Ssu-ma Hsiang-ju. The second of his poems in the old style in Chapter Five is modelled on Regret attributed to Lady Pan, translated in Chapter One, and the fourth, Unhappy parting, is modelled on the poet T'ang Seng-chi, also known as Hsiu Shang-jen.

Ch'in Chia, courtesy name Shih-hui, fl. c. AD 147, from Kansu. Later editors tacked a preface onto his three poems to his wife (in Chapter One) to provide a biographical context for them. It reads: 'Ch'in Chia, styled Shih-hui, was from Lunghsi. When he was promoted to commandery inspector at the capital, his wife, Hsü Shu, was ill and had returned home. Unable to say goodbye to her personally, Ch'in Chia had these poems conveyed to her'. Lunghsi is in Kansu. Prose letters linked to the poems survive. Ch'in Chia died young.

Ch'iu Ch'ih, courtesy name Hsi-fan, AD 464–508, from Chekiang. He served the Ch'i Dynasty and then the Liang under Emperor Wu, Hsiao Yen. He was a favourite at court. One volume of his work survives.

Ch'iu Chü-yüan, fl. c. 457, d. c. AD 484. Little is known about him. He served under the Liu-Sung Emperor Hsiao-wu, the poet Liu Chün.

?Fairy of Wuhsing, early sixth century AD, from Chekiang. Probably the name of a professional female entertainer. She presented a love poem to Hsieh Lan, perhaps when he was a senior official in Wuhsing.

Fan Ch'in, courtesy name Hsiu-po, ? d. AD 218, from Honan. Served under Ts'ao Ts'ao, founder of the Wei Dynasty.

Fei Ch'ang, *fl. c.* AD 510, from Hupei. Little is known about him today, but he was appreciated as an important poet in his own time.

Fu Hsüan, courtesy name Hsiu-i, AD 217–78, from Shensi. Rose from poverty and obscurity to wealth and fame through his literary talent. Served as censor and lord chamberlain under the Chin Emperor Wu. All that survives of his *oeuvre* of one hundred volumes are sixty-three poems, mostly folk-songs. His poem entitled *A pure wife* in Chapter Two of this translation is called in the original *Harmonising with Mr Pan's poem,* and is tradition-ally believed to refer to the Han historian, Pan Ku, to whom several other works are spuriously ascribed. But Pan Ku did not compose such a poem, and the only other piece by him to which Fu Hsüan's poem might refer is actually a piece on a filial daughter. Fu Hsüan's theme is on a chaste wife. Perhaps an earlier, unidentified narrative poem was the model. Later editors dubbed some of his folk-songs 'northern' because they were meant to contrast with the southern style that emerged after the partition of China into north and south after AD 317. One of his so-called imitations of northern folk-songs in Chapter Nine, translated under the title *Past autumn's nine,* is subtitled *Tung Cho's flight,* the name of a children's rhyme dating from the Later Han which tells of the eventual defeat of Tung Cho, who sacked Loyang in AD 190. But this subtitle bears no relation to the content of his poem.

Ho Man-ts'ai, ? mid-sixth century AD, biographical data scant.

Ho Ssu-ch'eng, courtesy name Wu-ching, ? AD 481–?534, from Kiangsu. Served the Prince of Nank'ang and the Prince of Wuling, the poet Hsiao Chi. His poem on Lady Pan in Chapter Six, commissioned by Hsiao I, may be compared with that of K'ung Weng-kuei, similarly commissioned and in the same chapter.

Ho Sun, courtesy name Chung-yen, d. *c.* AD 517, from Shantung. Served the Liang as the secretary of the Prince of Luling. The poet Shen Yüeh particularly admired his poetry, and contemporaries ranked him with Liu Hsiao-cho. Over one hundred of his poems survive. His imagination and artistry mark him as one of the major poets of the Southern Dynasties.

Ho Tzu-lang, courtesy name Shih-ming, b. *c.* AD 479, d. *c.* 522, from Shantung. With Ho Ssu-ch'eng and Ho Sun, he was called by the group name of 'The Three Ho of Tunghai'. His two poems in Chapter Five entitled *Bronze steps* and *A measure of wine* are probably modelled on poems by Hsieh T'iao and Yü Ch'ien.

?Hsi-chün, the Princess of the Wusun, ? 110 BC. Daughter of Liu Chien, the Prince of Chiangtu, and related to the Han Emperor Wu. She was sent in marriage to a chieftain of the Wusun tribe in the region of modern Lake Balkash (U.S.S.R.) and Sinkiang. Her poem translated as *Lost horizon* in Chapter Nine features the *hsi* sound-carrier particle in each line, reminiscent of the *sao*-song style of *The Songs of Ch'u.*

Hsiao Chi, AD 508–53. Eighth son of Emperor Wu of the Liang, Hsiao Yen. Enfeoffed as the Prince of Wuling. In AD 552 he proclaimed himself emperor, but within a year was assassinated by his brother, Hsiao I, who had meanwhile proclaimed himself Emperor Yüan.

Hsiao I, AD 507–55. Enfeoffed as the Prince of Hsiangtung. He proclaimed himself Emperor Yüan of the Liang in AD 552, a year after his older brother, Hsiao Kang, had been assassinated. He moved the capital from Chienk'ang to Chiangling. He was the seventh son of Hsiao Yen. While still a prince, he was served by several Liang poets, and many poem titles in this anthology are addressed to him as patron. He was well-known not only as a poet, but also as a fine painter. His brother, Hsiao Kang, called him 'my Tzu-chien', an eulogistic reference to a great poet of the third century, Ts'ao Chih, whose courtesy name was Tzu-chien. Two years after becoming emperor, Hsiao I was asphyxiated with a heavy sack of sand.

Hsiao Kang, AD 503–51. Became heir apparent in AD 531 when his brother Hsiao T'ung died. He was the third son of Hsiao Yen, and succeeded his father in AD 549 as Emperor Chienwen of the Liang. He was assassinated two years later by the Tartar general, Hou Ching. A statesman of great erudition and literary talent, he was interested in philosophy, religion, literary theory and composition, and surrounded himself with the outstanding literary personalities of the day. He was a believer in Buddhism. Hsü Ling's father was his tutor, as was Yü Chien-wu, a famous poet and father of the poet Yü Hsin. Hsiao Kang is credited with the development of a new form of love poetry called 'Palace Style Poetry', featuring a noblewoman languishing from unhappy love in a richly furnished boudoir. Its main characteristics, however, are now generally thought to have been elaborated by several poets in his entourage, including Hsü Ling's father, Hsü Ch'ih, and Yü Chien-wu. It is traditionally believed that Hsiao Kang commissioned Hsü Ling to compile *New Songs from a Jade Terrace* in order to immortalise the new type of love poem with the finest examples of his day. His own poetry reveals great artistry and a sensitive, individual imagination. The title *Night after night* in Chapter Ten is elsewhere listed as a composition by Shen Yüeh.

Hsiao Lin, ? *fl.* mid-sixth century AD, biographical data scant.

Hsiao Lun, AD 507–51. Enfeoffed as the Prince of Shaoling in AD 519. Younger brother of Hsiao Kang, sixth son of Hsiao Yen. In the histories he is presented as a base tyrant. In AD 532 he was temporarily reduced to the status of a commoner for his involvement in a brutal murder. Like many members of the Hsiao family, he participated in Buddhist ceremonial and attended services in many different Buddhist temples. His poem translated as *A pure wife* in Chapter Seven may be compared with poems treating the same theme of Ch'iu Hu by Fu Hsüan in Chapter Two and by Yen Yen-chih in Chapter Four.

Hsiao Tzu-hsien, courtesy name Ching-yang, AD 489–537, from Shantung. Grandson of the founder of the Ch'i Dynasty, Emperor Kai, and related to the Liang royal house. Enfeoffed as the Marquess of Ningtu. He wrote *The History of the Southern Ch'i Dynasty*, spanning the years AD 479-501. He became head of the Board of Civil Office and later served as governor of Wuhsing in Chekiang. His imitative folk-song, *Sunrise at the southeast corner,* in Chapter Eight, may be compared with the original, *Mulberry up the lane* in Chapter One. His other poem there may be compared with the same title by Ts'ao Chih in Chapter Two, *A beautiful woman.* Two of his poems in Chapter Nine, *No regrets* and *Tearstained mascara,* are elsewhere attributed to Hsiao I.

Hsiao Yen, courtesy name Shu-ta, AD 464–549, from Kiangsu. Founder of the Liang Dynasty, reigning as Emperor Wu from AD 502 until 549, the longest reign in the Southern Dynasties era. Though a distant relative of the Ch'i royal family, he took up arms against the last Ch'i emperor because he had executed Hsiao Yen's eldest brother. Shen Yüeh advised Hsiao Yen to found his own dynasty. A devout Buddhist, he became a monk twice, retiring to a monastery three times in his lifetime. He was a man of great learning and

353

considerable poetic ability, as were two of his sons, Hsiao T'ung, compiler of *Anthology of Literature*, and Hsiao Kang, poet and patron of *New Songs from a Jade Terrace*. Hsiao Yen formed a literary group called the 'Eight Comrades of Chingling', consisting of himself, Shen Yüeh, Hsieh T'iao, Wang Yung, Fan Yün, Hsiao Ch'in, Jen Fang, and Lu Ch'ui, the first three of whom are poets represented in this anthology. Some of the poems listed under his name in Chapter Ten are elsewhere attributed to other authors: some of his *Spring, Summer, and Autumn Songs*, the poems from *I can't resist* to *It's clear*, eleven in all, belong to the poems entitled *Tzu-yeh Seasonal Songs*, Tzu-yeh being the name of a professional singer of the fourth century AD. Another source lists *I can't resist* and *Sprays to send my darling* as compositions by a poet called Wang Chin-chu. Also, two poems entitled *Tzu-yeh Songs*, translated here as *Shy love* and *Morning sun*, are listed among the cycle of forty-two songs believed to have been composed by the singer Tzu-yeh, Child of Night, herself. *Richer than gold* is again attributed elsewhere to Wang Chin-chu, while *Jasper* is listed as anonymous in other anthologies.

Hsieh Hui-lien, AD 397–433. Younger cousin of Hsieh Ling-yün, from Honan. Served the Liu-Sung Dynasty as a top official in the judiciary under Prince I-k'ang of P'engch'eng. His poem in Chapter Three, translated as *A gown near my body*, is based on the early anonymous folk-song appearing in Chapter One, *Joy of Love quilt*, and may be compared with Pao Ling-hui's version in Chapter Four entitled *In the key of farewell*.

Hsieh Ling-yün, AD 385–433, from Honan. Came from a noble and famous family of distinguished statesmen, and was entitled Duke of K'anglo. At the fall of the Chin Dynasty he pledged support for the Liu-Sung in AD 419. Exiled because of envious enemies, he was forced to live in obscurity on his estate. He became a Buddhist convert and wrote religious treatises. While in Chekiang and Kiangsi he was influenced by the splendid scenery of hills and lakes, brilliantly describing them in his poems. With T'ao Ch'ien he is ranked as the earliest nature poet in Chinese literature. Admired by Li Po and Tu Fu. He was executed in Canton on false charges. Over a hundred poems survive.

Hsieh T'iao, courtesy name Hsüan-hui, AD 464–99, from Honan. Served the Ch'i Emperor Ming as head of the Bureau of Civil Offices. Later he was imprisoned for failing to support the rebellion of Lord Tung-hun, and died in prison. He was a distant relative of the Hsieh family famous in the annals of literature with such names as Hsieh Ling-yün and Hsieh Hui-lien. Shen Yüeh said in admiration of Hsieh T'iao's poetry, 'We have not had poetry like this for two hundred years!' He was one of the 'Eight Comrades', Hsiao Yen's literary group. He was also admired by Li Po. About 150 poems survive, mostly lyrics.

?Hsin Yen-nien, second century AD. Nothing is known of him. His poem in Chapter One, *The Imperial Guards officer*, apparently refers to the cavalry brigade patrolling the imperial palace called the *Yü-lin*, but the man featured in the poem is a slave.

Hsü Chün-ch'ien, courtesy name Huai-chien, early sixth century AD, from Shantung. Was administrative adviser to Hsiao I, when the latter was a general.

Hsü Fei, courtesy name Ching-yeh, d. AD 524. Second son of Hsü Mien who held high office under the Liang. He died eleven years before his father. He was a page to the heir apparent and later served as his equerry. Was a friend of Hsiao I. His wife was Liu Ling-hsien, younger sister of Liu Hsiao-cho, and a poetess in her own right. Examples of their letter-poems appear in Chapter Six.

Hsü Kan, courtesy name Wei-chang, AD 171–218. One of the 'Seven Masters of the Chien-an Era'. He came from Shantung. He served under Ts'ao Ts'ao. His set of six pieces entitled *Bedroom longing*, which appear in Chapter One, was greatly admired by generations of poets, and the third piece's last quatrain beginning with 'Ever since you went away' was frequently imitated. He was famous in his day for rendering Nâgârdjuna's *Pranyamûla Shâstra Tîkâ* into Chinese as *Essay on the Middle Way*.

Hsü Ling, courtesy name Hsiao-mu, AD 507–83, from Shantung. His father, Hsü Ch'ih, was tutor to Hsiao Kang while he was a young prince, and he introduced Hsü Ling to the prince's court. He showed a penchant for scholarship and literature from an early age. He served Hsiao Yen as a minister of state. He enjoyed Hsiao Kang's patronage, being included in his literary circle with many leading literary lights of the day. Between AD 531 and 549 – the precise date is not known – Hsiao Kang is traditionally believed to have commissioned Hsü Ling to compile *New Songs from a Jade Terrace*. He was one of the poets identified with the new form of love poetry known as 'Palace Style Poetry', which he well represented in his anthology. Later in his career, which outlasted the Liang Dynasty, he was sent as an envoy to the north and temporarily captured during dynastic upheavals. He eventually returned south to serve the new Ch'en Dynasty which had replaced the Liang in AD 557.

Hsü Shu, *fl. c.* mid-second century AD. Ch'in Chia's wife. One of her poems, *Response to my husband* in Chapter One, answers one of his letter-poems to her. Written in the *sao*-song metre (four syllables with an intervening *hsi* sound carrier particle), it barely qualifies as a poem for inclusion in that chapter, otherwise devoted to pentasyllabic poetry, but appears there alongside her husband's poem.

Hsü Yao, courtesy name ? Yao-chih, ? late fifth century AD. Little is known about him.

Hsün Ch'ang, courtesy name Mao-tsu, *c.* AD 420, from Honan. Became deputy head of an imperial secretariat under the Liu-Sung in the mid-420s. His two folk-songs in Chapter Three, *A grand house* and *Green, green riverside grass*, imitate the same titles among the anonymous series in Chapter One.

Juan Chi, courtesy name Ssu-tsung, AD 210–63, from Honan. Popularly known by his official title, Pu-ping, or chief of infantry. He was one of the 'Seven Sages of the Bamboo Grove', a literary-philosophical group given to discussing intellectual matters. He was a gifted poet, thinker, and musician. He is reputed to have drunk excessively, partly as a critical gesture against the political authorities. His literary legacy includes eighty-two poems in a series called *Poems from my Heart (Yung huai shih)*, numbers 2 and 12 of which appear in Chapter Two here. He was very much in vogue during the T'ang Dynasty.

Kao Shuang, *c.* AD 502, from Kiangsu. Served under the Ch'i and Liang Dynasties.

K'ung Weng-kuei, *fl. c.* AD 539, from Kweichi. Served as secretary to the Prince of Nanp'ing.

?Lady Pan, *fl. c.* 48–6 BC. Her first name is not known. Her official title, *chieh-yü*, or Beautiful Companion, indicates that she was a high-ranking lady in the palace. She entered the Han harem, becoming a favourite concubine of Emperor Ch'eng. Both her sons died in infancy. Later she was discarded by the emperor in favour of a girl dancer called Chao Feiyen. It was traditionally believed that Lady Pan composed *Regret*, popularly known as the *Round fan poem*, when she lost imperial favour. It has many imitators. Although she was a noted poetess in her day, none of her work survives.

Li Ch'ung, courtesy name Hung-tu, *fl. c.* AD 323, from Hupei. Served the Eastern Chin Dynasty as an imperial documents editor. Later he became a privy councillor. He was a noted calligrapher. Author of miscellaneous works, including poetry, a treatise on Buddhism and Taoism, and a satire on excessively bookish scholars.

Li Yen-nien, *c.* 140–87 BC. Court musician and entertainer in the reign of the Han Emperor Wu. He had a beautiful sister whose praises he sang in *A song*, Chapter One, before the emperor. The emperor was introduced to her and she became his favourite concubine. She received the title of *Fu-jen*, translated as 'Lady'. He was promoted to the rank of Harmoniser of the Tones. His poem is considered to be the earliest example of the five-syllable metre, and belongs to the *ko-shih*, sung poem, category.

Liu, Wang Shu-ying's wife, late fifth to early sixth century AD. Younger sister of Liu Hsiao-cho, and Liu Ling-hsien's sister. Little is known about her. Also see Liu Ling-hsien.

Liu Chün, courtesy name Hsui-lung, AD 430–64, from Kiangsu. Third son of Emperor Wen of the Liu-Sung Dynasty. He acceded to the throne in AD 454 as Emperor Hsiao-wu. Depicted in the histories as a pleasure-seeking spend-thrift. One of his poems imitates the latter part of Hsü Kan's *Bedroom longing* which appears in Chapter One; Liu Chün's version is translated as *Round and round* and appears in Chapter Ten.

Liu Hsiao-cho, courtesy name Hsiao-cho, AD 481–539, from Kiangsu. He enjoyed the patronage of both Emperor Wu of the Liang and of Hsiao T'ung while the latter was the Crown Prince Chao-ming. He held different governmental posts.

Liu Hsiao-i, courtesy name ? Hsiao-i, ? early to mid-sixth century AD. Younger brother of Liu Hsiao-cho and brother of Liu Hsiao-wei. Was well received by Hsiao Kang while he was crown prince. His short poem in Chapter Ten entitled *Weaver* is elsewhere attributed to Liu Hsiao-wei.

Liu Hsiao-wei, courtesy name Hsiao-wei, d. AD 548. Younger brother of Liu Hsiao-cho, and Liu Hsiao-i's brother. He enjoyed the patronage and friend-ship of Hsiao Kang, while he was crown prince, and of Hsiao I, the Prince of Hsiangtung. His two poems at the very end of Chapter Ten are clearly 'encores' added by later editors, since Liu appears earlier in that same chapter.

Liu Huan, courtesy name Han-tu, *c.* AD 549, from Shantung. Served Hsiao I as secretary. One of his poems was written in honour of a man called Liu who was a senior official in Hsiao I's service, and three others are modelled on Hsiao I's poems, all four poems appearing in Chapter Eight.

Liu Hung, ? mid-sixth century AD. Little is known about him.

Liu Ling-hsien, Hsü Fei's wife, Liu Hsiao-cho's sister, ? from late fifth century to early sixth century AD. She was the sister of the poetess listed as Liu, Wang Shu-ying's wife. Of Liu Hsiao-cho's three sisters, Ling-hsien was the most literary. When her husband, Hsü Fei, died in AD 524, his father, the man of letters and top official Hsü Mien, decided to compose a funerary oration, but when he saw Ling-hsien's funerary prayer he is said to have thrown down his pen in a gesture of defeat. Two of her poems in response to her husband appear in Chapter Six, where his to her also appear somewhat earlier. She also seems to be the author of the last poem in Chapter Six, which was written, according to some commentators, to her late husband's mistress named T'ang Niang. Either this was added by a later editor as another example of her poetry, or another example of Hsü Fei's, or else it is by neither of them, but by an unknown author. The same kind of confusion exists with poems tacked onto the end of Chapter Eight, where they clearly do not belong in chronological terms. Besides this temporal confusion, there is some doubt concerning the identity of the female poet called Liu, sometimes listed as Hsü Fei's wife, sometimes listed as Wang Shu-ying's wife.

Liu Miao, ? mid-sixth century AD, from Kiangsu. It seems he was taken prisoner by the Tartar general, Hou Ching, perhaps in AD 552 when the Liang capital of Chienk'ang had been captured.

Liu Shuo, courtesy name Hsiu-hsüan, AD 431–53, from Kiangsu. Fourth son of the Liu-Sung Emperor Wen. At the age of nine he was enfeoffed as the Prince of Nanp'ing. By the time he was twenty he had composed more than thirty imitations of old poems, a source of wonder among his contemporaries. He served as a general of the Army of the Centre, but was killed in his early twenties during the closing years of his father's reign. His poems at the end of Chapter Three are imitations of several of the anonymous old poems appearing in Chapter One.

Liu Tsun, courtesy name Hsiao-ling, d. AD 535, from Kiangsu. He was a cousin of Liu Hsiao-cho. While Hsiao Kang was still the Prince of Chinan (from AD 506 to 531), he was in his service as his secretary. Later, when Hsiao Kang became crown prince, he enjoyed a position of trust and favour at his court. Some of his poems were directly commissioned by Hsiao Kang, for example *Gay* in Chapter Eight.

Liu Yün, courtesy name Wen-ch'ang, AD 465–511, from Shantung. Held office under the first Liang Emperor as a senior official, and then as prefect of Wuhsing. His name is linked with that of Shen Yüeh in the formulation of the new tonal rules in poetry. His poems on fulling are based on a popular folk theme which many poets in this anthology imitated, such as Ts'ao P'i and Hsieh Hui-lien in Chapter Three, and Hsiao Yen in Chapter Seven.

Lu Chi, courtesy name Shih-heng, AD 261–303, from Kiangsu. His grandfather had helped to found the Wu kingdom, and when it was later conquered by the Chin Dynasty in AD 280, Lu Chi went into hiding. He went to Loyang ten years later and served the Chin. He was sponsored by the poet Chang Hua at the Chin court. Accused of treason, he and his two sons and brother were executed. His brother, Lu Yün, was also a famous poet. Hsiao T'ung included over one hundred of his poems in his *Anthology of Literature*. He is famous for his *Prose Poem on Literature,* a discursive, evaluative piece written in metaphorical language. His poems in Chapter Three are imitations of the anonymous *Nine Miscellaneous Poems* in Chapter One, followed by letter-poems written for a man called Ku Yen-hsien who also came from Wu. Lu Yün also composed letter-poems for this same Ku.

Lu Chüeh, courtesy name Han-ch'ing, AD 472–99, from Kiangsu. When his father and brother were executed, he was so heartbroken that he pined to death.

Lu Yün, courtesy name Shih-lung, AD 262–303. Younger brother of Lu Chi.

He also went to Loyang and served Ssu-ma Ying of the Chin royal house. Chang Hua was his sponsor, too, and secured a post for him at court. He was executed with his brother on charges of treason. They are known in literary history as 'the Two Lu'. The two brothers' poems may be compared in the epistolary style, poems written on behalf of Ku Yen-hsien, in Chapter Three.

Meng Chu, ? fifth century AD, from Tanyang in the region of Anhwei. Meng Chu was the name of a professional female singer.

P'an Yüeh, courtesy name An-jen, ? AD 247–300, from Honan. Served the Chin Dynasty as equerry and archivist to Grand Marshal Chia Ch'ung, and later served in the central secretariat. Famous for his poetry and his good looks. It was said that when he drove through Loyang women used to mob him, offering him peaches (the emblem of immortality, or eternal youth). He was a dominant figure in the literary group called 'Twenty-four Fellows'. Charged with treasonous involvement in the revolt of the Prince of Ch'i, he was executed. Of his fifteen extant poems those lamenting his dead wife are considered the finest. He was ranked in the Southern Dynasties as a major poet.

Pao Chao, courtesy name Ming-yüan, AD ?412–?66, from Kiangsu. Served in several posts under the Liu-Sung Emperor Hsiao-wu, the poet Liu Chün. He was assassinated by rioting soldiers when his patron, Liu Tzu-hsü, the Prince of Linhai, was forced to commit suicide for rebellion. Traditionally ranked with the poets Hsieh Ling-yün and Yen Yen-chih, he was esteemed by the T'ang poets, Li Po and Tu Fu. He is now generally regarded as a major poet of the Southern Dynasties, especially for his ballads and innovative developments in the folk-song genre. Of his surviving *oeuvre* of about two hundred poems, one-third are ballads, the best known ones being eighteen poems in the series *The road is hard*, four of which appear in Chapter Nine. Many other poets wrote on this theme, such as Shih Pao-yüeh, Wu Chün, Fei Ch'ang, and Wang Yün, all four of whom are also represented in Chapter Nine. One of Pao Chao's imitations of old ballads may be compared with the original, such as *Today a keg of wine*, the original on which *Jealous hate* in Chapter Four is based. His two poems in Chapter Four entitled *To my former love* go by the title *To Ma Tzu-ch'iao* in other editions. It is not clear who this person was, but it would be a man rather than a woman, and if this is the correct title, then Pao Chao probably wrote it for the man's wife, or former mistress.

Pao Ch'üan, courtesy name Jun-yüeh, d. AD 552, from Tunghai. Served Hsiao I when he was the Prince of Hsiangtung, and when he became Emperor Yüan continued in the imperial employ.

Pao Ling-hui, *fl. c.* AD 464. Younger sister of Pao Chao. Little else is known about her. Many of her poems imitate earlier models, particularly the anonymous old poems featured in Chapter One.

Pao Tzu-ch'ing, early sixth century AD. Little is known about him.

Shen Man-yüan, *c.* AD 540. She was Fan Ching's wife and Shen Yüeh's granddaughter. Her husband served the Liang Dynasty.

Shen Yüeh, courtesy name Hsiu-wen, AD 441–512, from Chekiang. Served three successive dynasties, the Liu-Sung, the Ch'i, and the Liang, achieving the rank of head of the imperial secretariat. Because his grandfather and father before him had been executed, he pursued a career in politics with utmost caution. He was one of the 'Eight Comrades', Hsiao Yen's literary group. He is credited with classifying, together with Liu Yün, the four tones of literary Chinese and of evolving a system of tonal harmony which were fully developed into basic prosodic rules in the T'ang. He was a great scholar, owning a reputed library of 20,000 books, including works on Confucianism, Buddhism, and Taoism. He wrote histories of the Chin (no longer extant), of the Liu-Sung, and of the Ch'i Dynasties. He developed the art of love poetry, capturing with sensitivity the feelings of lovers. His poetry was very popular in his own day. Two hundred or so of his poems survive.

Shih Ch'ung, courtesy name Chi-lun, AD 249–300, from Hopei. He was ennobled for his service to the Chin Dynasty, and was a favourite of Emperor Wu. He became extremely wealthy through maritime trade, and lived ostentatiously, having a well-known rivalry with Wang K'ai as to who could be more extravagant. He owned a magnificent park northwest of Loyang called Golden Vale where he used to entertain with lavish banquets. He was a member of the literary group called 'Twenty-four Fellows'. He had a concubine named Green Pearl, a beautiful entertainer who used to perform dance and music for his guests. Prince Lun of Chao wanted her for himself, but Shih Ch'ung refused to surrender her. Because that literary group was patronised by Chia Mi whose clan was purged, Shih Ch'ung was implicated and executed. His family was exterminated, and Green Pearl committed suicide by leaping from an upper storey of their mansion.

Shih Jung-t'ai, ? late fifth century AD. Little is known about him.

?Shih Pao-yüeh, late fifth century AD. A fine musician and poet in the reign of the Chin Emperor Wu. Biographical data are scant. Some commentators think that his poem in the middle of Chapter Nine was composed by Ch'ai Lang, based on information given by Chung Hung in his *Classification of Poets (Shih p'in)* in the sixth century AD.

Ssu-ma Hsiang-ju, courtesy name Ch'ang-ch'ing, c. 179–117 BC, from Ch'engtu, the old capital of Shu in modern Szechwan. Was very poor until his literary talent was recognised by the Han Emperor Wu. Author of several famous prose poems, a genre popular in the Han era, the best known being *Sir Fantasy* and *Shanglin Park*. Once when he travelled to Linch'iung he was invited to the home of a wealthy man called Cho Wang-sun. At a banquet there he sang songs of courtship intended for the ears of Cho's recently widowed daughter, Wen-chün, who was listening behind the door. She fell in love with the poet and they eloped that night. The courtship songs appear in Chapter Nine.

Su Hsiao-hsiao, fifth century AD, from Ch'ient'ang, modern Hangchow. She was a professional singer of the Chin and Ch'i Dynasties. A beautiful courtesan, she vowed to be true to her lover to the grave, beneath the 'pine and cypress'. She died young, and the legend arose that her spirit waited for her lover to join her in the next world.

?Su Po-yü's wife, ? third century AD. This attribution is given by one of Hsü Ling's eighteenth-century editors, Chi Jung-shu, who cited an earlier source-book on poetry, appearing to derive mainly from information given in the poem itself. Su Po-yü is said there to have lived in Shu, modern Szechwan, his wife in Ch'angan, the Han capital further in the north.

?Su Wu, 142–60 BC. The poem translated as *If I die* in Chapter One is traditionally attributed to him, partly because the theme of separation fits his historical life. Some editions have the title *My wife I left behind* tacked onto his poem to provide a pseudo-biographical context. The historical Su Wu was an envoy sent to the Hsiungnu by the Chinese court, but was held

359

captive by them for nineteen years. Later he was sent back to China, partly as the result of a ruse: the Hsiungnu were informed that a letter sent via a goose's foot had reached the Han court telling the emperor that Su Wu was still alive. The Hsiungnu, who had told the emperor that Su Wu had died, were so amazed by this feat that they set him free. Similarly, the belief arose that he had sent his wife a letter from captivity. The poem here is one of a set of four attributed to him.

Sun Cho, courtesy name Hsing-kung, AD 301–c. 380, from Shansi. For ten years he roamed the mountains and lakes of Chekiang. Later he served the Chin Dynasty in important posts. He was considered a major poet in his own day. Two of his poems were written on Green Jade, a favourite concubine of the Prince of Junan in the Chin Dynasty, translated in Chapter Ten as *A lower-class girl* and *She didn't feel shy*.

Sung Tzu-hou, from late second to third century AD. Probably lived in the Later Han and Wei Dynasties. Biographical data scant. His poem in Chapter One translated as *Flowers fall* has the title in the original *Tung Chiao-jao*, which may be the name of the girl speaking in the poem, or an old poem title, the meaning of which has been lost.

Tai Hao, ? mid-sixth century AD. Biographical data scant.

T'ang Seng-chi, ? personal name Hsiu, also called Hsiu Shang-jen and Yang Chi. The title *Seng* in a man's name meant that he was connected in some formal way with Buddhism, and *Shang-jen* is a similar religious title. His poem translated as *The glint of gold* in Chapter Eight expresses the theme of the vanity of human cares which might be construed as a Buddhist line of thought. The poet lived in the fifth century, his birthdate probably being AD 464.

T'ao Ch'ien, courtesy name Yüan-ming, AD 365–427, from Kiangsi. In his youth the family wealth was diminished. Much of his early adult life was spent in unsuccessful efforts to secure a post at court or in an office at the capital. Later he retired to the country, still only in his forties. Much of his poetry reflects a philosophical view of life. He is admired as a nature poet and, though rated in the Southern Dynasties as a second-rank poet, was fully recognised in the T'ang and is acknowledged today as one of China's major poets.

?T'ao-yeh (Peachleaf), *fl.* fourth century AD. Favourite concubine of the painter and writer Wang Hsien-chih, son of Wang Hsi-chih, the famous painter and calligrapher. Her three poems on a round fan were written, it is thought, in answer to Wang Hsien-chih's letter-poems. They appear in Chapter Ten.

Teng K'eng, c. AD 502. Enfeoffed as the Marquess of Sung-tzu. His father was from Hupei. Biographical data are scant.

?Ts'ai Yung, courtesy name Po-chieh, AD 133–92, from Honan. Was a well-known poet, musician, and calligrapher. He was well versed in astronomy and musical theory. He wrote the authorised version of the *Six Classics* (the five *Confucian Classics*). Later he incurred the displeasure of the authorities and was condemned to death, sentence being commuted to having his hair pulled out. He became a recluse, but when the warlord Tung Cho challenged the Han Dynasty he summoned Ts'ai Yung to court, inviting him to take office and ennobling him as a Marquess. When Tung Cho was defeated, Ts'ai Yung was again imprisoned for an indiscreet remark, and he died in jail. Known as Drunken Dragon for his drinking bouts. He was the subject of a play by the fourteenth-century playwright Kao Ming, who portrayed him in less than flattering terms; the title of the play is *The Lute*. His poem in Chapter One is elsewhere listed as anonymous, and its attribution remains doubtful.

Ts'ao Chih, courtesy name Tzu-chien, entitled the Prince of Ch'en, and also known as the Prince of Yung-ch'iu (he was enfeoffed ten times), AD 192–232. Third son of Ts'ao Ts'ao. He was passed over as heir to the Wei throne in favour of his brother Ts'ao P'ei. The bitter rivalry in power and in love between the two brothers is legendary. Ts'ao Chih wrote in a variety of styles and adopted many different, sometimes contradictory, literary poses, such as a Confucian statesman, a Taoist immortal, or *bon viveur*. The view that persists of his tragic life is partly fictional. Efforts to reconstruct a chronology of his poems, arguing a descent from happy youth to tragic manhood are erroneous. Ts'ao Chih was the most gifted of a family of literary men. He was particularly successful in using existing folk-song themes in new ways, and in establishing the new five-word metre as an expressive art form. His *Prose Poem on the Goddess of Lo River* was greatly admired, and is frequently referred to in the poems of this anthology.

Ts'ao Jui, courtesy name Yüan-chung, AD 204–39. Acceded to the Wei throne as Emperor Ming on the death of his father, Ts'ao P'ei, in AD 226. His mother, Empress Chen, was deposed and committed suicide in AD 221, so he temporarily forfeited the right to succession. Later he was reinstated. The three imperial Ts'ao – Ts'ao Ts'ao, Ts'ao P'ei, and Ts'ao Jui – are known in literary history as the 'Three Imperial Ancestors'. His poem *Dull nights* in Chapter Two is elsewhere listed as an anonymous old lyric entitled *Song of anguish*.

Ts'ao P'ei, courtesy name Tzu-huan, AD 187–226. Acceded to the Wei throne in AD 220 as the first Emperor Wen on the death of his father, Ts'ao Ts'ao, founder of the Wei. He established his capital at Loyang. Patron of the arts, he gathered a select group of writers to his court called 'Seven Masters of the Chien-an Era'. He wrote *Essay on Literature* (*Lun wen*), one of the earliest pieces of Chinese literary criticism. His brother, Ts'ao Chih, and son, Ts'ao Jui, are also represented in this anthology. There is some controversy about the authorship of the poem entitled *Empress Chen* listed either under his name or after his name in Chapter Two. In some collections this poem is attributed to his wife, Empress Chen, or to Ts'ao Ts'ao, or treated as anonymous. Similarly, the next two poems entitled *Bedcurtains* and attributed to Wang Sung are also ascribed to Ts'ao P'ei, who is believed to have written them on behalf of Wang Sung.

Ts'ao P'i, courtesy name Fu-tao, *fl. c.* AD 317, from Anhwei. Related to the Ts'ao family of the Wei Dynasty. Served the Eastern Chin as a scholar in the Grand Academy, holding several minor posts and rising to the rank of Great Officer of Brilliant Favour. His cycle of songs to Orchid Fragrance, a nymph, were greatly admired in his day, but have not survived.

Tso Ssu, courtesy name T'ai-ch'ung, b. ? AD 250, d. ? AD 306, from Shantung. Ridiculed by local girls because he was ugly and stammered. Devoted himself to scholarship. Served as secretary to Chia Mi, nephew of Empress Chia, but retired from office when the Chia clan was purged. His sister became an imperial concubine, which rank brought wealth and status to his family. Famous for his *Three Prose Poems on the Three Capitals*, a literary endeavour that took him ten years to complete. It was so popular that paper was scarce in Loyang when it was circulated. His poems often contain colloquialisms which may have been erroneously copied and misinterpreted in transmission, making some passages very problematical.

Wang Chien, courtesy name Mao-kao, *c.* AD 277–322, from Kiangsu. Served the Eastern Chin Dynasty as secretary to the heir apparent. Said to have become the son-in-law of the imperial family. The last few lines of his poem are construed by some as his flattering reference to the empress, mother of his wife the princess; it appears in Chapter Three entitled *Seventh Night*.

?Wang Hsien-chih, courtesy name Tzu-ching, AD 344–88, from Kweichi in Chekiang. Son of the famous painter and calligrapher Wang Hsi-chih (AD 321–79). Hsien-chih was also a famous calligrapher, scholar, and writer. He served the Eastern Chin Dynasty in the archive department. He had a concubine called T'ao-yeh, Peachleaf, for whom he is thought to have written two songs, *I won't need oars* and *It takes two*, appearing in Chapter Ten. In some anthologies, however, his poems are attributed to Peachleaf herself.

Wang Hsün, courtesy name Huai-fan, AD 511–36, from Shantung. Became a head of a department in the imperial chancellory, and served Hsiao Kang when he was crown prince. His literary talent was considered exceptionally fine, and he attracted a number of devotees. One of his poems in Chapter Eight, *If only*, is modelled on Hsiao Kang's *Goddess or painting?* in Chapter Seven.

Wang Huan, from late fifth to early sixth century AD. Little is known of his life.

Wang Seng-ju, courtesy name Seng-ju, personal name unknown, AD 465–522, from Shantung. Devoted himself to literature and scholarship from early youth. Though from a poor family, he rose in office to serve the Liang as prefect of Nanhai, and later became a deputy of the Board of Censors. The title *Seng* in a man's name meant some formal connection with the religious life of a Buddhist, either as a monk or lay religious. His poem *Spring regrets* in Chapter Six is listed elsewhere as a composition by Wu Chün.

Wang Seng-ta, AD 423–58, from Shantung. Served one of the Liu-Sung princes as an administrator, prefect, and departmental head of an imperial secretariat. He was eventually thrown into prison for his blunt memorials and he died there.

Wang Shu, ? from late fifth to early sixth century AD. Biographical data scant. One poem title indicates that his poetry had attracted the attention of Hsiao Yen's brother. Another title shows that he attended a banquet given by a ministerial head, probably the illustrious Hsü Mien, all of which suggests that he moved in the top circles.

Wang Su, courtesy name Hsiu-yeh, AD 418–71, from Shantung. When his mother died, he became a recluse and lived in the country. On the accession of the Liu-Sung Emperor Hsiao-wu, Wang Su was often summoned to court. The emperor was the poet Liu Chün.

?Wang Sung, wife of General Liu Hsün, ? from late second to early third century AD. A favourite official of Ts'ao Ts'ao, her husband was later killed. There is some doubt about the attribution of her poem. Some ascribe it to Ts'ao P'ei.

Wang T'ai-ch'ing, courtesy name T'ai-ch'ing, ? from late fifth to mid-sixth century AD. Served the Liang administration and was well received by members of the royal family.

Wang Wei, courtesy name Ching-hsüan, AD 415–43, from Kiangsu. (Not to be confused with the T'ang poet Wang Wei.) He served the Liu-Sung Dynasty as administrative advisor to the Army of the Right for Prince Shuo of Nanp'ing. Disliking official duties, he retired on the grounds of ill health. He died young.

362

Wang Yün, courtesy names Yüan-li and Te-jou, AD 481–549, from Shantung. Grandson of Wang Seng-ta. Admired in his day for his literary talent, especially by Shen Yüeh and Hsiao T'ung. He died from misadventure, leaping into a well to escape from rebels. His six poems in Chapter Eight harmonise with Registry Officer Wu's poems (probably Wu Chün the poet). Thirty-nine of his poems are extant.

Wang Yung, courtesy name Yüan-chang, AD 468–94, from Nanking. He was Wang Seng-ta's grandson. Served the Ch'i Dynasty in the departments of astronomy and receptions. Because his personal name was the same as the taboo name of the Ch'i Emperor Ho, his courtesy name was used instead. He was imprisoned because of political intrigue at the time of Emperor Hsiao-wu's illness, and seems to have died there. His poem *Ever since you went away* in Chapter Ten is modelled on Hsü Kan's *Bedroom longing* in Chapter One.

Wen-jen Ch'ien, personal name Ch'ien, ? *fl.* mid-sixth century AD. Biographical data scant.

Wu Chün, also known as Wu Yün, courtesy name Shu-hsiang, AD 469–520, from Chekiang. Prince Wei of Chien-an appointed him as his secretary and as governor of Yangchou. Later he attended court with the honorary title *Ch'ao-ch'ing*, by which he is sometimes known. He did some editorial work on the *Annals of the Ch'i Dynasty*, but was dismissed for inaccuracies. He also worked on a general history, but died before its completion. His poetic artistry was generally acclaimed and there were many imitators of the 'Wu Chün style'. He is one of the earliest poets to have used the term *chüeh-chü* for a short, four-line verse.

Wu Man-yüan, *fl. c.* AD 471. Biographical data are scant. His poem *Two white geese* in Chapter Four is based on the old anonymous ballad of the same title in Chapter One.

Wu Tzu, ? sixth century AD. Little is known about him.

Yang Fang, courtesy name Kung-hui, *fl. c.* AD 317, from Chekiang. Served the Western Chin Dynasty in various prefectural posts, and finally retired to the countryside. His five epithalamia which appear in Chapter Three have attracted different theories concerning their composition: (1) all five are love-songs or wedding songs; (2) the first two are wedding songs, the last three miscellaneous poems; (3) all five are on the *ho-huan,* or joy of love flower; (4) all five are allegorical, two describing deep devotion, one estrangement, and two unrequited love; (5) all five are letter-poems between a man and woman, of which the sixth is missing.

Yao Fan, ? *fl.* early sixth century AD. Little is known about him.

Yen Yen-chih, courtesy name Yen-nien, AD 384–456, from Shantung. Orphaned and impoverished in his youth. Given to drink. Became a page to the heir apparent and was promoted to deputy head of an imperial secretariat. Served the first four Liu-Sung emperors. Demoted to governor of a district in Chekiang. Nicknamed Yen the Clown for being outspoken and bibulous. Was protected by the Liu-Sung Emperor Wen's bemused favour. His poetry is often compared with that of Hsieh Ling-yün. His narrative poem *A pure wife* may be compared with Fu Hsüan's version in Chapter Two. Yen's poem in Chapter Four has nine stanzas of ten lines each, with a change of rhyme in each stanza.

Yü Chien-wu, courtesy name Tzu-shen, AD 487–550, from Honan. From a poor family. Father of the famous poet Yü Hsin. While Hsiao Kang was Prince of Chinan, he and Liu Hsiao-wei, together with eight others, were known as the 'Ten Scholars of the Lofty Studio'. At the age of twenty he served Hsiao Kang the infant and stayed with him when he became the Crown Prince, enjoying over thirty years of royal favour. Enfeoffed as the Marquess of Wuk'ang. Both Yü and later Hsü Ch'ih shaped Hsiao Kang's literary taste. Both men, and others, are identified with 'Palace Style Poetry', but Hsiao Kang is more popularly accredited with immortalising this new verse form. Almost a hundred of his poems survive, many of which illustrate the new poetic style.

Yü Hsin, courtesy name Tzu-shan, AD 512–80, from Honan. His father was Yü Chien-wu, who was tutor to Hsiao Kang. During his lifetime the Tartar general Hou Ching captured Chienk'ang. The Liang ruler moved his capital to Chiangling. The Liang foundered in AD 556, and was replaced by the Ch'en Dynasty. When Yü Hsin was sent as an envoy to the north, the northern dynasty of the Western Wei invaded the south and captured Chiangling. Western Wei was in turn defeated by the Northern Chou Dynasty. The poet was in virtual exile during all these upheavals, and while still in the north wrote a famous prose poem *Lament for South of the River*, meaning the old southern region of the Yangtze of his birth. He was greatly admired as a poet in his own time, especially by his conquerors. Later Tu Fu expressed the highest praise for his verse.

Yü Tan, ? from late fifth to early sixth century. A scholar. He served as governor of a district in Kwangsi, and as secretary to Hsiao Wang.

Yü Yen, *fl. c.* AD 488, from Kweichi in Chekiang. A contemporary of Shen Yüeh. Served in a military capacity.

Poem Titles

(The poem's original title appears in parentheses)

A beautiful woman 68

A beautiful woman (Imitation of) 209

A beauty admires herself in a painting (by royal commission) 215

A blur of blooms (Four miscellaneous *Chüeh-chü*, 2) 279

A border guard 282

A boy 165

A dainty girl 85

A dropped earring 211

A dull ache (Another Ch'ingho composition) 64

A few days (Six poems answering Liu Yün's letter-poems, 6) 163

A former palace lady marries a supplies sergeant (A former palace lady, a singer from Hantan, marries a supplies sergeant) 128

A gown near my body (Imitation of an ancient style poem) 106

A grand house (We met in a narrow alley) 34

A grand house (Imitation of We met in a narrow alley) 102

A grand house (Imitation of In Ch'angan there's a narrow alley) 182

A hint of shadow (A hint of shadow darkens the sunshine) 67

A jade dish (Four summer songs, 3) 283

A lovely woman's morning make-up 199

A lower-class girl (Two songs for darling Green Jade, 1) 265

A maid's thanks for a mirror (For Yang Kan's maid, thanking him on her behalf for his gift of a mirror) 227

A measure of wine (Harmonising with Yü Ch'ien's old theme) 150

A melody so sad (East city wall high and long) 38

A merchant (Five Modern Western Songs, 2, Merchant's music) 269

A newly wed knight parts from his bride (At Ch'ingho I saw a newly wed knight in a tow-boat part from his bride) 64

A party at Golden Vale 274

A peacock southeast flew (An Old Poem written for Chiao Chung-ch'ing's wife) 53

A pity I didn't (Song of Meng Chu of Tanyang) 272

A pledge with wine 287

A poem on sweet promise sent to my mistress (A poem on sweet promise written in front of a peach-tree near my bedroom and sent to my mistress) 173

A poet meets his former mistress at a party (On Liu Hsiao-cho meeting his former mistress, a singer, at Yüan Ching-chung's party) 260

A prince went wandering 274

A promise (Two Rejoice to hear songs, 1) 285

A pure wife (Harmonising with Mr Pan's poem) 77

A pure wife (Ch'iu Hu) 113

A pure wife (Imitation of the Boudoir regrets of Ch'iu Hu's wife) 201

A rose 148

A round fan 285

A satire on the poet Liu Hsiao-cho 155

A secret palace (Four poems on spring parting, 2) 258

A singer's frustration 192

A soldier departs (Three White-brass-shoes songs, Hsiangyang, 1) 285

A song 41

A sweet thought (Three spring songs, 2) 283

A throne crumbles away (Song of Lady Li and her palace attendant) 248

A twin-stemmed gardenia (Picking a twin-stemmed gardenia, I presented it to Hsieh Niao with this poem attached) 280

A wanderer's wife (Bright the moon shines on a tall house) 66

A weaving wife (Northwest there is a weaving wife) 66

A woman strolling in the park 289

A wool-weave screen (Four A crow perched tunes, 4) 255

Admiring from a distance 288

Admiring the moon from the west city gate 115

Adorable (At Chancellor Hsü's banquet I was assigned the theme Adorable) 156

Alone, I never see him (Two songs for drum and flute, 1) 145

Along the bank (Three ballads, 3) 93